HUNTING
NORTH AMERICAN
BIG GAME

Durwood Hollis

© 2002 by

Durwood Hollis

Published by

krause
publications

700 East State Street • Iola, WI 54990-0001
715/445-2214 • FAX: 715/445-4087   www.krause.com

Please call or write for our free catalog of publications.
Our toll-free number to place an order or obtain a free catalog is 800-258-0929.

Library of Congress Catalog Number: 2002105756
ISBN: 0-87349-383-4
Printed in the United States of America

DEDICATION

This book is dedicated to the memory of Donald S. Pine (1932-1991), a career wildlife biologist with the California Department of Fish and Game. For many years, we hunted big game—especially deer and wild boar—together. His knowledge of the outdoors made him an exceptional mentor. A fine companion in the field, Don had an uncommon mastery of the hunt. Many of the hunting skills I acquired were learned at his side. Way too early, my good friend quietly slipped away from the campfire of life. His presence on the trail has been missed ever since.

Photo by Durwood Hollis

Don Pine had a real passion for the hunt, especially the pursuit of big wild hogs.

ABOUT THE AUTHOR

Durwood Hollis was born and raised in southern California. He attended universities in Utah and California, graduating with a major in anthropology and minors in biology and education. For more than 20 years, his work has been published in most major outdoor sporting magazines. During the 1980s, Durwood wrote a regular column on knives in Petersen's Hunting magazine. For a time during the 1990s, he also authored a similar column in Blackpowder Hunting magazine. In 1988, Durwood served as the editorial director for The Complete Book of Knives (Petersen's Publishing, 1988). More recently, he authored the Complete Game Care Guide (Brunton, 1995), Elk: Strategies For The Hunter (Krause Publications, 2000), The Complete Book of Hunting Knives (Krause Publications, 2001), and Hunting Monster Mule Deer in Arizona's Kaibab Region (Arizona Big Game Hunting, 2001). This is his fifth book. Durwood's interest in hunting has taken him to Africa, Europe, Latin America and throughout the United States. Despite an abiding interest in all game species, the pursuit of wild boar holds a special place in Durwood's personal pantheon of hunting activities. Durwood continues to reside in his native California. There, in a home filled with trophies of the hunt, he lives with his wife, teenage son and young daughter.

Photo by Durwood Hollis

The bucks don't have to be huge to get the author's hunting instincts fired up. He took this 3x2 blacktail in the heat of August on the central California coast.

ACKNOWLEDGMENTS

Many have contributed to the development and production of this work. First and foremost is friend and fellow outdoor scribe, Bob Robb. For last decade, Bob has been an Alaskan resident. During those years, he has hunted all of the various species of northern game extensively. Many of us have pursued this category of game on occasion and taken a representative specimen. Bob, on the other hand, has hunted them repeatedly and taken some of the most impressive trophies imaginable. Simply put, his experience hunting the big bears, wild sheep, mountain goat, caribou, moose, musk oxen and Sitka blacktail deer are without a peer in the outdoor writing community. For all of these reasons, I turned to him for consultation and assistance in the development of material on those species. Many of his first-hand experiences pursuing the game of the Far North can be found within these pages, as well as countless photos. Thanks my friend, I couldn't have completed this effort without your assistance.

Also, I am indebted to outdoor writers John Higley and Jim Matthews for the use of many of their photographs. Both men are longtime friends and accomplished photographers. In this profession, good friends are hard to come by. These two individuals are the best of the best of that category. My gratitude also goes out to associates Kevin Howard and Matt Foster, as well as my good friends Frank Baratti and Charlie Merritt, for the use of their photos. Thank you my compatriots for your assistance.

Several outfitters and guides, including John R. Winter, Tim Doud and Duwane Adams deserve a generous "thank you" for sharing their camps with me. Much of the material recounted in this book has come from those times.

My gratitude is extended to hunting guides Craig Rossier and Doug Roth of Camp 5 on the California central coast, as well as to game manager Don Givet and his staff on the famed Tejon Ranch in southern California. The generosity of these individuals in opening their properties to me is deeply appreciated. And to all of the other guides and outfitters mentioned in this tome, from the most renown to the least known, thank you very much.

I am also appreciative of the assistance provided by Dan Herring of Herring's Taxidermy in Thermopolis, Wyoming. Dan has been an occasional hunting companion and a regular consultant on matters involving trophy work. His experience was a valuable contribution in areas within this book that touched on that subject. And I appreciate being to able to use many of his fine photos. Thanks Dan for your support with this project.

My wife Anita deserves humble thanks for just putting up with a jumble of photographs on the floor, research papers scattered about the house and me being absent from home all too often on hunting trips. A marvelous companion, through it all she was a staunch supporter of this effort. Thank you my love for being there.

And to the folks at Krause Publication, including Senior Acquisitions Editor, Don Gulbrandsen, and editor Kevin Michalowski for all of the help they provided in bringing this book to fruition. And to you the reader, thanks for supporting my efforts, and good hunting.

Durwood Hollis
Rancho Cucamonga, California
2002

CONTENTS

PREFACE

When I learned that Durwood Hollis was putting the finishing touches on his latest book, *Hunting North American Big Game*, I couldn't think of anyone more qualified to tackle that particular subject. I started hunting California's coastal mountain range for deer and wild pigs with Durwood back in the late 1970s. Since those years, the scope of his big game adventures, both in terms of geography and actual species, has increased exponentially. Even so, his near-obsessive dedication to hunting is every bit as keen now as it was then.

In those days, I would often get a phone call at 9:00 p.m. on a Friday after a tough work week, to hear an urgent sales pitch along these lines:

"Hey, it's Durwood. How soon can you get ready to roll? There's a really good place I want to try that's got hot-and-cold running hogs. It's about a five-hour drive. Don't bother eating, we'll grab something on the way . . ."

What invariably followed was a hell-bent-for-leather drive out of the Los Angeles Basin, followed by a full-day death march through the scrub oak and chaparral of lower Monterey County. More often, than not, we got skunked. But no matter how grim the going, how hot or cold the weather, or what piece of essential gear we'd forgotten, Durwood was always upbeat, always the consummate hunter.

Whenever a piece of hunting strategy worked Durwood was always suitably modest ("I do this stuff a lot," or "I'd rather be lucky than good," are often-used rejoinders of his that spring to mind).

Although a rifle crank of the first magnitude, once away from the bench, Durwood's surprisingly democratic about his choice of hunting tools. He's equally conversant with iron-sighted lever guns in chamberings that would excite the envy of Cowboy Action shooters; customized bolt-actions in magnum calibers that would elicit the concern of a chiropractor; big-bore handguns, archery tackle or muzzleloaders. He really doesn't care what he uses as long as he's hunting. And his skills at field dressing, skinning, game care and cooking are equal to his skill at finding an animal and putting it on the ground. (Someone once jokingly suggested that he write a book about game care. He did.)

Since those days on the Coast Range, he's been around plenty. I've heard his name bandied about in hunting camps from Texas to Wyoming to Alberta. Elk, antelope, mule deer, whitetail, bear, sheep and wild boar fill his wall space. In the old days, he'd grouse about the rising price of ammunition; now he discusses his yearly taxidermy bill in hushed tones.

Durwood still finds time to chase wild hogs and mule deer in our old Central California stomping grounds. And to this day, I'm only half-dreading one of those Friday evening phone calls.

Payton Miller
Executive Editor
Guns & Ammo magazine

Photo by Durwood Hollis

Guns & Ammo *Executive Editor, Payton Miller, has hunted with the author on many occasions. If they were out for tender venison, it certainly didn't take a big buck to draw their interest.*

FOREWORD

North American hunters can pursue several species of deer, elk, moose, caribou, sheep and bear. Bison, musk ox, wild sheep, mountain goat, pronghorn antelope, javelina and wild boar make big hunting on this continent all that more interesting.

In many areas, species that are primarily predatory may also be considered game animals. Most certainly, all of the varieties of bears, as well as mountain lions and wolves fall into this category. You will note that with the exception of the chapters on bears, there is an absence of commentary on the other predators. The whole issue of hunting mountain lions and wolves has gained too much political baggage for this author. Likewise, there will be no mention of hunting polar bear or walrus, which are protected by the Marine Mammal Protection Act of 1972. Even if it were legal to take these arctic animals, importing trophies would present difficulties.

To avoid unnecessary controversy, I have chosen to comment only on what are viewed as mainstream big game hunting activities. The reason behind writing about the pursuit of some animals, while excluding others, is based mainly on a shift in public acceptance regarding the hunting of predators. In many areas, trapping, baiting and the use of dogs to pursue and take these animals have become severely restricted or eliminated. Even bear hunting, particularly with hounds, has fallen under close scrutiny.

You will also note that there's almost no discussion about trophy scoring. While the term "trophy" will be found, references to particular record book scores will be few and far between. While I have no point of contention with the various big game trophy record-keeping organizations, some writers have put too much emphasis on this subject. Which one of us can say that a first-time hunter's smallish forked-horn buck isn't a trophy? In my mind, the first little buck I ever shot was most definitely a trophy of considerable significance. If that doesn't qualify as a trophy, then you tell me what does! Even more difficult, try explaining to a youngster that whatever they've just shot isn't a trophy.

Some may take issue with hunting musk oxen and bison. While these species may not be as wary as other big game animals, such endeavors can be an exciting and challenging experience. If you really hunt these animals the right way, not just chase them in a snowmobile or pickup truck in order to "bail and blaze," you can expect a real hunt. In fact, creeping up on a herd of shaggy musk oxen on the frozen tundra of the Far North is something that must be experienced to fully comprehend.

The vast majority of North American big game hunters are deer hunters, plain and simple. From the Northwoods to the Eastern Seaboard, all across the Great Plains, well below the Mason-Dixon line and in the desert mountain ranges of the Southwest, whitetail deer both large and small will be found. Mule deer are residents of the western third of the continent, all the way down into northern Mexico. Possessing the largest antlers of any species that are called deer, a trophy class mule deer is a highly coveted prize. Along the Pacific coast, from central California to Alaska, you'll find the blacktail deer. Scientists now believe that only two core deer species—the blacktail deer and the whitetail deer—migrated from Asia to North America. The meaning of this is that the mule deer is a subspecies of the blacktail, rather than the other way around as was previously thought.

Three primary species of elk—Rocky Mountain, Roosevelt and tule elk—can also lay claim to North American residency. Hunting the dark timber and grassy meadows for these large cervids is a sport that's purely addictive. Likewise, three species of moose—Alaska-Yukon, Canadian and the Shiras moose—are all residents of this continent. Unusual in appearance and phlegmatic in behavior, moose have their own following of hunters.

Mountain game—wild sheep and the white goat—have become some of the most highly coveted of trophy animals. The environment in which these high country inhabitants reside is clearly demanding and potentially life threatening. One wrong step on a glacier or cliff and you'll find that your hunt can turn into a personal survival experience. Obviously, going after Dall's sheep, Rocky Mountain bighorn, Stone's sheep, desert bighorn sheep and mountain goat is a sport for those with a sound heart and substantial funds.

Bears of every kind—hump-backed and otherwise—have always intrigued the hunter. The pursuit of both the grizzly and coastal brown bears has an element of danger that is absent in most other big game pursuits. Indeed, one of these big bears may well start hunting you, while you're hunting him. The black bear is no slouch either. Possibly the single most widely distributed game animal on the continent, black bears can be found from Mexico to Canada and Alaska, and from the Pacific to the Atlantic coasts. While most specimens will run 200 to 300 pounds, some exceptional black bears can outweigh the largest grizzly.

Vast numbers of caribou wander across Alaska, Canada, the Northwest Territories and the Yukon Territory annually. Waiting patiently for these animals are both native and sport hunters. You'll find that the most difficult part of the pursuit of these tundra wanderers is timing your hunt to intersect herd movement and then selecting which bull to take. And even if you take the bull of your dreams, an even larger animal might just happen by when you're elbow-deep in primary field care. That's the way it goes when caribou are on the agenda.

Often, finding pronghorn antelope isn't any more difficult than locating caribou. Judging the trophy potential of an antelope's horns, however, can be just as challenging. Such an undertaking is a matter of patience and requires a trained eye. Despite substantial pronghorn populations in some areas, locating a trophy buck may take a dedicated hunter several years.

Where they occur, wild boar and javelina are readily available game animals. Short of the big bears, wild hogs of every genetic make up are next on the list of most dangerous animals on this continent. Similarly, getting in the way of a highly agitated herd of javelina isn't any joke. Despite the inherent peril, stalking large tuskers and small ones is great fun.

My own introduction to big game hunting consisted of nothing more than a borrowed rifle, a handful of shells, a sharp knife and marginal knowledge of deer hunting basics. Two days into the hunt, I came across a forked-horn buck. Quite frankly, the encounter was more accidental, than on purpose. It certainly was a toss-up as to which of the two of us was more surprised. At this moment, I can't even recall where the crosshairs of my scope came to rest (read that as a serious case of "buck fever"). However, it must have been a vital spot, since the little forked-horn collapsed in a heap at the shot. With only a meager grasp of appropriate field care, somehow I managed to gut the animal and drag it back to camp.

Over the years, I've learned a lot more about the pursuit of big game than I ever dreamed existed. In the pages that follow you'll find descriptive information on the various big game species. I've also shared several experiences of my own, as well as those of others, that occurred during the pursuit of these animals. There's plenty of information about hunting strategies that have worked and some that haven't. To keep the hunting camp conversation lively, you'll find lots of salient detail on calibers, guns and archery gear for big game. Furthermore, entire chapters have been devoted to the importance of selecting the right gear, gadgets and optics. And there's a separate chapter on the significant aspects of game care. To assist readers in accessing various resources, a listing of the names, mailing addresses, telephone numbers and Internet web addresses of game departments, governmental and private agencies and hunting organizations has been provided.

To say that this book contains everything you need to know about hunting big game on the North American continent would be stretching the truth beyond creditability. However, I am sure you'll find something here that will make your own hunting efforts more enjoyable and successful. And that, my friend, is what hunting should be all about. Read on!

Durwood Hollis
2002

Photo by Bob Robb

Usually in the shadows and never far from cover, the whitetail deer is this continent's favorite big game quarry.

THE DISAPPEARING ACT: WHITETAIL DEER

A master of cover and concealment, the whitetail deer is North America's favorite game animal.

Parts of South Fox Island were obviously slowly disappearing under the sand. Every windward opening to the interior held massive concave troughs of the white granular material. Thankfully, the steep shoreline quieted the wind and protected the island interior. At the low-lying southern end, however, several hundred yards of open sand now blanketed the ground like a shroud. Barren and desolate, this end of the Lake Michigan island was about as attractive as the surface of the moon.

A few stunted trees, growing together in a thin line, were situated midway across the expanse of sand that separated the main island from an abandoned lighthouse at the extreme south end. Like soldiers holding their ground in the face of enemy fire, the twisted trunks and tangled branches had somehow remained long after their brethren no longer found root. It was apparent that this tiny strip of green, growing just below a sandy berm and scant yards from the lakeshore, was also slowly giving way to the stark reality of the sand.

Interestingly, whitetail deer tracks criss-crossed this arid landscape as silent evidence that there was more here than met the eye. My curiosity piqued, I wandered across the sand to see if there was any meaningful pattern to the tracks. After several minutes, I came abreast of the cluster of trees. There was no way that this pitiful cover could conceal anything, let alone a whitetail deer. To my surprise, a 10-point buck and two does were suddenly manifest out

Photo by Durwood Hollis

Here's a South Fox Island whitetail that didn't get away.

While several other North American big game species have vanished, whitetail deer have managed to successfully co-exist with man.

Whitetail deer are far more numerous and widely distributed than any other big game species in North America.

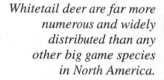

of the greenery. With the deer running along the edge of the lake, on the other side of the trees and just below a sandy berm, there was no shot in the offering. In fact, the only things I could see were antler tips and several streaks of brown.

At a good 250 yards, the trio crossed in front me and headed for a timbered ridge in the distance. Dropping down to a sitting position, I draped the rifle across my knees and tried to impart some meaning to this unexpected opportunity. It just wasn't to be. The challenge of computing range, trajectory and target speed was beyond my ability. I could only watch as a fine whitetail buck once again disappeared into the distance.

Whitetail deer are true lords of their own lair. Even if it's nothing more than a sparse line of shriveled trees on a sandy spit in the middle of Lake Michigan. The buck and his cohorts had obviously seen my approach. Using the limited concealment available, the deer had apparently hidden themselves on the other side of the trees. When I came too close, they simply used that scattering of limbs and leaves to cover their departure.

Wherever you find them, whitetail deer are all about cover and concealment. No matter how proficient at the game you may have become, in this particular arena we are all amateurs. This is not to say these deer are men-

Characterized by their sweeping antlers (all tines rise from a single main beam) and prominent white throat patch, the whitetail deer is sought by hunters in all but a few states and Canadian provinces.

tal giants. They aren't! What gives these deer the edge is they have full knowledge concerning their environment. And this includes every tree, limb, leaf and vine. Even though you may have pursued deer on the same parcel for several seasons, your human understanding of that domain is no more than superficial. The difference is that the deer live there. You are only an occasional visitor in that realm.

Each of us could probably walk around our own homes in the dark without any more illumination than that provided by outside street lights. Each room has its own "feel." And it is our sensory perception that provides this information. With their superior sensory acuity, whitetail deer are no less competent on their own home turf. My experience on Michigan's South Fox Island certainly confirmed the ability of these animals to use what little cover existed to their advantage.

In the beginning: When Europeans first crossed the Atlantic and settled in North America they encountered eastern elk, moose, black bear and whitetail deer. In Europe, big game usually belonged to the crown. Members of the royal court, or commoners willing to risk their heads by poaching, did what little hunting occurred. When confronted with a bounty of game on this continent, without restrictions regarding what and how many they could take, the new Americans set out to fill their larders. With an "I am going to get mine before someone else gets theirs" attitude, everyone from Pilgrims to pioneers had an impact on the game. First to feel the effect was the eastern elk. These stately animals were hunted to extinction in a matter of a few short years. Shortly thereafter, moose could only be found in the most remote regions. Even black bear retreated to the deep woods. Whitetail

Photo by Durwood Hollis

From fawn to mature adult in a matter of months, it still takes several seasons before a buck produces trophy-quality antlers.

about a 100-mile drive north and west of New York City. An area of mountains and vast forests, cut by the Hudson River, it is majestic in its beauty and grandeur. Before European settlement, historic records indicate that the area supported a limited population of deer. Today, however, whitetail can be found everywhere. When I flew into one of the small airports in the area, the number of deer that could be seen at dusk on that property was astonishing. And since nearly every home is adjacent forestland, whitetail deer consider flowerbeds and vegetable gardens their own personal delicatessens. Simply put, the deer were a nuisance. This same situation is repeated throughout the East, Northeast, New England and in Michigan, Minnesota and Wisconsin. Even in the South, whitetail deer are so numerous that the seasons stretch on for months and there is only a daily bag limit. In every state and province, thousands of deer are killed on the roadways annually. Likewise, a staggering number of whitetails are taken during each hunting season. Even so, these animals continue to thrive and do so in far greater numbers than ever before.

deer, however, seemed less affected by contact with their new neighbors. No doubt many deer were shot for food, buckskin leather and glue. Nevertheless, for every whitetail that perished by the gun, far more benefited from the endeavors of the new settlers—particularly the farming.

While American Indians participated in limited agricultural pursuits, those actions paled in contrast to the activities of the European settlers. Huge tracts of land were cleared, not only for farming, but also for homesteads and townships. Thoroughfares were cut out of the forest to allow contact between settlements. Cut, burn and plow were the watchwords of the immigrants. With every acre cleared, the deer population grew correspondingly. And since they were smaller than the regal elk or the phlegmatic moose, whitetail deer were less demanding in their habitat needs. Likewise, these deer were far more difficult to hunt. Where other big game had struggled for existence, the whitetail deer managed to survive and even flourish.

Today: Recently, I toured the Imperial-Schrade cutlery plant in Ellenville, New York. This location is

Photo by Jim Matthews

Whitetail hunters count all the antler tines, including the eye-guards. Here's a really nice 10-point buck (one tine is hidden).

Photo by Bob Robb

Whitetail deer can use a wide range of habitat, including deciduous forests, river breaks, stream courses, shelterbelts and agricultural holdings.

Wherever mankind has spread across North America—the Great Plains, Canada, the Rocky Mountains and onto the Pacific Northwest—whitetail deer have also come. Under the plow, vast prairie lands have long since given way to fields of corn, wheat and sorghum. Having riparian roots, whitetail simply followed the major watercourses west. Once in a region to their liking, the deer spread up and down every tributary until they too could call this new land home. And westward movement continues unabated to the present.

Whitetails are the most numerous and widely distributed big game animal on the North American continent. Far more abundant than either the mule deer or the blacktail deer, these animals can be found in all but two of the lower 48 states. I am sure that it's only a matter of time before these highly adaptable animals

spread into northern Nevada and northeastern California. Once in the Golden State, only the deserts in the lower half of California will stop their progress. The prospect of whitetail deer living in suburban San Francisco, Los Angeles and even Hollywood isn't such a stretch of the imagination. And if those same deer discover California's fertile central valley with its burgeoning agriculture, then it's game over. Won't happen, you say? The state legislature will pass bills allowing hunters to shoot whitetail deer of any age or sex on sight. Don't bet on it—not in California.

The look: Whitetail, or white-tailed deer are more correctly known by their scientific name, *Odocoileus virginianus*. Depending on where they are found, there are several subspecies that basically differ only in size. The largest representative of this group will be found in Canada, the Northeast, Midwest, Minnesota,

Wisconsin and the far West. Whitetail deer found in the South, Southwest, Texas and northern Mexico are considerably smaller in size.

Depending on age, subspecies under discussion and available nutrition sources, a mature whitetail buck will weigh from 110 to more than 300 pounds on the hoof. Does are slightly smaller weighing 85 to 225 pounds. In comparison to a mule deer, whitetails are a little shorter in height and less angular in appearance.

While mule deer tend to be grayish in color, whitetail deer are more reddish-brown in the summer and buff-color in the winter. A prominent white throat patch is characteristic of this species. The belly and underside of the tail are also white. The white under hair on the tail is quite visible (flagging) when the deer runs. In some populations, pure white and piebald (white patches) deer are occasionally seen.

Whitetail fawns are colored like adult deer, with the exception of a covering of white spots on the back, chest and sides that provide camouflage. In addition, fawns have no scent during the first few weeks of their lives. This, along with their spotted pelage provides a measure of protection from predation. The spots usually disappear as the deer matures and are completely absent by 4 months of age.

Life cycle: Whitetails produce far more fawns annually than do both mule deer and blacktail deer. In prime habitat, more than half of the does and a significant number of buck fawns are able, and do breed when they are just 6 months of age. Furthermore, nearly all

In some Midwestern states, corn is an important staple in the whitetail deer diet.

Photo by Bob Robb

An elevated deer stand, situated along an active trail, is a proven whitetail hunting strategy.

that other deer eat. To be sure, disease, injury and predators take nearly one third of all the fawns born in a single year. Those that survive, absent some adverse contact (vehicular incident, bullet or broadhead) with man, generally live to about 10 years of age.

Antler logic: Whitetail antlers sweep out and around, with all of the tines rising from a single main beam. Deer hunters count all of the points on a whitetail rack. What a mule deer hunter would call a 4-point (4x4) buck, the whitetail hunter refers to as an 8-pointer. And if the deer has eye guards, they are generally thrown into the mix. Unusual antler formations are seen with some frequency, including drop tines, extra points, and forked eye guards. Like most other species of deer, whitetail deer shed their antlers each year, usually during the months of January and February. In April or early May, new antlers will begin to develop. Most yearling mule deer bucks only produce a pair of single spikes, or at best tiny forked antlers. Well-nourished whitetail yearlings are more likely to have at least three individual tines on each main antler beam. Newly formed antlers are relatively soft and covered with soft, short, dense hair (velvet). As the antlers harden, most bucks will have rubbed this velvet covering loose. An occasional buck, usually one with underdeveloped or damaged testes, will retain this velvet covering until the antlers are shed. A few does have even been known to grow antlers. With whitetail, you can always expect the unexpected.

Habitat: The best whitetail habitat consists of deciduous trees. Among the many towering species, the deer prefer living in the shadows of ash, box elder, cottonwood, elm, oak, and red cedar. Many varieties of shrubs, including buck brush, chokecherry, wild plum and sumac are often found in the same locales. The breaks of rivers and stream courses, with their plunging gullies and prominent ridges can also hold vegetation that whitetail like. In many parts of the Midwest and Great Plains you'll find shelterbelts. Where these protective woodlands are found in close proximity to agriculture, you'll also find whitetail there. While these deer would prefer the safety of dense woods, when marshes and abandoned farmlands provide suitable cover, deer will be found there, too.

During the growing months, farm country offers everything a whitetail deer could ever want. Food, water and shelter are only a few bounds away from each other. After fields are harvested, the deer will simply melt away into nearby woodlots, marshes and other suitable refuge. In some areas, that sanctuary may well be the empty lot across from the local Wal-Mart, the median of an interstate, a golf course or even a city park. Like I said, whitetail deer have become so numerous that they are, in some instances, a nuisance.

of the healthy adult females also produce fawns annually. The beginning of the rut varies depending on how far north or south a particular whitetail population is found. In the north, the rut usually commences in October and runs through November. In places like Texas and northern Mexico the rut will not hit full swing until December and may carry over into early January.

Whitetail fawns are born in late spring through early fall, after a gestation period of approximately 6-1/2 months. Younger deer generally produce a single fawn, while older does will give birth to twins and even triplets. In any whitetail population, more fawns are produced than the total number of does. When compared with mule deer or even blacktail deer, the reproductive rate of whitetail in both live births and number of fawns born to a single doe is far greater.

Shortly after birth, the whitetail fawn is up on its feet and walking. Within a couple of weeks the newborn deer will begin to sample greenery. By 4 months of age the fawn is usually off the teat and eating everything

A deer scrape is a sure sign that a dominant buck is in the area, keep on the lookout for them.

Photo by Bob Robb

Food sources: While many naturally occurring foods, including the buds of dogwood, chokecherry, wild plum, buck brush, and wild rose, as well as oak mast, forbs and to a lesser degree some grasses and sedges, are utilized by whitetail, most of their diet is composed of various agricultural crops. This food preference alone presents one of the biggest conflicts between man and deer. And it has become a management problem for which there is no easy answer. There is a constant political struggle to meet the demands of the hunter, while somehow gaining landowner acceptance of a certain level of crop depredations. If the landowner is also a hunter, then the whole matter is less of a problem. Corporate farming presents another entirely different paradigm. Large commercial farming interests want the "most bang, for the least amount of powder." When it comes to game management, it's the last thing on any agricul-

tural CFO's (Chief Financial Officer) mind. Despite all of this, in some states like Kansas, Iowa and Nebraska, corn alone still comprises nearly half of a whitetail deer's diet. All I can say about this is, "Hallelujah for corn!"

Movement: Whitetail deer are more elegant in movement than a mule deer. While they cannot bounce stiff-legged (stott) into the air like a mule deer (a curious behavior that allows the mule deer to momentarily rise above thick sage and high grass as a predator avoidance mechanism), they can bound across wide distances in a continuous fluid movement. Furthermore, these deer can swim with ease and often will be found right deep in a swamp on a dry hammock, or on a tiny island in the middle of a river. In areas where both food and protective cover are readily available, a deer may live and die within one or two square miles. Conversely, deer living along a

Photo by Durwood Hollis

Even a solo hunter can be effective in moving deer out of cover.

narrow strip of riparian habitat may move extreme distances from their place of birth.

Just stand: A successful whitetail hunter will generally know the habits of his quarry and recognize the signs of a buck in a particular area. Whitetails are almost completely nocturnal in their behavior. This is particularly true after the opening day of deer season. What daytime movement occurs usually happens under cover of concealment. Understanding movement patterns can put the hunter in the right spot at the right time. Hunting on a stand or stationary location, is a proven whitetail hunting strategy. Elevated stands are popular in some areas. This is particularly true in the state of Texas where these raised hunting perches range from bare bones metal pipe tripods, to penthouse-deluxe box blinds. Situated above low-lying brush, the hunter is in a better position to see approaching deer. Furthermore, tree stands can be positioned high enough to get above ground level air movement, which prevents the deer from scenting the hunter.

Picking a stand location is a science in and of itself. An active deer scrape is always a good bet. Scrapes are made by rutting bucks as sign to any doe that he is in the area and ready for love. It also serves as a warning notice to other bucks that a trespasser will be in for a fight. Most bucks have more than one scrape, which they check and renew with some regularity. A fresh scrape is a sure sign that a buck is working the area. Sooner, or later, the owner of that urine soaked bare

ground will come along. Remember, he who waits is most likely to bring home the venison.

Deer sign: Tracks, beds and droppings are all solid indicators of deer activity. Fresh tracks will have sharp edges and be quite distinct in appearance. In the open, tracks deteriorate quite rapidly. When shaded, however, tracks may look fresh when they are actually hours old. Knowledgeable hunters generally discount the difference between the tracks of a buck and some larger does. If you run across some tracks of various sizes, then for sure it'll be a doe with a yearling or fawn(s). A single large set of solitary tracks was usually left by a buck—or not! And if those tracks visit a scrape, you can be sure there are antlers somewhere ahead of you. In the northeast, where the ground is generally covered with snow during deer season, tracking has become a real art. Those that are good at it kill some huge bucks. Others seem to just stumble around in the cold and wet! If I encounter a solitary track, I like to loop around ahead of the direction the tracks are leading. This enables me to get in front of the buck. Whatever method you use, don't get so involved in the track that you forget to use your eyes. There may just be a buck standing in those same tracks looking back at you!

Deer scat, or droppings are good indicators of deer activity in an area. A deer will defecate a number of times during a 24-hour period. Biologists use the number of droppings in a particular area to determine the size of the deer population. You can also use those tiny oblong pieces of digested food material as an aid in your hunt. Hard, dry scat is at least a day or so old. Soft droppings are usually several minutes to hours old. And soft, slick scat may be seconds old. How can you determine when the scat was put down? Pick up a couple and feel the texture. I don't know that scat has ever been totally responsible for filling my deer license, but I have used that knowledge to focus my hunting efforts in a specific area. A good deer hunter must be part scatologist. Like it, or not!

Like any other deer species, whitetail deer move regularly between bedding areas, feeding locations and water sources. Unlike the mule deer, whose movement patterns may be random in nature, whitetail deer use the same trails with great frequency. Furthermore, a whitetail doesn't like to be exposed anytime during daylight hours. This means that deer trails will keep inside of cover when possible. The secret here is to locate a pinch point and wait for a buck to pass. Patience, absolute silence and a cover scent should be your primary tools. Get comfortable and wait it out. An old deer hunting adage states, "the hunter who waits the longest gets the buck." It may be the last hour of the last day, but if you can gut-it-out, the best may be yet to come.

In the driver's seat: Another successful whitetail hunting tactic is the ever-popular deer drive. When pushed, however, most whitetails will "go to ground." I've seen bucks lay flat-out and remain so even when a

---

CHRONIC WASTING DISEASE (CWD)

Chronic wasting disease (CWD) has been known to exist in deer, elk, moose and caribou for some time. Originally identified in Colorado elk some 30 years ago, it now exists in both elk and deer in at least eight states, as well as parts of Canada. CWD creates tiny sponge-like holes in brain tissue and is related to mad cow disease in cattle and Creutzfeldt-Jakob disease in humans. Several individuals in Europe have contracted Creutzfeldt-Jakob disease after consuming beef infected with mad cow disease. While CWD is related to mad cow disease, no scientific evidence has yet been found that proves eating venison from deer, elk and other game could have a similar effect on humans.

Three Wisconsin men, who knew each other and ate elk and deer at wild game dinners put on by one of the men, have died of brain-destroying illnesses. Two of these individuals were confirmed to have had Creutzfeldt-Jakob disease, one passed away as a result of Pick's disease; a similar yet more common disorder. In addition to the fact that all three men were big game hunters, the only other common factor in all three deaths was their attendance at the same wild game banquets. Authorities are looking into these deaths for a possible connection to CWD.

---

hunter nearly steps on them. One thing that always seems to spook a hidden buck is to stop frequently. Then it becomes a question of whether you'll move before the whitetail breaks from cover—or not. Another whitetail deer drive avoidance tactic is doubling-back and then fleeing from cover after the hunters have passed. A well-planned whitetail deer drive not only includes standees and drivers, but also a few hunters on the outside to catch those deer that sneak by the initial drive line. When a manageable piece of cover is selected, I've seen effective deer drives conducted by as few as two hunters. Conversely, an army of orange vested Nimrods can have difficulty when it comes to pushing a buck out of quarter section of standing corn. Believe me. There's real science in an effective deer drive. Furthermore, some smart old bucks just won't be driven anywhere.

Pillow talk: Many hunters wouldn't even think of stalking whitetails in their bedding grounds. In my experience, a buck is far more alert when he's on the prowl, than when he's bedded. In the middle of the day, most hunters are back in camp, at their truck or napping. In short, the woods have quieted down and things are beginning to return to normal. This is when I want to be out hunting. Think about it for a minute. When are you most alert? I don't know about you, but when I am out and about my senses are at high alert. Strange foot steps in the hallway, a screech of tires, a distant siren, a cough in the shadows is reason for concern. In the sanctity of my own bedroom, however, nothing short of a SWAT team entry is going to get my attention. In this regard, deer aren't any different. Find where a buck beds and you're half way to filling your license.

Deer can bed in some really out-of-the-way places. While hunting along the margin of a small stretch of cultivated ground, I noticed lots of deer tracks disappearing into a stand of cattails that spread across the shallow end of an adjacent lake. These tules spread for hundreds of yards in either direction and extended well out into the lake. My curiosity got the best of me and I returned to the truck for some hip boots. Looking more like a swamp rat than a deer hunter, I braved the ankle deep mud and trudged out into the sea of waving greenery. It didn't take too long to figure things out. All of the tracks lead to various muskrat houses scattered throughout the cattails. Built sturdy enough to hold the weight of a deer, the top of one of those thrown together tangles of twigs and sticks made for a dry and secure whitetail bed. It was then just a simple matter of checking out as many of those locations as possible.

About the time the mud started to take its toll on my leg muscles, I caught sight of a 10-point buck as he splashed out of the water onto one of those oversize rodent residences. A short stalk put me into position for

Blackpowder whitetail hunters can reap significant benefits from a slow, silent hunting approach.

Photo by Bob Robb

a shot. Fortunately, the constant movement of the cattails covered my approach. When I pulled the trigger, the buck bailed off the opposite side of the muskrat house into the water. At first, I thought that somehow my bullet had gone astray. Further checking found the heavy-antlered buck lying dead in the shallow water. Then the real work began. Dragging a wet deer carcass across a broad stretch of muddy marsh, through head-high tules is enough to put anyone into cardiac arrest. It was a relief to make it back to dry land.

Not all muskrat dens have 10-point bucks bedded on them, but if there's enough evidence of deer activity in such an area, don't overlook what that sign may suggest. Since it was difficult to map out all of the muskrat houses in the marsh by sloshing around aimlessly, I hired a private pilot to fly me over the area in a small plane. From the air, I could pinpoint each location on a map. Afterwards, it was just a matter of using my compass and GPS unit to plan out a hunting strategy. Hiring a pilot and a small aircraft isn't something I'd recommend for everybody. That was a decision that cost me the better part of a week's salary. When you consider how much easier it was to plot out each location from the air, rather than spending countless hours wading around in the mud, then the cost was well worth it (at least that's what I told my wife!).

In the zone: Other bedding grounds can be just as productive. In many areas cottonwood trees grow along the course of meandering streams. Under the shade of these trees, it's hard for other vegetation to gain a foothold. And while much of the bottomland may be clogged with brush and chest-high sages, along the cottonwoods you can often see for a considerable distance. Equipped with binoculars, you can still-hunt your way right into a bedded buck. As well, it's possible to have a buck drift right in front of you.

While still-hunting some cottonwood-shaded bottom-land late one morning, I glassed a buck bedded just inside of some brushy cover. At first, only the white tips of his antlers were visible. Even though the deer was reasonably close, it took several minutes to finally put all of the visual information together (binoculars are essential in this game). Interestingly, the deer was fast asleep with his nose tucked into his tail. All it took was one well-placed shot. When I looked at my watch, the time was just past noon. On another occasion, still-hunting in the same locale, a whitetail doe emerged from cover and crossed in front of me. On her way from somewhere to somewhere else, this old girl never sensed my presence. Right behind her was a 13-point buck. The end result was one of the largest whitetail bucks I've ever taken. Was this a lucky break? Maybe. I'd much rather think that it was the product of proven hunting strategy. Still-hunting deer in bedding zones is not only possible; it has proven to be one of my most often used and effective whitetail hunting tactics. Luck? I don't think so!

Bare fisted: The sound of clashing antlers and one buck shoving another around often brings other competitors to the scene. While the literature is silent on rat-tling mule deer, it is replete with commentary on using this technique for whitetail deer. Most horn rattling takes place in Texas, but that doesn't mean it won't work elsewhere. The rub is that you have to hit the peak of the rut just right, as well as having appropriate buck-to-doe deer ratios. When it all comes together, however, a big buck can blow into you like a hurricane. Horn rattling has risen to a true art form in south Texas, with each hunter having their own preferences in tools and techniques. It's easy to get discouraged when a buck doesn't show up, but if conditions are right you're sure to produce results. Most guys use antlers from a deer they've taken in a previous season, or a pair of cast off antlers that have been picked-up off of the ground. Some may purchase a set of artificial antlers for this purpose, or utilize a bag full of sticks that when rubbed together to produce the sound of two bucks fighting. While I am not an expert at this game, in my opinion the most realistic rattling sound comes from a set of antlers that haven't completely dried out. While there is no set pattern to rattling, most guys use a combination of tine ticking mixed with hard clashing and grinding. For added emphasis, you can use the antlers to thump, rake

The author took this 13-point whitetail buck while still-hunting along a cottonwood-lined Wyoming creek.

Photo by Durwood Hollis

Photo by Bob Robb

Fights between whitetail bucks are commonplace during the rut. The sound of this combat can be imitated by rattling a set of cast-off antlers together.

and scrape the ground. Before you begin to rattle, make sure you're hidden from view. Since a buck can appear from any direction, you'll need to remain flexible. I usually rattle for at least 15 minutes at each selected location. Don't be discouraged if you fail to get results. Rattling isn't an absolute science. Sometimes it works. Sometimes it doesn't.

Whitetail calibers and guns: Western hunters are likely to choose a bolt-action rifle, chambered in .270 Win., .280 Rem., .30-06 Spfd. or 7mm Rem. Mag. for their rifle of choice. Since predominate deer of the West are mule deer, which are generally inhabitants of the open sage, rimrock country or oak grassland, such a selection makes real sense. Likewise, western whitetail hunters can rest assured that the same calibers they use for mule deer will work equally as well on whitetail. While there are some whitetail hunting venues—many of our Western states, Midwestern bean fields and Texas *senderos*—that can offer long shots, most of these deer are taken in relatively short to medium-range shooting situations. And those environments can necessitate a quick follow-up shot. This being true, you're apt to find a significant number of lever-action, pump-action and semiautomatic rifles in the hands of whitetail hunters. One of my favorite whitetail rifles is a Savage Model 99 lever gun. Other solid choices are the Browning BLR lever gun, BPR pump gun, and BAR autoloader, as well as the Remington Model 7400™ autoloader, and the Remington Model 7600™ pump.

No matter how quick you can get follow-up shot out of a lever-action, pump-gun or automatic, I'll still put my money on a boltgun. Since most of my whitetail hunting is in mixed cover, the Remington Model Seven™ makes the perfect whitetail rifle. Chambered in .260 Rem., 7mm-08 Rem. or the dependable .308 Win., this handy carbine-length boltgun can get the job done no matter where you hunt. The fact that this little rifle is now chambered in a couple of Remington short-action Ultra-Mag™ calibers, makes it an unbeatable choice. Other fast-handling selections that you might want to consider are the Savage Model 10FM Sierra or the 10FCM Scout short-action boltguns, the Sako Model 75 *Battue*, as well as the Browning, Winchester (U.S. Repeating Arms), and Weatherby short-action carbines.

LYME DISEASE

Lyme disease is caused by a tick-borne spirochete (bacteria) known as *Borrelia burgdorferi* and is the most common vector-borne disease in the United States. Vector-borne diseases are those spread by a vector such as a mosquito, tick or rodent. In the early stages, the illness may include symptoms such as a rash, fever, fatigue, headache, stiff neck, and swollen lymph glands. Weeks to months after disease onset, facial nerve palsy may be experienced. Furthermore, the heart and joints (particularly the knees) may also become involved.

In 1991, the nationwide total number of reported cases of Lyme disease was 9,470 cases. However, this number rose to 17,730 cases in 2000. Most of the disease incidents were concentrated in the Northeast (Connecticut, Maryland, Massachusetts), Mid-Atlantic (Delaware, New Jersey, New York, Pennsylvania and Rhode Island) and the upper Midwest (Minnesota and Wisconsin). However, a significant number of cases were reported in California. Obviously, this disease presents a significant threat to hunters in the primary areas of epidemic focuses.

Since hunters regularly enter tick-infested habitats, those who pursue deer are at particular risk for this disease. No matter when during the year hunters enter the woods, it is recommended that a tick repellant be used; elbow length plastic or rubber gloves should be employed during field dressing and skinning procedures; and any ticks seen on your body or clothes must be promptly removed. A Lyme disease vaccine was licensed in 1998 and should be considered as preventive treatment by those frequenting tick-infected areas.

When it comes to caliber selection, any chambering based on the venerable .30-06 Springfield (.25-06 Rem., .270 Win., and .280 Rem.) are all solid whitetail medicine. Likewise, those based on the .308 Winchester (.243 Win., .260 Rem., 7mm-08 Rem., and the .358 Win.) are good short-action choices. The 6.5x55 Swedish Mauser is another favorite whitetail caliber. For close cover work, the .30-30 Win. and .35 Rem. are popular in some regions. And for those demanding bean-field and *sendero* whitetail shots, you can't beat the .264 Win., 7mm Rem. Mag., or any of the Remington Ultra-Mag™ chamberings. Likewise, the Winchester .270, 7mm or .30 Short Magnums, 7mm Shooting Times Westerner, and any of the Lazzeroni or Weatherby magnum numbers are equally as flat-shooting.

Shotgunners have a wide range of big game scatterguns to choose from. Most manufacturers make shotguns specifically designed for deer hunting, in both bolt-action, pump-action and autoloaders. And interchangeable rifled barrels or screw-in rifled choke tubes make it a snap to convert your bird whacker into a deer gun.

In most close cover whitetail hunting venues, a blackpowder hunter can be as successful as a center-fire rifle shooter. Either a .45- or .50-caliber blackpowder rifle can be used on whitetail, with the nod going to the larger caliber. Traditional blackpowder deer hunters are usually fans of flintlock or percussion rifles. Center-fire riflemen who take advantage of blackpowder hunting seasons often select an inline design. Furthermore, Savage makes a front-loading rifle that can use smokeless propellants. And hunters can choose between blued steel rifles with hardwood stocks and brass furniture, or all-stainless steel models with molded synthetic stocks. Sight choices include classic open iron sights, rear peeps, light pipe front and rear sights and low magnification scopes. Propellant choices are equally as diverse with your choice of granulated blackpowder (Elephant, Goex, etc.), blackpowder substitute (Pyrodex) in granulated and pellet form, and clean-burning non-blackpowder alternatives. As well, a wide range of projectiles—balls, sabots, conicals—are also available for the front-loader. Blackpowder deer hunting regulations vary from state-to-state and province-to-province, so check the regulations carefully in your hunting area.

Sticks and strings: Bowhunters are right at home hunting whitetail deer. Most will select one of the modern

Photo by Durwood Hollis

In wide-open spaces, a flat-shooting rifle is the best key to whitetail success.

Photo by Bob Robb

Obviously, the use of a bow isn't a hindrance to whitetail success.

compound bow designs that offers enhanced arrow speed for flatter shooting trajectory. Either aluminum and graphite arrows are popular. Aluminum shafts are the most economical, but graphite offers deeper penetration. Both feather fletch and soft plastic stabilizer vanes can be found on arrows. I've used both and have found that the plastic holds up better in inclement weather. Equally as diverse is your choice of broadhead designs. Broadheads kill by cutting through and interrupting the blood supply. Select a broadhead that can provide the ultimate in edge sharpness. Forget about price, it's performance that counts. Of course, there is a whole host of other gear (sights, string silencers, release mechanisms, arrow quivers, etc.) that will become part of your kit. While there are lots of archery gear choices, nothing is more important than arrow placement. And the key to bowhunting success is practice, practice and more practice.

The bottom line: In recent years, whitetail hunting has become overburdened with gear and gadgets. Some writers would have you believe that to be successful you must acquire all of the leading edge technology. I am reminded that most of the companies producing all of that stuff are also outdoor magazine advertisers. A whitetail hunter needs a rifle (maybe a handgun) or a bow, a handful of shells or a quiver full of arrows, a good pair boots, a sharp knife and a solid mastery of basic hunting skills. Does this mean that cover scent, game calls, and all the rest aren't necessary? Everything has its place in the scheme of things. Just remember it's the magician, not all the bells and whistles, that produces the magic of successful whitetail hunting.

Photo by Durwood Hollis

It's your ability as a hunter, not gear and gadgets, which gets the job done.

The Coues deer may not seem like much of a whitetail, but it's unique enough to have its own record book classification. Mario Palacio (left) took this fine desert whitetail with guide Duwane Adams (right).

DESERT DWARFS: COUES DEER

The Coues deer may just be another ordinary whitetail subspecies, but hunting these tiny desert deer is an extraordinary experience.

The sun had almost completed its daily sojourn across the sky, when I noticed a flicker of movement at the top of a distant ridge. Even with binoculars, in the failing light I could barely make out the image of a deer. Whether or not it was a buck, let alone the kind of buck I wanted, was beyond the ability of my moderate magnification optical instrument. It would take the extreme visual enhancement of guide Duwane Adams's tripod-mounted 15x60 binoculars to confirm this particular sighting.

"It's a whitetail buck all right. There are three good points on each antler beam and nice eye guards. Let's move to the edge of this canyon quickly while we still have enough daylight to shoot," Duwane said with authority.

What is a Coues deer? Hunting whitetail deer in the Arizona desert seemed somehow out of place. Yet, the tiny Coues deer is definitely a whitetail. Interestingly, this is the only whitetail subspecies that merits its own category in the record books. A U.S. Army quartermaster, Lt. Elliot Coues, first identified these deer during the Apache wars in the 19th century. Initially, the minuscule deer were thought to be a unique species. Today, scientists know more about this animal and have classified it as *Odocoileus virginianus couesi*, which makes it just one of the many whitetail subspecies. Even so, the Coues deer is so unique that it has retained its own distinct record book classification.

The range of the Coues deer includes southern Arizona, southwestern New Mexico and across the border into the northern Mexican states of Sonora, Sinaloa and western Chihuahua. While these deer are desert dwellers, they reside only in isolated mountain ranges where

Photo by Bob Robb

Coues deer country is extremely rugged. Just getting to where the deer live can be a real chore.

suitable food and water can be found. Most are thinly distributed in pockets between 3,000 and 8,000 feet in elevation. It is here in the stands of manzanita, mountain mahogany, scrub oak and the desert grasses that are found on many south-facing slopes that the Coues deer makes its home. Good bets for stateside Coues deer hunting are the Chiricahua, Catalina, Dragoon, Galiuro, Peloncillo and Santa Rita mountains, as well as the Canelo Hills. In Old Mexico, the lower Sierra Madres in the state of Sonora have a sizeable population of these tiny deer. While both the Coues deer and desert mule deer range overlaps, the little whitetail will be found at higher elevations and in regions of predictable summer rain.

Well suited to the southwestern desert country, the Coues deer is slate gray in color, with white underparts. White circles around the eyes and a band of white across the muzzle distinguish the Coues deer face. The usual white throat patch, so prominent on whitetail found in other parts of the country, is barely discernible. Both the ears and the tail are larger than would be expected, rivaling that of the mule deer found on the desert floor. The tail is gray to reddish-black on top, with a completely white underside. The tail is quite prominent and when these animals are surprised they will "flag" (wave the tail from side-to-side) their tail as they flee. These are particularly petite animals, with bucks measuring just over 30 inches in height at the shoulders. Even in the best of condition, a Coues deer will only field dress out at about 75 pounds. The small size of the Coues deer turns out to be an advantage, however, when you have to pack one out of the backcountry. Boned-out, you'll only have 35 to 40 pounds of useable meat. Add the head skin cape and antlers to that load and you can easily understand why I like to hunt these little deer.

Why Coues deer?: What is so special about the Coues deer? Since the antlers of a "shootable" buck will only measure about 12 to 14 inches in outside spread, with three main tines and an eye guard on each antler beam, this is a question that begs for an answer. The explanation can be found in the Boone and Crockett record book. The minimum qualifying score (the score needed to put an animal in the book) for a typical whitetail is 170 points; the same minimum for Coues deer is just 120 points. While finding a record book Coues buck isn't easy, someone who is willing to invest the time and boot leather can be successful. In fact, this may be the easiest whitetail for a dedicated hunter to receive record book recognition.

Hunting the desert whitetail: It took a solid eight hours to drive from my home in southern California to the town of San Manuel (one flashing stop sign and a convenience store) in southern Arizona. It was here, that guide Duwane Adams makes his home. This tall

and lanky outdoorsman has earned a reputation as one of the southwest's top big game guides and can boast of several record book entries with clients. Highly recommend by several friends who had previously hunted with him, Duwane is "the man" when it comes to Coues deer hunting.

When the alarm woke me at 2:00 a.m., I had a hard time shaking the cobwebs from my sleep-deprived brain. Shortly thereafter, Duwane and I piled into his truck and set off for a nearby mountain range. In the dark, it was difficult to realize just how steep the terrain we would be hunting really was. Later, after about an hour of straight uphill hiking, my legs let me know that this was tough country.

One of the hinge pins of Duwane Adams's hunting strategy is to get high early and settle in before daylight. To understand this philosophy, you need to know that

From sunup to sundown, it will take dedication and hours sitting behind high-magnification binoculars to score on a trophy Coues deer buck.

Duwane uses his eyes, rather than his feet, to find deer. Most of the time that (read that as all day long if necessary) he's in the field hunting, he'll be sitting behind tripod-mounted, high-magnification binoculars. This isn't just casual glassing. Duwane actually scrutinizes every square inch of the vista under examination.

The eastern horizon was just starting to "pink up" by the time we made it to where Duwane wanted to be. Quietly, we moved in below the ridgeline and found a comfortable position from which to glass. I knew it was going to be a long day when Duwane pulled a fanny cushion out of his backpack. I made a mental note to acquire something more comfortable than the rolled-up jacket stuffed under my posterior. We had to wait almost an hour before it was light enough to start glassing, but Duwane emphatically stated that it's "better to be early, than late."

When the first rays of the newborn sun ripped the curtain of darkness from the landscape, I counted 18 deer scattered out across the east-facing slope below us. Amazingly, half of the animals were bucks! I could only guess at what lingered in the scrub oak and manzanita tangles at the top of the slope. Later on in the day, Duwane would tell me that typically the Coues deer buck-to-doe ratio is quite high. A good thing, because just finding these little deer isn't all that easy.

For the rest of the morning, I sat quietly next to Duwane as he continued to glass. He looked over the bucks that were out in the open, but without exception they were all small six-pointers (forked horns with eye guards). About 10:00 a.m., he nudged my shoulder and told me to look through his binoculars. At first, the only thing I could see was a distant hillside. After a while I noticed what looked like several ants in the field of view.

"Those are Coues deer about a mile and a half away from where we are located," Duwane explained.

Before I could even reply, Duwane was packing up his gear. A sure sign that we were going to change locations, I followed suit. It was then that I noticed that the truck was barely visible in the distance. Oh well, I didn't come all the way to Arizona for a stroll in the

Obviously, Robert Finilli (left) is pleased with the nine-point Coues deer buck that guide Duwane Adams (right) found for him.

park. It took us about an hour to get back to where the vehicle was parked. In the rugged arid terrain, hiking down was almost as difficult as our predawn uphill march. To say my feet were sore and legs ached would have been an understatement. The morning's hunt made me realize just how physically demanding hunting desert whitetail can be.

While we were driving, Duwane explained his plan for the afternoon. After looking the situation over where we had spent the morning, it was obvious that a good buck wasn't to be found. Curious about the handful of deer we'd glassed several ridges over, Duwane wanted to see if we couldn't find something more promising in that area. Getting there, however, wasn't all that easy. After about an hour of driving, the road (if you can call it that) we were on simply vanished. Pulling into a narrow canyon, Duwane announced, "We're here."

Photo by Durwood Hollis

The author learned that it takes a backpack and boot leather to be successful on Coues deer. He took this eight-point buck in Arizona's Catalina Mountains.

Once again, it was backpack and boot leather time. Straight up a long and winding ridge we went, taking care not to stumble on the fist-size rocks that blanketed the terrain. Another hour passed before Duwane announced, "This is it!" To me, it all looked like the rest of the country—rough, dry and foreboding. Flopping down on a narrow game trail, we did our best to get comfortable. It was going to be a long wait until the shadows started to lengthen. Still tired from my long drive to Arizona, as well as all of the activities of the day, I dozed off like a drunk after a Saturday-night binge.

When I awoke, Duwane was already glassing the opposite slope. And so it went for the rest of the afternoon. Even though we had spotted several deer in this location earlier in the day, they were noticeably absent now.

Just as the sun started to slip behind the mountains, Duwane leaned back and asked, "Hungry?" Since the only meal we'd eaten was a meager breakfast more than 12 hours earlier, the answer was obvious. Besides, I think he heard my stomach growl.

"It's going to be hard working our way down to the truck by flashlight, so let's start back while we can still see," Duwane said.

It was at that moment, I noted the deer drop over the top of the ridge mentioned at the outset of this chapter. The animal started to work its way down the slope, feeding as it went. Once Duwane clearly identified it as the category of buck he'd been looking for, it was time to shoot, or go home.

"It's a long way across this canyon, so break a little daylight over that buck's shoulders. Give me all of your extra shells. If you run your rifle dry, I'll hand them to you one at a time. That buck is so far away he'll never know we're shooting at him," Duwane whispered in my ear.

My shooting rig, a Browning A-Bolt chambered in .243 Winchester and topped with a 2x7 scope, had never been proven on game. During several previous sessions at the range, however, I had gained confidence in its ability to print minute-of-angle groups. Since I knew that most shots at Coues deer might wring the best out of the rifle, I had sighted the rifle in to hit 3 inches high at 100 yards. I was to discover that every bit of elevation, both from range work and manual target acquisition, would be necessary to put my bullet on target. Taking up the slack in the trigger, I said a silent prayer for a clean sear break.

At the shot, the deer bolted down the slope a few yards, then stopped and stood still.

"Shoot again, but hold just below the spine" Duwane instructed. The second shot was a repeat of my first attempt, but this time I could see dust fly up from behind the deer. Working the bolt for the third time, I settled in again on the animal.

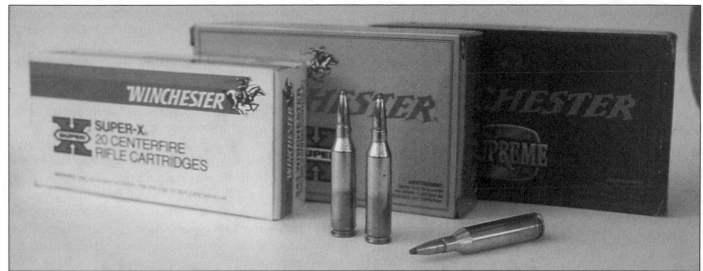

The .243 Winchester is a fine Coues deer caliber. With a good assortment of bullet styles, this reliable 6mm can be counted on even at the 300-yard mark.

"He's history," Duwane said as he put his glasses down.

Indeed, the buck stumbled a few feet and collapsed in a heap. There was no need for a third shot. The hunt was over.

"It's getting dark fast. You better get over there to where the deer went down before we lose daylight. I'll stay here and direct you with hand signals," Duwane said.

By the time I made it to where the buck lay, daylight was gone. Examining the deer, I discovered that my first shot had hit just below the spine, missing the lungs entirely. That explained the sudden reaction when the animal bolted down the slope. I could also see that my second bullet had struck lower, rupturing both lungs and exiting on the far side. This was a real testimony to the ability of a 100-grain Nosler® Partition® bullet to get the job done—even at the ragged edge of ballistic performance.

The little buck was a fine representative of his species. His antlers carried a total of eight-points and the outside spread measured a tad beyond 13 inches. Whitetail hunters from other parts of the country wouldn't have been impressed with what they would consider a smallish buck. If you have a passing understanding of what Coues deer are supposed to look like, then the buck at my feet would have drawn several compliments.

After I field dressed the deer, Duwane volunteered to carry it back to the truck. Absent its entrails and bodily fluids, the diminutive buck weighed only about 70 pounds. Duwane just picked the carcass up off of the ground and tossed it onto his shoulders. All the way back to the truck, the extra weight of the deer didn't even cause Duwane to breathe hard. Like I said, Coues deer aren't very large.

Hunting tactics: Both javelina and Coues deer are hard to see in their desert habitat. Constant herd movement is what reveals the presence of javelina, but the desert whitetail isn't a herd animal. The camouflage color of the pelage, as well as the slow feeding movement, makes Coues deer almost invisible to the naked

For handloaders, the Nosler® 6mm, Ballistic Tip®, 90-grain bullet is a great choice for desert whitetails.

Photo by Duwane Adams

It took guide Duwane Adams (front) hours of glassing to locate this nice eight-point Coues deer buck. Craig Hayward (rear) brought the hunt to a close when he put his bullet on the mark.

eye. The only way to effectively hunt these deer is to use high-magnification binoculars and glass from a prominent location. The three cardinal rules of Coues deer hunting are: get high early, get comfortable and use a lot of glass.

When Duwane and I hunted together, our assent into whitetail country began well before first light. After getting out of bed, we ate breakfast and packed our gear (every Coues deer hunter will need to carry a backpack). Our plan also had to include extra time to allow for driving to the hunting area, as well as hiking into the backcountry. The best time to catch Coues deer out in the open is the first hour or so of daylight. After that, you'll have to really search for the animals. As Duwane said earlier, "better to be early, than late."

If you intend on spending lots of time behind a pair of tripod-mounted binoculars, you must be comfortable. All of the cactus spines and tiny rocks typically found in desert terrain don't make for a cozy sitting. Without some type of cushion under your posterior, after a few minutes you'll wiggle like a coon dog with a tick. An old-time minister once remarked that his "congregation would maintain interest in my sermon as long as long as the pews were comfortable." If a hard church bench can make one's interest wane, then just think what sitting on a rock-strewn ridge in some remote desert mountain range will do to your enthusiasm for an extended glassing sesssion. Do yourself a favor and purchase some kind of fanny cushion.

What's a lot of glass? Most Coues deer guides use 15x60 (5mm exit pupil) porro prim binoculars. This

Photo by Jim Matthews

It can take all day behind a pair of tripod-mounted, high-power binoculars to find the caliber of Coues deer buck you're looking for.

When it comes to the pursuit of Coues deer, well-broken-in boots, a sturdy backpack and a pair of big binoculars are essential tools of the hunt.

Photo by Durwood Hollis

offers both the magnification and light transmission necessary to be useful throughout the entire day. Zeiss binoculars seem to be the instruments of choice, but other optical firms also make similar quality products. Some guys use 20x80 instruments, but they're really bothersome to carry. I've used a pair of Bushnell Elite 12x50 binoculars when hunting and found them about the right combination of magnification and carrying size. I've even seen some 10x40 and 10x50 binoculars in the field, but they're just about entry-level magnification in this game.

If you're used to a pair of shirt pocket or compact binoculars, then hauling a high-magnification instrument around will make you feel like someone has strapped a millstone around your neck. Guides who use outsize binoculars carry them in their packs, which makes good sense. However, it is possible to carry large binoculars across your body, slung under your left or right armpit. Substitute a wide neoprene carrying strap for the narrow one that often comes on some models, then the extra weight won't cut into your neck. The later chapter on optics has a lot more information about using binoculars, so I won't pursue this subject any deeper here. Suffice it to say, consistent glassing is the best way to find a good desert whitetail buck.

Clothing, boots and gear: While the desert may be the desert, don't fool yourself into thinking that the ambient temperature can't get uncomfortably cold. While I've never had to wear long underwear on a Coues deer hunt, packing a sweater, jacket and a pair of gloves is a good idea. This is especially true early when you're hiking into and out of any desert mountain range. A sweater or jacket will ward off the early morning or late afternoon chill. And gloves will protect your hands from sharp rocks and cactus spines.

You'll definitely need a pair of well broken-in boots. You may have to splash across an infrequent desert creek, but ultra-waterproof boots aren't really necessary for desert hiking. Leather, or leather and fabric combination boot construction can handle an occasional dousing without getting your feet wet. Since ankle support is an important consideration when hiking over rough terrain, I like boots that are 7 to 9 inches in height. Whatever kind of boots you wear, don't fail to wear two pairs of socks. This will prevent sore spots and blisters from plaguing your feet.

You'll need a good pack. External frame packs are the best choice for carrying heavy loads, but the boned-out venison; antlers and a head skin cape from a Coues deer won't weigh any more than about 50 pounds. I've used several different internal frame packs and found them easy to manage and completely capable of hauling weights of up to 75 pounds comfortably. One thing for sure, you'll need more than a day pack and less than a full-size external frame pack. Now, you decide!

Most Coues deer hunts are conducted from a base camp. You'll hike deep into a designated mountain

Hunter and guide have hiked deep into Coues deer country. Now, it's a matter of intense glassing and patience.

This Winchester Model 70 bolt-action rifle, chambered in .264 Win. magnum and topped with a Bushnell Elite 4x16 scope can handle any shot in the rugged desert country that Coues deer call home.

range, and then spend most of the day glassing for deer. Dehydration in the desert is a very real possibility, so carry a canteen of water (sometimes two are necessary) with you at all times. A topographical map of the hunting area, a flashlight (extra batteries and bulb) and a couple of heavyweight plastic bags for boned-out venison are other essential items to carry in your pack. And don't forget your knife, blade sharpener and hunting license.

A word of caution: Two potential dangers can be encountered in desert mountain ranges—bad falls and rattlesnakes. Most of the spills I've seen have happened to hunters who couldn't handle the demands of a Coues deer hunt. A lack of prior physical conditioning combined with fatigue usually was the combined cause of most serious injuries. Coues deer country can be hard on you. If you accidentally fall, the resultant injury can range from just a scrape to a broken bone—or worse! Don't expect to step from your every day urban existence into a desert mountain range without putting in some earnest physical conditioning ahead of time. Start well before hunting season and continue right up to the time you leave for hunting camp. Activities like distance walking, hiking, jogging, bicycling and swimming will serve to tone your body. Even an aerobic class at your local health club is well worth the effort.

Rattlesnakes are really more of a nuisance than a danger. However, the poisonous serpents are well distributed throughout the lower elevations of most Coues deer habitats. When you're hiking in the dark, use a flashlight to illuminate your path. Once, while working our way into the Catalina Mountains, north of Tucson, Arizona, Duwane Adams and I blundered into a rattlesnake convention. Since there was plenty of moonlight, we didn't use our flashlights—not a good idea. Without adequate light, there was no way we could have seen the nasty vipers before stepping into their realm. Duwane was the first one to encounter a snake. His reaction was complete with Pogo stick leaps, punctuated with four-letter words. It seemed like everywhere he jumped, he landed close to a rattler. Before long, the entire hillside was alive with the sound of agitated snakes. I thought it was humorous, until I took a step backwards and heard one of the reptiles sound off right at my feet. Needless to say, the flashlights immediately came out of our packs. Neither of us got bitten, but that possibility existed. A rattlesnake bite may not kill you, but the venom can do extensive muscle damage. Wherever you are in the desert, watch where you put your hands and your feet.

Coues deer calibers: Since Coues deer aren't very large; it doesn't take a whole heap of bullet weight to put one on the ground. Projectiles weighing 100 to

120 grains are more than enough to churn up the insides of a dinky desert whitetail. This is where calibers like the .243 Win., 6mm Rem., .250 Sav., .257 Roberts, .260 Rem., .25-06 Rem., .270 Win., 7mm-08 Rem., and the .280 Remington really shine. For those that want the flattest trajectory possible the .240 Wby., .264 Win. Mag. or the Lazzeroni .257 Scramjet® are all solid choices

I like lightweight, short-action boltguns for this assignment, so my caliber preferences lean toward the .243 Win, 7mm-08 Rem. and the .260 Remington. All three of these chamberings are available in the handy little Remington Model Seven, which weighs only about 6 pounds. Another rifle that seems made for this kind of hunting is the Remington titanium boltgun. Chambered in .260 Rem., .270 Win. and .30-06 Spfd. this lightweight pill-thrower weighs in at slightly more than 5 pounds.

Do you need a guide? Desert mountain ranges are some of the roughest country you'll encounter. While Coues deer are well distributed in the southwest and northern Mexico, they are not particularly in abundance anywhere. Scattered in sparse numbers across an expansive range of desert mountains, the diminutive deer can be hard to locate—especially for the uninitiated. While it's possible to find these deer on your own, unless you live in close proximity to Coues deer country such an endeavor may take several trips. Just mastering the art of glassing with high-magnification binoculars will necessitate lots of serious work before it becomes second nature. Most hunters simply don't have the time it takes to find pockets of deer and then locate a trophy buck.

Those who are looking for a "book" on Coues deer should consider engaging the services of a guide. Guides spend months scouting out remote canyons in search of quality animals. They can hike into and out of any desert mountain range in the dark without getting lost. Most importantly, a guide will be far more able to judge trophy antlers than most of us. An experienced hunting guide should be able to estimate antler width within an inch or two, even at considerable distance. Rather than trying to go it on your own, a Coues deer hunter (especially an out-of-state hunter) is always better off with a guide.

What about licenses? Southeastern Arizona probably has the largest concentration of Coues anywhere in the West. At one time, licenses to hunt Coues deer in

Rugged, vast and seemingly empty, Coues deer country is demanding to hunt, even for those experienced at the game.

Arizona were fairly easy to acquire. This situation has changed over the years and getting a license isn't always a sure thing. You can avoid the license draw by hunting on an Indian Reservation, but permits are costly. New Mexico has a smaller population of these animals, with their range restricted to the extreme southwestern corner of the state. Like Arizona, there's a license drawing, but outfitters can obtain private land hunting permits. Once again, don't expect these permits to come without substantial cost.

Coues deer can also be hunted in Mexico, but that is an expensive undertaking. You'll either have to negotiate the tangle of Mexican bureaucracy to obtain a hunting license, gun permit and a visa, or utilize the services of an outfitter. Believe me, trying to deal with Mexican authorities can be a real hassle. Furthermore, you can't hunt south of the border without a licensed guide. You're better off booking a hunt with an outfitter and letting him deal with all of the headaches.

The least expensive way to obtain a Coues deer license is participation in the Arizona drawing. You may not score on your first try, but most applicants are able to get a license within three years. Who knows? You might be lucky and pull a license the first time you submit an application. Once you have that coveted document in hand, then the planning begins.

The last word: Since I've spent much of my life in southern California, the desert has always been one of my favorite hunting grounds. I like to see farther than just few yards ahead and the wide-open arid country provides a broad vista for viewing. Even where there is some cover, it's never so thick that you can't find deer with the right visual tools. Besides, there's just something about the optical search that has always been exciting. In my book, Coues deer hunting has what I am looking for and in equal proportion to my own abilities. If it wasn't so, then it wouldn't be called hunting!

High, wide and handsome can all be attributes of a trophy mule deer buck.

ALL EYES AND EARS: MULE DEER

*Well adapted for life in the broad expanses of the North American West,
the magnificent mule deer can be found from the desert floor to well above the timberline.*

The sun was well past its zenith by the time we had hunted to the extreme western end of Two-Ocean plateau. A promontory of nearly 10 miles in length, characterized by the near absence of vegetation along the top of its entire length, the movement of an ancient glacier had formed this bulge in the earth. At an altitude of nearly 10,000 feet above sea level, from the top of the winding plateau one could see as far west as the jagged

Tetons and north into the wild expanse of Yellowstone National Park. A lush valley, from which both creeks eventually leading to both the Pacific and Atlantic oceans bubbled forth in a single spring, lay to the south. And to the east, the verdant Yellowstone meadows could be seen in the distance. With such a panorama, one was left with a breathtaking view of Wyoming's Bridger-Teton Wilderness.

The right place, at the right time is what mule deer hunting is all about.

Photo by Dwane Adams

A successful hunt is over.
Now the real work begins!

Photo by Jim Matthews

On the previous day, outfitter and guide, John Winter, had brought us by horseback to his Atlantic Creek elk camp. The more than 20 miles of trail and six hours in the saddle had extracted its toll from all of us. Sore muscles, little sleep and a slight touch of altitude sickness were enough to sap the energy from any would-be hunter. Now, some 24 hours later, my lower extremities should have been getting used to the saddle. No such luck.

For much of the morning and throughout the early afternoon, my guide and I had ridden along the top of Two-Ocean Plateau. When we came to a likely overlook, the horses were tied up and the serious work of glassing for elk and looking for fresh sign was undertaken. It had all been in vain. I was sore and tired and my eyes ached from hours of glassing alpine meadows.

The heat of the sun, initially tempered by an early morning mist rising out of the bottoms, had long since pushed the elk deep into the surrounding timber. And with the exception of a solitary covey of blue grouse, our hunting efforts had proved fruitless.

A well-worn phrase states that, "Opening day of elk season is worth the rest of the season." Unfortunately, this particular opening day hadn't proved to be worth spit! With the sun fast slipping toward the horizon, thoughts of a hot meal and a warm sleeping bag began to invade conscious thought. To say that my attention span had begun to slip a bit was an understatement.

Riding just below the crest of the plateau, we followed a faint game trail along a narrow bench. A massive set of jagged rocks, long ago weathered-out from the soil, formed the lower lip of the bench. Below the rocks, the plateau continued its downward drop nearly 2,000 feet toward Pacific Creek. Suddenly, the guide turned in his saddle, looked in my direction and silently mouthed the words, "big buck." Following the guide's lead, I pulled my rifle from the scabbard and swung out of the saddle in one fluid motion.

"I saw a huge mule deer buck just below us on the next bench. Let's tie the horses up and have a look," my guide whispered.

It only took a minute to secure the saddle stock to a cluster of stunted trees. Walking quietly, we moved down the slope to a break in the rocky lip of the bench. It didn't take a pair of binoculars and hours of glassing to find the buck. He was right out in the open with his head buried in a bush. Apparently, the hormonal urge of the rut was wreaking havoc with his emotions. This old boy was in the process of assaulting the vegetation with his antlers in a manner that

questioned the sanity of the moment. First he'd move one way, and then the other as the tattered bush took the brunt of his vengeance.

Initially, I couldn't get a sense of this mule-eared old bruiser's headgear. Sure, I could see antlers, but the bush obscured my view. Long seconds added up to several minutes before I could even get a glimpse of his cranial protrusions. Finally, the buck took a couple of steps backward and pulled his head out of the bush. Now, there was no doubt as to the caliber of this particular animal. Heavy and wide, the deer's antlers were impressive—to say the least.

If one could pick a definitive oxymoronic hunting moment, then this was it! I had come to Two-Ocean Plateau for elk and now was looking at the biggest mule deer of my entire hunting career. With a valid deer license in my pocket, the decision was easy. I quietly chambered a round, found the buck in my

Photo by Durwood Hollis

It can happen just like this almost anywhere in the West.

The black-tipped tail, slopping nasal ridge and characteristic antler configuration identify this buck as a mule deer.

Photo by Jim Matthews

scope and took up the slack in the trigger. The distance that separated us wasn't far; nonetheless, I still had to compensate for the extreme down slope target presentation. Finding my point of aim slightly below and just behind the point-of-the-shoulder, I squeezed the trigger. At the shot, the buck sagged but still remained on his feet. However, sanguine evidence of a well-place bullet was clearly evident at my point-of-aim.

"Shoot again," my guide hissed through his teeth.

I slammed another round in the chamber and started to make target acquisition, but before I could even bring the rifle to bear, the mortally wounded deer took a couple steps forward and collapsed. In that instant, the entire paradigm shifted from hunting to game recovery and trophy work.

It was almost dark before we finished field dressing the animal. I did, however, measure the antlers. If outside antler width of 30 inches is the holy grail of mule deer hunters, this buck certainly qualified as worthy of any Crusader's effort. Add to this five separate, equal and distinct antler points arising from a pair of heavy main beams, it was a sure bet that my taxidermist would be sending me another bill.

While elk and deer can often be found in the same area, both species prefer different kinds of food and cover. However, where a small stretch of deer habitat exists, sometimes a hunter can get lucky. This is just what happened in the above-cited instance. Since few license holders were willing to hunt deer 20 miles from the nearest road head, the isolated nature of Two-Ocean Plateau had allowed the buck to reach full maturity. Obviously, the animal possessed the right genetic potential. This combined with the right nutrients had produced a magnificent set of antlers. When opportunity presented itself, we were in the right place, at the right time.

Mule deer range: Mule deer, known by the scientific designation as *Odocoileus hemionus*, can be found in all of the Western states, including Califor-

nia, eastern Oregon, eastern Washington, Idaho, Montana, Wyoming, Nevada, Colorado, New Mexico, Arizona and the Dakotas. These deer can also be found along the western fringe of Kansas, Nebraska, Oklahoma and Texas. Western Canada, northern Mexico and the Mexican state of Baja, California can also boast of their own mule deer populations. Lower ambient temperatures, intense weather fronts and snow depth stimulate vertical movement between summer and winter ranges. When access to food supplies becomes difficult, the deer are forced to migrate to lower elevations. While mule deer can be found in many parts of their vast range, these animals prefer areas of high sage plains or rolling oak grassland, characterized by rocky outcroppings and deep canyons. And depending on the time of the year, mule

Photo by John Higley

This 4x4 buck, taken by outdoor writer John Higley, exhibits the typical mule deer antler configuration.

This 3x4 buck is a good example of uneven antler development.

deer can be found in any of these regions from above timberline to right down on the desert floor.

Family ties: The mule deer is a member of the family *Cervidae*, which interestingly enough also includes moose, elk and caribou. Segments of this family grouping can be found worldwide and in a variety of habitats—from the arctic to tropics. While related to the whitetail, mule deer are quite distinct in appearance and behavior. Nevertheless, where mule deer are found in riparian habitats, their behavior is almost identical to that of the whitetail. Conversely, the Coues whitetail of the Southwest and northern Mexico manifests behavior patterns not unlike the mule deer. Obviously, the elements of terrain and vegetation have as much to do with deer behavior as do inherited genetic influences.

It's all in the looks: The characteristic name, "mule deer," came about because of the overly large "mule-like" ears of this species. These animals also tend to have curved, or "Roman" nose bridge (apology to members of the Italian community that may take offense), which also contributes to the equine similarity. At the shoulder, a mature mule deer stands 36 to 42 inches in height and can weigh from 150 to over 300

pounds on the hoof. In the wild, mule deer life expectancy is about 10 years. The male, or buck, is somewhat larger than the female, or doe. These animals are generally dark gray-brown in color, with a distinctive white rump patch and a black-tipped tail. However, a wide range of color variation occurs within the various mule subspecies. Furthermore, the appearance of these deer changes as the dark, thick winter pelage is shed and the lighter color of the summer coat is manifest. And where these deer come into contact with certain kinds of vegetation, oils from leaves and stems can discolor the hair to the point that it can appear almost black.

Antler wisdom: Mature male mule deer antlers branch to form two equal forks, from which additional tines can arise. Unlike whitetail hunters, who count the total number of antler tines (i.e., 6-point, 8-point, 10-point buck, etc.), mule deer hunters only count the tines on a single antler side (i.e., forked-horn, 3-point or 3x3, 4-point or 4x4, etc.). Antlers are shed each year, generally in late winter. Within a matter of weeks, new antler buds (pedicles) will appear. Antler growths is entirely dependent on genetic predisposition, available food resources and age. As the buck matures, the antlers will increase in number of points, width and mass. The Rocky Mountain mule deer, the major mule species found throughout much of the West, is known to produce the largest antlers. Some individual animals have been taken with antlers measuring more than 40-inches in width. However, an outside antler measurement of 24 to 28 inches, with four or five points on each side, is typical of a mature Rocky Mountain mule deer.

Out of the ordinary: Atypical mule deer antler formations are also possible. Some of these anomalies are due to injury. When antlers are in the formative stage, they are relatively malleable. Should a buck fall, inadvertently run into something or experience a similar accident, an antler tine may become damaged. Even an injury to a leg can result in antler malformation (usually the antler on the opposite side of the injured appendage). Bucks can also produce asymmetrical racks. I've seen spike/forked-horn, 3x4, 4x5 and a host of other lopsided antler formations. Drop-points are another antler abnormality. These tines drop down and away from the main antler beam. Most often a single drop-tine is produced. And occasionally there are antlers with double drop-points, one situated on each side. The most unusual mule deer antler configuration can be found in the famous "Cactus" bucks of the Southwest. These deer have a whole head full of antler points, without any seeming regularity to their formation.

The mid-point of life and beyond: Deer antler formation really comes into its own when a buck hits the 5- to 7-year bracket. At this midpoint of life, the deer is fully mature and produces his largest set of antlers. Beyond this stage, antler size will diminish in all aspects. As an example of what advancing years can do to antler growth, let me share with you an experience from a few seasons back. Hunting in the high plains of Wyoming, I had located a huge buck bedded in the bottom of a sage-choked ravine. The deer was about 400 yards away from my vantage point. Quickly, I worked out a strategy with my hunting buddy. He would loop around out of sight and drop well below the deer. Using the winding ravine for cover, he'd try to get close enough to the buck for a clear shot. If the deer caught his scent, then the only possible escape route was along the bottom of the ravine. This would bring the animal right past me at scant yardage. No matter how things turned out, we just knew that one of us was about to put venison in the freezer and antlers on the wall.

My hunting companion never got close enough to even see the deer. Having survived enough seasons to know when danger was near, the buck slipped out of his bed and headed in my direction. Predictably, the deer ran along the bottom of the ravine and held his head low and out of sight. And it wasn't until he was nearly on top of me, that I got a clear look at his antlers.

Astonishingly, that old boy had the heaviest and widest set of forked-horn headgear I'd ever seen. One look at his shrunken muscle mass and protruding ribs let me know that he was well beyond his prime. Obviously in physical decline, the buck no longer possessed the hormonal ability to produce trophy quality antlers. I never even touched the trigger. Besides, venison from that old buck would have been as tough as shoe leather.

Battle weapons: Mule deer antlers serve as both an offensive and defensive weapons. During the rut, bucks will spar with each other to exert their sexual dominance. Even immature bucks will "learn the ropes" by challenging one another in mock battles. It's here, in these early contests that young bucks learn fighting strategy. I once watched three bucks, a forked-horn and two three-pointers, square off with one another. Despite the fact that the forked-horn was the smallest of the trio, he quickly learned how to use terrain to his advantage. One after another, he upset his mock rivals by working around to an uphill position and then pushing them off balance. When he achieved maturity, there was doubt that he was going to be the dominant buck.

Photo by Bob Robb

This 5x5 buck is what mule deer hunters dream about. Taken by outdoor writer Bob Robb, the deer's antlers measure a whopping 35 inches wide.

Photo by Jim Matthews

This buck's posture indicates that he's definitely on the trail of his true love.

Mule deer have been known to not only use their antlers on rival bucks, but also to ward off predators. Believe me, a coyote, or even a mountain lion on the receiving end of a multi-tined antler thrust would be in a world of hurt. Even a wounded deer is capable of inflicting serious injury. I once grabbed a "dead" deer by the antlers to turn it over for field dressing. To my surprise, the deer was instantly on its feet. Had I not released my grip, the animal could have easily flipped me over its head—or worse! It took another bullet to settle the matter. In the interim, I had learned a serious lesson. Never assume that any animal has expired until you are certain that all life signs have stopped.

Time for love: The start of mule deer mating season, also known as the rut, varies depending on the particular region where the animals are found. On the California central coast, the rut generally begins in mid-September and runs through early October. In other Western areas, the rut often doesn't begin until late October and runs right on through to November. It is during this time that even a well-seasoned buck can abandon his normal caution behavior in exchange for a go at the ladies. Each year, one to two fawns are born to those mule deer does that were bred the previous fall. Interestingly, multiple births of up to four individual fawns have been recorded. The gestation period lasts an average of seven months, with most fawns being born in the late spring or early summer. By the time the yearling buck is twelve months of age he will have achieved sexual maturity. With the approaching of the rut, other more mature bucks seeking

Photo by Durwood Hollis

Taken during an early season, this buck was headed for his bed when the author intercepted him.

Photo by Bob Robb

A mule deer buck of this caliber isn't easy to come by no matter where you hunt.

to breed the doe will drive away any lingering male off-spring. Failing that, the doe herself will drive the yearling off. In this way, genetic diversity in the mule deer population is enhanced.

Behavior: Mule deer activity begins just before dark and can continue well into the night. When there is sufficient moonlight, these deer may feed for an extended period, only lying down for a short period just before dawn. At first light, however, the deer are already moving toward their daytime bedding grounds. Stopping to feed and water, some animals may still be out in the open late into the morning. No matter what the weather, deer will generally bed down during midday. During hot weather, the animals will tend to bed earlier and remain until just before sundown. Even so, bedded animals may get up and move short distances. Furthermore, just before an approaching change of weather a spurt of feeding energy is often manifest. Likewise, immediately following a storm the deer will move out from cover to fill their empty stomachs. In arid regions, mule deer can move considerable distances between feed, water and bedding areas. Moreover, the presence or absence of snow can also influence movement, as well as stimulate wholesale migration. Mule deer follow traditional migration patterns year-after-year. A fortunate hunter in the path of such a movement can witness a remarkable phenomenon.

Are they easy? Many hunters are of the opinion the mule deer are easy to hunt. No doubt, part of this belief is based on the fact that mule deer are often found in open county. Although you will see more mule deer during daylight hours than whitetail, most of those animals will be smallish bucks and does. This fact alone makes the mule deer, particularly young bucks, considerably more vulnerable to hunting than whitetail. Most hunters just want to fill their deer license. In areas where both mule deer and whitetail are found, hunters generally will take a young mule deer buck, rather than spend the time it can take to put some whitetail venison in the freezer.

Any mule deer that has survived four or five hunting seasons, of necessity, has become wise to the ways of man. You may catch a glimpse of one of these old bruisers during the late summer, or in your headlights on a country road after dark. When leaves begin to turn, that same deer will somehow vanish from the face of the earth. Even if you know where he generally hangs out, getting a shot at a wise old devil can be next too impossible. And you can forget about the so-called "classic" mule deer behavior of running a short distance when disturbed, then stopping briefly to look back. Big mule deer, even in open country, don't stop to look back. If they did, they would've never made it past those first couple of hunting seasons.

Let me share with you just how hard it can be to catch a big mule deer buck unaware. While hunting along the base of a rim that overlooked a deep river canyon, I accidentally pushed a nice 4x4 buck out of his bed. An investigation of the area revealed several old beds and enough deer scat and tracks to confirm in my mind that the buck had been using the same spot for a considerable time. Since the deer was bedded up against the rim, there was no way for me to come at him from behind. And the lip of the bench prevented a clear shot from below. The only way to get at this buck was a lateral approach from one of two directions. For nearly a week, I focused my attention on this one animal. Only a couple of shooting opportunities presented themselves, both of which was nothing more than fleet-

ing seconds before the deer disappear from sight. By using that particular bedding site, the deer was able to foil every one of my hunting strategies. And this isn't the only occasion when I've encountered a mature mule deer buck pulling off the same maneuver with equal success. Are mule deer easy? That depends on what you're looking for!

Glass your way to success: Arizona big game guide, Duwane Adams, has put his clients on more outsize bucks than he can remember. This includes 15 Boone & Crockett Club record book mule deer entries, as well as a host of similar Safari Club records. His strategy is simple and involves high-magnification binoculars. "Get high before first light, glass the south, southeast and east facing slopes for the first two hours,

Mule deer tend to live in open country, which makes it no simple matter to take a big buck with a short-range muzzleloader.

Guide Duwane Adams (rear) found this huge mule deer buck for client Russ Schulpetz by using tripod-mounted, high-magnification binoculars.

Photo by Duwane Adams

then switch to the north, northwest and west-facing slopes for the remainder of the day. Find the buck you want before he knows you're in the area, and then plan out a stalk that puts you in position for a clear shot. Before I knew how to

use binoculars, most of my hunting efforts involved boot leather and sweat. Sure, I saw lots of deer, but very few big bucks. When I did occasionally run into a good buck, that old boy was already in gear hightailing it out of the country. After a while, I just got tired of literally spinning my wheels. I just knew if a buck could be located before he sensed my presence, then I could control the situation. Big binoculars (15x60 Zeiss) on a tripod were the logical choice in putting me in the driver's seat. After that, it was just a matter of patience

and persistent glassing," Adams advised. Does glassing work? You bet it does!

Still hunting: There are occasions when persistent glassing isn't entirely practical. This is especially true in areas with mixed cover and few vantage points from which to effectively use binoculars. In these regions still-hunting is the best option. Wear quiet clothing (wool, fleece or Saddle Cloth®), hunt into the wind, put the sun at your back (the glare makes it difficult for deer to see you coming) and don't hurry. Following the course of a game trail or old vehicle track—where the ground has been softened by use—will help to muffle your footfalls. Carefully scan the area before you move (7x and 8x wide-angle binoculars work well here), then try to avoid making any unnatural sound. If you're hunting with someone else, don't ever talk above a quiet whisper. Work out a system of hand signals so you can communicate with each other without making any noise. The use of a cover scent (I like skunk) is another tool that can be of assistance, especially for bowhunters and blackpowder enthusiasts.

There is a particular river canyon that I've still-hunted for years with considerable success. If I am by myself, then the plan consists of getting as high as possible on the south-facing slope where the cover is open enough to see deer at a distance. When someone else accompanies me, then that person is positioned about halfway up the slope. Hunting at the same pace, we move along the canyon face slowly, stopping to glass any open areas. If there are three hunters, then one departs from camp well before light. While it's still dark, this person finds a vantage point a mile or two up the canyon. This is where he'll make his stand. What generally happens is that deer are caught in the open as they move toward daytime bedding areas. Should a buck move out in front of the slowly moving hunters, then the hunter on the stand usually has a shooting opportunity. Basically, this is nothing more than a modified deer drive.

The same still-hunting techniques that I use on mule deer usually don't work very well with white-tail. Those masters of cover and concealment will hunker-down and either let the hunter walk right past, or slip around behind you. A mule deer, however, usually reacts differently when pushed. With their excellent hearing and exceptional eyesight, a mule deer buck can detect danger at a considerable distance. When he realizes that you're in his domain, he'll just move out ahead of you. If you're in the right place when this occurs, than you might just find yourself elbow-deep into primary field care.

Hot weather hunting tips: In some states, bow season and even some rifle seasons open while the weather is still warm. On the California central coast, the bow season opener is near the first of July. In this same area, the rifle season opens the initial weekend of August and runs through the third week of September. With daytime temperatures running in the triple-digit range, you can imagine just how tough it is to fill your deer

A combination of glassing and still-hunting put the author's tag on this 3x3 California mule deer.

Photo by Durwood Hollis

In the flat, desert country of northern Mexico, outdoor writer, Bob Robb, had few vantage points from which to use his binoculars. No matter, he's an accomplished still-hunter.

A late season provided the opportunity for the author to take this buck during the rut.

Photo by Durwood Hollis

On the high plains, it takes a flat-shooting rifle to make the long shots. In this instance the author used a Savage bolt-gun chambered in .300 Win. Magnum.

tag. Some warm-weather hunting tips can tilt the odds in your favor, no matter whether it's an early mule deer season in California, eastern Oregon, Nevada or any place else. During hot weather, mule deer will bed down early, sometimes even before the sun comes up. Furthermore, they are likely to stay in their beds until just before dark. This is particularly true when the moon is full. During the dark of the moon, the morning feeding period tends to be longer and the deer will move out in the afternoon earlier. When the hot weather abates, you can then expect less crepuscular activity and more daytime movement. My suggestion is to forget about the opener and hunt the last few days of the season. Most deer hunters are opening day specialists, after that only the die-hards will keep coming back. In hot weather, you might score on a forked-horn or a smallish three-point on opening weekend. If you're interested in a bigger buck, then grit your teeth and hold out until the closing days of the season.

Hunt the rut: Hunting the rut is the best way I know to score on a big buck. Unfortunately, mule deer seasons throughout the West are generally situated somewhere in the month of October. While some initial rutting activity will begin by the end of October, most seasons will close well before it hits its peak. If you can select from more than one hunting period (depending on the region within a particular state, you may have such an option), then going late is always better than early. That said, a late-season hunt in the Rocky Mountains might put you right in the middle of bad weather. This can make getting away from a paved road nearly impossible. Furthermore, camping out in the miserable weather isn't my idea of a good time. Absent a heavy snowstorm (always a possibility), however, you may find yourself right in the middle of the rut. The best mule deer hunting advice I know is that if a late season is available in your hunting area—go for it!

Calibers and guns: Mule deer aren't particularly tough animals. Almost any caliber, from the minuscule .243 Win, to the ever-popular .30-06 Spfd., within their respective performance envelopes will work. The advantage gained from the flatter trajectories of the several hot-stepping magnum chamberings, both proprietary and factory-developed, can make a real difference in some target presentations. The real key to success lies with bullet adequacy, particularly the right combination of projectile weight and sectional density. The minimal mule deer bullet starts at the 100-grain mark, with most deer hunters seldom using anything heavier than a 180-grain pill. The mid-range of bullet weights—130- to 165-grain—usually offers the best combination of useable trajectory and suitable penetration.

Since mule deer frequent open country, the bolt-action rifle is preferred because it offers the best accuracy potential. A barrel length of 22 inches is standard on non-magnum calibers, although some carbine-length boltguns feature 20- and 18-1/2-inch barrels. For optimal velocity, magnum chamberings usually feature 24- or 26-inch barrels. The average standard caliber mule deer rifle will weigh somewhere between 7 and 8 pounds. Abbreviated bolt-action carbines will tip the scales at just a tad over 6 pounds. Remington recently brought out a titanium boltgun, chambered in either .270 Win. or .30-06 Spfd., with a 22-inch barrel that weighs a feathery 5-1/2 pounds. The laws of physics being what they are, however, the lighter the rifle and the heavier the bullet, the greater the recoil.

What about the future? Beginning with the settlement of the West, mule deer populations flourished with changes brought about by the impact of livestock. In the late 1800s, as the existing grassland was

Photo by Dwayne Oberhoff

In the future, bowhunting for mule deer will continue to provide solid hunting opportunities. Dwayne Oberhoff took this fine buck in the Kaibab.

overgrazed by cattle and sheep, the subsequent growth of other preferred mule deer foods provided unanticipated habitat expansion. Subsequent fire suppression efforts further allowed these shrubs and brush to proliferate. By the 1930s, mule deer began to demonstrate unparalleled herd growth that continued well into the 1960s. However, by the 1970s, mule deer populations everywhere began to exhibit signs of weakening. In the sagebrush-steppe regions, continued overgrazing by livestock along with aggressive fire suppression led to the expansion of Juniper forest which provided little deer forage. Several tough winters during the 1970s and 1980s extracted their toll from the already vulnerable mule deer herds. And in many areas, these winters were followed by extended periods of drought.

To be sure, the recent habitat decline isn't entirely to blame. Increases in human population (the United States ranks third in total population, after China and India) are also part of the problem. More and more homes are being built in foothill regions. This alone has an adverse impact on deer migration routes and winter range. Power and gas lines also bring their own disruption through construction and maintenance activities. Interstate freeways crisscross both summer and winter deer range, which results in an ever-growing number of vehicle-deer incidents. And there continues to be greater numbers of hunters, backpackers, snowmobile and ATV users, as well as campers in the woods each year.

Whitetail deer also share some of the blame in this situation. A more aggressive deer species, with the ability to produce a greater number of offspring in a shorter period of time, in riparian areas competition with this species has also reduced mule deer numbers. How this will affect mule deer over time is not known. One thing is for sure, whitetail are continuing their westward expansion unabated.

Finally, the lack unanimity between the various Western states, as well as the federal government, on predator control, or the lack thereof, also has an impact on mule deer populations. The data on the effect of predators, especially mountain lions and coyotes, is inconclusive. Even an aggressive program to reduce the

Mule deer populations may be in decline, but there are still a few awesome bucks to be found.

Photo by Bob Robb

Photo by Jim Matthews

Game departments need to make the hard decisions about mule deer management before it's too late.

number of predators, which may not be politically acceptable in these times, cannot make up for the continued loss of habitat. To the knowledgeable observer, it becomes patently obvious that the biggest problems mule deer have are people!

When this country was first developed, the westward movement of human population artificially inflated mule deer numbers. What we are seeing currently may be nothing more than the return of the deer population pendulum to more pre-settlement proportions. Furthermore,

any population, from sand fleas to humans, will experience boom and bust cycles. Are mule deer populations on the skids? Certainly, some herds are experiencing decreases in fawn recruitment. How well mule deer populations respond to the changes in habitat that have occurred over the last two centuries remains to be seen. Hopefully, game managers throughout the West will step beyond turf and political issues and make the right decisions before we are left with nothing more than scattered relic populations of these magnificent creatures.

Photo by Bob Robb

Secretive and elusive, the blacktail deer (Columbian blacktail pictured) find the dense chaparral of the central California coast and the rainforest of coastal northern California, Oregon, Washington and British Columbia much to their liking.

THE PACIFIC GHOST: BLACKTAIL DEER

As elusive as a wisp of smoke, the secretive blacktail deer is perhaps the most challenging of all North American deer to hunt

Hunting blacktail deer was responsible for my early big game education. To say it was a school of "blood, sweat and tears" would be less than candid. Those initial hunts were pure misery. Punctuated with triple-digit temperatures, impenetrably thick chaparral, rattlesnakes and poison oak, a blacktail deer hunt was as much pain as it was pleasure. Yet, I always returned every August through September to pursue what locals often reverently refer to as the "Pacific Ghost."

With few exceptions, these secretive deer spend their entire lives drifting invisibly through the thick brush, old-growth timber, thorny berry vine tangles and coastal rain forest jungles from the central California coast north to Alaska. This means that scoring on a true trophy-class blacktail buck will take as much skill, patience and pure hard work as any North American deer subspecies, bar none.

Two is better than one: There are two subspecies of blacktail, the more primitive Sitka blacktail (*Odocoileus hemionus sitkensis*) of the coast of Alaska and British Columbia, and the more genetically evolved Columbian blacktail (*Odocoileus hemionus columbianus*) that is found from coastal central California north throughout the coast of British Columbia.

For many years, it was thought that the blacktail was a subspecies of the mule deer. Recent scientific thinking suggests that the blacktail and whitetail deer were the only two core deer species to enter into North America from Siberia. Apparently, the mule deer evolved from a cross between ancient blacktail and primitive whitetail deer some two million years ago. Today, blacktail and mule deer interbreed wherever

Photo by Bob Robb

Columbian blacktail have the same bifurcated antler formation as a mule deer. A 4x4 like this buck is an outstanding trophy animal.

their ranges overlap, creating several different hybrid mule deer subspecies.

What they look like: A mature Columbian blacktail will stand some 33 to 36 inches tall at the shoulders and weigh between 110 and 225 pounds. A Sitka blacktail is a bit shorter and somewhat blockier in appearance. Both Columbian and Sitka blacktail deer are easily distinguished from their mule deer cousins by their tail, which is solid black on the topside. Mule deer only have a black stripe running down the center of an otherwise light tan or brown tail.

Blacktail deer have the same bifurcated antler configuration as the mule deer. For record book purposes, however, they are scored exactly the same. Blacktail deer just have smaller antlers. The classic trophy-class Columbian blacktail has heavy antler bases and beams, four tines (points) measuring 4 to 5 inches in length per antler beam, noticeable eye guards and an inside antler spread of at least ear-width. On the other hand, a *whopper* Sitka buck will have the same antler configuration, though the tines will be much shorter. It should be noted that many

Photo by Bob Robb

When it comes to Kodiak Island Sitka blacktail, this 4x4 is a real trophy.

Photo by Bob Robb

On the California central coast, hunting old burns is one of the most effective methods to find Columbian blacktail deer.

large blacktail bucks, both Columbia and Sitka, often only have three tines on one or both main antler beams, with or without one or both eye guards. This results in an antler configuration that looks more like classic whitetail antlers, than mule deer cranial protuberances. While they won't score high enough to make the record book, heavy-antlered bucks of this type are nonetheless still trophy animals.

The record books: For the purposes of the Boone & Crockett and Pope & Young record books, the range of the Columbian blacktail extends from the Pacific coastline in the west, to Interstate 5 in the east. Monterey County, California, forms the southern boundary, while to the north these deer can be found along a short stretch of the southern British Columbia coast and onto Vancouver Island. Sitka blacktail will be found north of this line of demarcation and all along the western coast of Alaska and many of the offshore islands—including Kodiak Island.

In the still of the night: Blacktail deer have habits more like whitetail than mule deer. This seems to be a function of both the habitat in which they live and their extremely nocturnal nature. A 1996 study by the Oregon Department of Fish and Wildlife demonstrated just how nocturnal mature blacktail bucks really are. In this pre-rut inquiry, special cameras were placed on six fall migration trails that vacated the high Cascade Mountain Range and lead to low-elevation wintering grounds. The cameras were triggered when an animal passed a beam of infrared light, which also registered the date and time the photograph was taken. The results of this study were eye-opening. Of the 606 deer caught on the camera, 87% of the bucks and 42% of does and fawns traveled entirely after dark. Interestingly, 42% of the bucks had four or more points on each antler beam. This investigation into blacktail deer movement confirmed what those who have pursued these animals for a long time have known all along—to score on a buck during

No matter where you pursue blacktail deer, both still-hunting and glassing are important components of the hunt.

Photo by Bob Robb

Charles Barnum took this huge Columbian blacktail in northern California, near the town of Eureka.

legal shooting hours you'll have to root him out of his jungle home. How you do this depends on both the time of year and the region you're hunting.

Hunting Columbian blacktail: Along the central California coast there isn't much old-growth forest, but the mountains have substantial stands of chaparral brush (a dense covering of mixed species of thorny bushes, shrubs and evergreen oaks). During the

August general rifle season (the bow season opens in July), the daytime temperatures can reach 100 degrees, or higher. In this environment, it's best to glass open meadow pockets and visible trails right at dawn and again just before sundown. Farther up the coast in northern California, Oregon and Washington it can also be swelteringly hot. In these regions, the country is interspersed with expansive stands of old-growth timber. About the only way to spot a buck is cross-canyon glassing into the thick cover. Some hunters eschew binoculars and use traditional "whitetail" hunting tactics. The dedicated hunters scout trails and bedding areas and when they find evidence of a buck, then it's tree stand time. Others use a ground blind or make a stand along the edge of a clear cut where they can watch for deer leaving the forest to feed on succulent new growth.

Still-hunting is quite popular among forest blacktail hunters who have the patience of the Biblical Job and move like an overweight snail. No doubt, this is a response to the thick cover, which inhibits effective work with binoculars. To their hunting advantage, the ever-present rainy weather that dominates the Pacific Northwest can quiet the woods to a church-like silence. Sneaking along a deer trail that winds through chest-high ferns, thick berry tangles and ancient trees is as exciting hunting as you could ever experience. Blacktail deer often have a relatively small home range and the bigger bucks are famous for lying low while you

walk right past them. Still-hunters often shoot bucks right in their beds.

I once caught a blacktail buck sound asleep, with his nose tucked into his tail. It was early afternoon and the temperature was soaring well above the triple-digit mark. Still hunting along a barely visible game trail, I only took a couple steps at a time. Peering into every brush pocket, vine tangle and under overhanging limbs, I just knew that the shape of a deer would materialize. Then it happened. The faint track led to a small grass-covered opening, at the far edge of which a buck was curled up in the shade of an overhanging bush. The wind was right and my approach was quiet enough that the deer wasn't aware of my presence. Needless to say, I ate deer liver and onions that evening.

Outdoor writer and friend, Bob Robb, is well acquainted with still-hunting Columbia blacktail deer. His adventures with these animals have taken him all along the California, Oregon and Washington coast. A hunt he took in northern California a few

Photo by Bob Robb

Hunting guide, Doug Gattis scored on this magnificent Columbian blacktail near his home in Medford, Oregon.

Photo by Bob Robb

Taken by outdoor writer, Bob Robb with a Remington in-line blackpowder rifle, this 4x4 Columbian blacktail buck qualified for entry into the Boone & Crockett record book.

years back exhibits the fruits of still-hunting the Pacific Ghost.

"I took my very first *whopper* blacktail buck in the thick old-growth forest of northern California. The area near Eureka, on the coast, is known for producing some of the biggest blacktails of all time. "Sneak and peek" hunting here among the redwoods is one of my favorite pursuits. That morning, my friend Charles Barnum and I were slipping through the tall trees, along an old logging road. The steep mountain forest was dotted with tiny, grassy meadows, excellent places to catch a buck out feeding early and late in the day.

"As it often is, it was incredibly foggy that morning. It was difficult to see more than 100 yards in any direction. Charles and I crept up to the edge of one meadow where we caught sight of two deer feeding on the other side. Wisps of fog were rolling in and out of the opening, so we used it for concealment. Moving to within 75 yards of where we last had seen

the animals, we waited for the mist to clear. Suddenly, as the fog evaporated, a buck materialized. He was a dandy, with three antler points on one side, four on the other. I could see dual eye guards with my binoculars and antlers were slightly wider than his ears. In blacktail hunting, if there ever is such a thing as a "keeper," then this was it! I was shooting my battered old boltgun, chambered in .243 Winchester. The 100-grain Remington CoreLoc® bullet flipped the deer over in his tracks. That was my first-ever record-book qualifying blacktail. A couple of years later, Charles and I hunted together again. Using the same "sneak and peek" methodology, I shot another four-point blacktail that also easily made the record book."

Unlike many other forms of deer hunting, serious blacktail hunters drop everything and head for the woods when it's misting, raining, foggy or a combination thereof. When it's wet outside, the chance of seeing a good blacktail buck can increase immeasurably.

The author took this nice forked-horn Columbian blacktail with a .50 caliber percussion frontloader.

Photo by Durwood Hollis

This is particularly true when the rut is on. Once again, Bob Robb describes one of his memorable blacktail hunts and this time the damp weather played an important role.

"Medford, Oregon hunting guide, Doug Gattis, is as wise a blacktail hunter as I've ever met. Since I had drawn a special late-season Oregon muzzle-loader blacktail permit, arranging a hunt with Doug seemed like the best way to put another blacktail in the record book.

"Doug had previously scouted out what he called the 'Gate Buck.' Doug and a client had seen the deer several times during the previous season. The buck seemed to always hang out by an old gate on the dirt road. When you hear a story like that from a hunting guide who has personally taken five record-book bucks and literally dozens of heart-stoppers over the years, your ears perk right up! If the deer was still around that area, according to Doug's description he was the buck of my dreams.

"The big problem, according to Gattis, was the unseasonably hot, dry November weather in southwestern Oregon. Rain, he felt would bring the bucks out in the open. Mix a little fog with the rain and Doug felt that the deer would be really fired up.

"We woke the next-to-the-last day of my hunt to a falling barometer, drizzling mist, plenty of fog and a forecast of rain. Doug was pumped and so was I. We set up to glass an old dirt track where we'd seen some big tracks and several does earlier in the hunt. After a quarter of an hour and no deer in sight, we decided to take a gamble and check down by the old gate. A short time later, we peeked around the corner and got lucky. A doe was placidly feeding while being tended by two bucks. One of the bucks was a very large 3x3, which would have been a nice deer on any other day. His saving grace was the other deer, a perfectly symmetrical 4x4 that was the largest blacktail buck I'd ever seen. At only 60 yards, it was easy to settle the front sight bead on the deer's shoulder and squeeze the trigger on my .50 caliber in-line muzzleloader. Sped on its way by two 50-grain Pyrodex® pellets, the 250-grain Nosler® Partition® HG Hunting Sabot made the tracking job a short one.

"As the rain finally began to fall hard, I let out a war whoop that would have awakened the dead. Had someone called and told me I won the lottery, the only catch being that I had to trade this deer in for the check, there was no way such a swap would have ever been made. The buck's tall, heavy and well-balanced antlers were a blacktail hunter's most heartfelt wishes come true. Later, Medford Taxidermist, Dennis King, would officially score the buck at 154-1/2 points. This meant that the deer would place number 58 in the all-time Boone & Crockett record book listing of blacktail deer.

"Snuggling under the covers later that night, I thought back more than 25 years of blacktail hunting. There was a big 4x4 buck that gave me the slip in the Trinity Alps of California one weekend. The deer vanished like a ghost just when I was sure that I had him cold. And I could still see the arrow I shot flying over the back of another 4x4 buck one evening along California's north coast. After weeks of scouting and

A small, but hard-earned Columbian blacktail buck. With a bow, any buck taken in the heat of late summer is a trophy.

Photo by Bob Robb

When you hunt blacktail in triple-digit temperatures, immediate field dressing and skinning are all-important to prevent meat spoilage.

deer again. When I checked his tracks, he apparently turned at the last minute and dropped down in a nearby canyon. Who knows what spooked that buck? He might have intended on following that particular course of travel in the first place (who knows the mind of a deer?). Most likely, a faint breeze brought my scent to his nostrils and it was game over. Either way, he simply vanished. That's one blacktail deer I'll never forget.

For a number of years, I had the good fortune to be a part owner in a Monterey Country, California ranch. The holding was about 1,000 acres and consisted of some oak flats and a deep south sloping river canyon. The ranch was excellent blacktail country. Deer didn't always come easy, but if you were willing to work at it, one could usually score. Over the 25 years I held ownership in that ranch, I never failed to punch both of my deer tags annually. Bob Robb was a regular companion on many of those hunts and on one occasion he pulled off a double play. Since Bob was the one to "hit the home run" on that trip, I'll let him tell the story.

"Durwood and I awoke long before dawn, had a quick bite to eat, checked our gear and headed out the ranch house door. The sky was as clear as a bell; the stars as bright as city lights and the shape of the moon

planning, I had set up a tree stand right where I knew the deer pass. He did. I missed. And that was that! There were so many more special blacktail memories, but none of them would be replaced by the buck I'd taken earlier in the day. He will always be extra special because he's a superb blacktail trophy and deer of that caliber are hard to come by."

I can certainly understand the disappointment of both having a big buck get away from you and missing an easy shot. Both events have happened to me and on more than one occasion. Once while glassing a broad draw from a fire road, I saw a great 4x4 blacktail buck headed in my direction. Watching the deer come put my senses into overdrive. By the time the buck had closed the gap to under 100 yards, I had him cut, wrapped and in the freezer—or so I thought!

The cover was heavy and the deer moving rather fast, so I reasoned that my best shooting opportunity would be when he crossed the open dirt track. When the buck started up the hill toward my position, I temporarily lost sight of him. Waiting anxiously, I was fully prepared to make the shot. In fact, I never saw the

Photo by Bob Robb

This 3x2 Columbian blacktail buck fell to a long cross-canyon shot.

Photo by Bob Robb

Rain, fog and bone-chilling cold are typical weather components when hunting Sitka blacktail on Kodiak Island.

told me it was in its first quarter. It was nippy enough for a light sweatshirt, but we both had to pack a quart of water to help us through the morning that would soon turn hot.

"We headed out in different directions. Durwood took a stand overlooking the river where he had taken several decent bucks previously. I chose to hike a couple of miles up the canyon to a rocky ridge that over-looked the south-facing slope of the river canyon. Several fingers of brush trailed up from the river below for the deer to hide in. Here and there were plenty of stands of acorn-laden oaks for the right kind of deer

Photo by Bob Robb

Taken on Kodiak Island, this 4x4 Sitka blacktail is a Boone & Crockett record book qualifier.

Larry Suiter (left) and Chris Batin (right) teamed up to take this Sitka blacktail buck on remote Kodiak Island.

buffet. I was hoping to catch a buck slipping back to bed after a predawn drink at the river and a breakfast of succulent acorns.

"After an hour of hard hiking, using only the moonlight as my guide, I made my way to the prearranged location. A large boulder afforded a commanding view of the canyon below, so I got set and waited. The predawn chill made me glad that I'd packed along a light jacket. As the sky began to change from pitch black to gray, I began glassing. Soon the horizon was a deep orange and purple. The sound of the wilderness coming alive began to fill my ears. Owls hooted, coyotes howled and a covey of California quail called sharply from an acorn flat to my right.

"I knew that Durwood would be coming along below in about an hour, so if I couldn't glass up a buck, maybe he would push one in my direction. After considerable time optically searching the terrain, I noticed something out of place in the thick chaparral. Closer visual inspection showed it was a forked-horn buck feeding calmly as he worked his way up the canyon. Immediately, I was down off of the boulder and moving to the edge of the rocky outcropping. At the cliff, I stopped to glass the buck again. Amazingly, another deer had joined him and it too, was a legal forked-horn buck. This may not sound like much, but in this area of California you could hunt the entire six-week long season and never see a buck, let alone two at the same time (the legal season limit in that particular hunting zone was two bucks).

"The distance from my position to the deer was about 250 yards. I had plenty of time to get set for what would occur next. Laying prone at the cliff edge, I rested the rifle over the top of my pack. The variable scope was turned to 8X for a clear sight picture. Quickly, I found the larger of the two bucks in the scope, took a deep breath, slowly exhaled and squeezed the trigger. The .280 Rem. boltgun barked and the forked-horn went down in a heap. I worked the bolt in a hurry and started to look for the other deer. Interestingly, the second buck had only ran off a short distance and was now standing still. Obviously, he was trying to figure out what was going on and why his buddy had hit the dirt. Momentarily, he too, went down quickly.

"It was one of the most memorable and satisfying hunting trips I've ever been on. Taking two legal blacktail bucks in one morning and in thick cover on rugged public land was indeed an incredible experience. Durwood and I had been hunting here together every season for nearly ten years. While we had taken our fair share of bucks, none were ever easy. Two bucks, together, at the same time were like frosting on a cake. There was a sweet taste in my mouth. Sadly, it would be my last hunt here. Shortly, I would be moving from California to Alaska, following another dream. Though this experience took place more than a decade ago, I still hold the memories of this special place and that final day, as dearly as any hunting experiences I have had around the world."

Like Bob, I too miss the old ranch and the deer hunting it afforded. My heart is filled with memories of a quarter of a century of blacktail pursuit on the place. While I've hunted nearly every species of North American deer, none were any tougher to come by than those August and September blacktails on the California coast.

Hunting Sitka blacktail: The pursuit of Sitka blacktail is one of the most exciting and enjoyable forms of deer hunting you could ever participate in. From Kodiak Island in the north, down to Prince William Sound and throughout the panhandle of the Alaskan mainland and its associated islands, Sitka blacktail hunting opportunities are excellent. Deer numbers are high; and except immediately following years of higher than average winter kill, the hunting is superb.

Sitka deer seasons are long, opening up in early August and extending into December. In the early season, when the bucks are still in velvet, they can be found in the high, lush alpine bowls above the timber and brush lines. The summer days are almost never-ending and the weather is as good as it gets in the Far North. Hunting this time of year can be beyond imagination. This is when spot-and-stalk hunting works best. Later on, from mid-October through November, the bucks go into the rut. At this time of the year, the leaves are off of the alders and other brush, making it a lot easier to see the animals. And besides spot-and-stalk hunting, Sitka bucks can be called using both fawn and doe bleats, as well as grunt calls. The "kicker" when it comes to call-

Photo by Durwood Hollis

The author used a Remington Model 600 rifle, chambered in .308 Winchester, to take this young Columbian blacktail buck.

ing Sitka deer is the giant coastal brown bear. These carnivores thrive in the same areas and prey on Sitka deer whenever they can catch them. Hunters who used deer calls sometime have been surprised when the animal that comes to the call is a hungry bear instead of a big buck. When a bear is intent on making a meal out of you, it's best not to facilitate those intentions.

On one of Bob Robb's Kodiak Island hunts, he shot a really nice Sitka blacktail. Leaving the deer for just a few minutes, Bob wanted to try for another bigger buck (multiple tags are available for hunts on Kodiak Island) that had appeared just over a nearby rise. He spent about 10 minutes trying to find the other animal, then abandoned the project and returned to where the first deer had dropped. Surprisingly, the only thing he found was a lot of bear tracks. Apparently, a brown bear had picked the buck up in his jaws and carried it off into the dense cover. Bob tried to follow, but he realized that there was no way that bear was going to give up a meal of fresh venison. Any deer you take in brown bear country must immediately be field dressed and removed from the kill site. Let the bruin feed on the gut pile and maybe he won't track you down and take your venison.

Sitka deer hunters can approach the sport in several ways. One is by boat. Large charter boats take hunters to remote mainland and island covers, where they can then go ashore in skiffs and climb the hills in search of deer. These roving aquatic camps have several advantages. For one thing, you can hunt different country every day. Second, they provide a safe, warm and comfortable place to sleep and dry out when the inevitable rains come. And third, you can bring plenty of gear aboard, as well as store lots of venison in a cool, dry place.

Another way to hunt these deer is to access remote areas by aircraft. A small airplane can land you on a lake with floats, or on the tundra with oversize tires. Airplane hunting is a great way to pursue Sitka deer, however, your gear will be limited by the carrying capacity of the aircraft. When you go by airplane, you'll only be able to carry the bare essentials.

Some hunters even use a vehicle to go after Sitka blacktails. On the huge Prince of Wales Island, hunters can fly into Ketchikan, rent a vehicle and take a ferry over to the island. Prince of Wales Island is covered with old logging roads. Using the roads as access, hunters follow them until they find an area where a short hike puts them into good deer country. It sounds easier than it really is, but using a vehicle will save you miles of walking through unproductive country.

Limited-entry hunts, key to big bucks: The best opportunities at true trophy-class blacktail bucks can be found after obtaining a limited-entry permit. Sure, you'll have to participate in a drawing along with all of the rest of the prospective blacktail hunters. However, that's just the way the game is played these days. After a few attempts, some applicants will get discouraged and quit submitting applications. It's necessary to stay the course for a hunting permit to end up in your mailbox. If you don't submit, you'll never pull a tag. Patience and persistence are what limited-entry buck permits are all about. Should you be one of the lucky ones, the limited-entry permit will allow you to hunt the rut when older, mature bucks are more active during legal shooting hours.

Oregon's late muzzleloader hunts—especially those located in the southwest area of the state—are the best limited-entry blacktail hunts. This is a region where the largest concentrations of trophy Columbia blacktail deer exist today. The Willamette Valley also offers good late season muzzleloader hunting. As well, California has a handful of excellent limited-entry, late-season blacktail hunts that are conducted on public lands.

Photo by Bob Robb

Taken on the California coast during the July archery season, this 3x2 Columbian blacktail was the result of three days of serious hunting.

Application submission deadlines for the Oregon and California hunts fall in May and June, respectively.

Blacktail calibers: Either blacktail species are no more difficult to bring down than any other North American deer species. In fact, most blacktail are smaller than either mule deer or whitetail. Centerfire chamberings from .243 Win. to .30-06 Spfd. are more than adequate in any blacktail environment. In the more open country found in parts of the central California coast, the 7mm Rem. Mag. is favored by some hunters. The .356 Win. and the .358 Win. are other good choices for shots under 250 yards. Those who stalk the rainforest for the Pacific Northwest often use chamberings like the .375 Win., .444 Marlin and the .45-70 Gov't for close cover work.

Blackpowder hunters usually stick with .50 caliber frontloaders. When hunting blacktail in wet weather, an in-line rifle and Pyrodex are more reliable, than external-hammer percussion long guns and blackpowder. Blackpowder regulations vary from state to state, so read the hunting regulations carefully. Bowhunters use a variety of stick and string combinations, all of which will work on blacktail deer. Solidly constructed, razor-sharp broadheads are the most important consideration in this arena.

Planning Your Hunt: Putting together a public land blacktail hunt requires considerable research. A good place to begin is with maps, lots of maps! The U.S. Forest Service regional office (Region 5, California, 600 Sansome St., San Francisco, CA 94111, 415/705-2874, and Region 6, Oregon and Washington, 319 SW Pine St., Portland, OR 97208, 503/221-2877) can help you get started with locations of public land tracts, access points and maps. As well, inquiries at the Bureau of Land Management (BLM) regional office (Alaska, 701 "C" St., Box 13, Anchorage, AK 99513, 907/271-5076; Oregon and Washington, 333 SW 1st Ave., Portland, OR 97208, 503/808-6002; California, Federal Bldg., 2800 Cottage Way, Sacramento, CA 95825, 916/978-4743) are helpful. Of course, contacting the fish and game department, public information officer in each state will also yield important and valuable information regarding seasons; limited-entry hunts and tag applications and licensing procedures.

There are also some excellent guided blacktail hunting opportunities. Two well-respected Sitka blacktail outfitters are James and Susan Boyce owners of Baranof Expeditions and Scott Newman, another Alaskan resident. For guided Columbian blacktail hunting none are better than Doug & Janet Gattis who operate Southern Oregon Game Busters. And Multiple Use Managers in northern California are another outfit that offers some great blacktail deer hunting.

Read On: To learn more about blacktail hunting, I can recommend a couple of good books. *Hunting*

Photo by Bob Robb

Hunting the "Pacific Ghost" will demand every ounce of hunting skill you can muster. And even a forked-horn buck will bring a smile to your face.

Blacktail Deer, by John Higley (176 pages, 15 chapters, with an appendix, $16.25 ppd., John Higley, P. O. Box 120, Palo Cedro, CA 96073) is an excellent primer for the sport. John Higley has been a serious blacktail hunter for more than 40 years and is the former Outdoor Life California editor. When it comes to blacktail deer, this man knows where of he speaks. *Blacktail Trophy Tactics*, by Boyd Iverson (168 pages, 15 chapters, $14.95 plus $2.50 shipping and handling, Grassroots Publishing, 84453 Murdock Rd., Eugene, OR 97405) has a lot of information on Columbian blacktail hunting and is written by a hunter who knows the secret to success.

Let's go: Most North American hunters don't even know what a blacktail deer is, much less how to or where to hunt them. However, I promise that once you get started, the "Pacific Ghost" will find a way into your soul. These deer are challenging to hunt and mature bucks are as difficult to take as any animal on the continent. And why, after all these years, do I feel that something is missing if there's no blacktail hunt in the offering?

Photo by J. Mark Higley

Here he is, now it's all up to you.

FOREST MONARCHS: ELK

One of this continent's greatest big game animals, the elk has rebounded from the ashes of near extinction.

The movement of air currents, from an insignificant mountain zephyr to a steady wind, can be a hunter's blessing or bane. Before leaving my truck, I confirmed the origin of the afternoon draft was somewhere west of where the truck finally came to rest. To prevent the steady breeze from giving away my presence, I carefully selected which direction to hunt. Even the faintest

suggestion of man scent would spook any elk long before a shot was possible. And it wasn't just any elk I was looking for. No, that wouldn't do. The bull I wanted had to wear a suitable set of antlers on the crown of his head.

A couple miles and several hundred feet of elevation later, the only animal that I had seen was a 3x3 mule

Photo by Durwood Hollis

Elk country is big, really big. Most veteran hunters use horses.

Rocky Mountain elk can be found in all of the western United States, as well as parts of Canada.

Photo by Bob Robb

deer buck. Since all of my energies were focused on searching for a bull, deer hunting was no more than a back-burner interest. When elk hunting success came, there would be plenty of opportunity to look for a buck. I sidestepped past the deer, keeping out of sight. While I was sure that the buck had probably seen me, it didn't seem to register on his internal protective alarm system (the wind was a blessing in this instance). Almost immediately, the deer returned to feeding. With the breeze blowing steadily in my face, I pushed on toward the top of the nearest ridge.

Nothing outdoors is completely predictable. Just when you think you're in the right position, conditions can change. And where you are can quickly change to where you don't want to be. Influenced by the terrain, ambient pressure and a decline in temperature, the steady current of air, which had been my comrade, now threatened to become my worst enemy. Swirling impet-

uously, the wind carried my scent forward at a most inopportune moment.

Just in front of me, a big bull elk burst from a clump of cedars and streaked along the top of the ridge. With the elk mostly hidden by a lush screen of greenery, a shooting opportunity wasn't possible. Even so, I immediately sat down and tried to find the animal in my scope. Rather than continuing on his initial path, the bull suddenly changed direction about 250 yards away and started down the crest of a distant draw. It seemed the situation had turned in my favor. With few obstacles between me and the bull, I took the logical course of action.

My first shot struck right behind the bull's nearside shoulder, but he never faltered in his downward flight. Cycling the boltgun, I chambered another round and tried again. This time my bullet went over the animal's back. The third and final round would have to do the trick, because the elk wasn't slowing down at all. Placing the scope crosshairs about even with the bull's nose and a little lower than my previous shot, I squeezed the trigger. I would later discover that the 230-grain Winchester Fail-Safe® bullet took the bull right through the neck, severing the carotid artery.

I watched the elk disappear into a group of three small cedar trees. Quickly stuffing three fresh shells into the magazine of my rifle, I waited for the animal to reappear. Seconds gave way to minutes as the tension grew. Nothing happened. I knew that at least my first bullet had hit the bull squarely. The second shot missed. And I wasn't sure about the last attempt. After 10 anxious minutes of waiting and watching, I decided enough was enough.

Watching the place where the elk had disappeared, I crossed the heads of both draws and cut the fresh tracks. There wasn't any blood, cut hair or other clear evidence of a successful bullet placement. When I was within spitting distance of the tiny clump of cedars where the bull vanished, the first sanguine evidence became manifest. There in a small skiff of snow, three tiny drops of blood held the promise of conquest. A

few feet farther, I found the elk all crumpled up under a screen of cedar boughs. The bull was mine. Best of all, he had six long tines on one antler branch, and five on the other—a good elk in anyone's book.

Whether you hunt elk all by yourself, or stalk these majestic animals in the company of a guide, it's demanding in its reality and exhilarating beyond imagination. Hunting elk is like nothing else you can ever experience. The sheer size of a mature bull is overwhelming. Moreover, the absolute tenacity of these animals cannot be easily fathomed. Elk are tough. They are tough to hunt and tough to take cleanly with a single bullet, ball or broadhead.

What and where: There are four distinct varieties of elk that currently roam this continent. All are directly related to the same genus and species—*Cervus elaphus*. Members of this scientific grouping can be found worldwide in the northern hemisphere. The red deer of mainland Europe, the stags of the British Islands and Mongolian elk are all cousins of our own North American elk.

Those in the scientific community think that there were at least 10 subspecies of elk on this continent dur-

Photo by Jim Matthews

Tule elk are found only in California. This herd of young bulls was photographed in the Owens Valley, about 200 miles northeast of Los Angeles.

Roosevelt elk are huge, with some bulls weighing more than 1,000 pounds on the hoof.

ing the Pleistocene Epoch. The fossil record tells us of four of these ancient subspecies, which were discovered in Wisconsin (*Cervis Whitneyi Allen*), New Mexico (*Cervis lascrucensis*), California (*Cervis aguangae Frick*) and Alaska (Murie, 1951), respectively. When European settlers first arrived, only six subspecies were left. The eastern elk (*Cervis canadensis*) and the Merriam elk (*Cervis canadensis merriami*) were quickly ravaged to extinction by early European settlers. This left only four subspecies, which remain to this day.

The largest elk subspecies is the Roosevelt elk (*Cervis elaphus roosevelti*) that can be found in the Pacific rain forests of northern California, Oregon, Washington, British Columbia and a few of Alaska's offshore islands. Roosevelt bulls can weigh upwards of 1,000 pounds, or more on the hoof. Next in size is the Manitoba elk (*Cervis elaphus manitobensis*), which is found in southwestern Manitoba, parts of Saskatchewan and eastern Alberta, Canada. Slightly smaller in size, the live weight of a mature Manitoba bull is 800 to 900 pounds. This subspecies is only slightly larger than the Rocky Mountain elk (*Cervis elaphus nelsoni*). A Rocky Mountain bull elk will weigh 700 to 850 pounds on the hoof. Found in all of our Western states, Rocky Mountain elk make up the largest contingent of any North American elk subspecies. Our smallest elk is the tule elk (*Cervis elaphus nannodes*). One of these little bulls will only weigh about 400 to 450 pounds. Found only in California, where it was almost hunted to extinction in the 19th century, this minuscule elk produces antlers that have a tendency to "crown point" (multiple antler tines) at the very top. It's not uncommon to see a tule elk bull with an inordinate number of tines on each antler branch.

Most certainly the number of subspecies is nothing more than genetic adaptation in response to specific environmental conditions. The farther south in the hemisphere where you find game animals, the smaller the body size. Small bodies more easily radiate heat, making survival in triple-digit temperatures more favorable. With the exception of the Roosevelt elk, which seem to grow overly large in their coastal Pacific rain forest environment, the farther south elk are found, the smaller they will be. Hence, the tule elk of the central California valley is a midget when compared to the Rocky Mountain subspecies. And the Manitoba elk, whose range is farther to the north, is somewhat larger than the Rocky Mountain elk.

A crowning achievement: Elk antlers begin to emerge from a bull's skull cap sometime in April. Velvet-soft, blood-rich coverings encase the new antlers until they reach full growth. By late August or early September, the velvet sheath will be rubbed off in preparation for the coming breeding season. A bull elk in his first year of life will produce a slender, solitary unbranched antler on each side. These so-called "spike" bulls are not fully mature and can often be found still running with a group of cow elk. In its second and third years of life, a bull will often sport multi-tined antlers, with three or four points on each side. These young bulls are called "raghorns," or "brush bulls." While they are able to breed, most are kept on the fringe of elk society by more dominant bulls. Because these animals are constantly on the move, revolving around other elk herds, they are referred to as "satellite" bulls. By their fourth year, bulls will have five, six or more tines on each antler branch, with bases of up to 12 inches or more in circumference. When mature, most bulls are rather solitary, associating with other elk only during the rut and on traditional wintering grounds. Antlers are finally shed in February or March, with a new set surfacing almost immediately.

Hunting elk: Just like hunting other members of the *Cervis* genus, there's the rut—and everything else. During the rut, a bull abandons all of his usual clandestine feeding and bedding activities and is as freewheeling as a Las Vegas lounge lizard. Protective behaviors give way to a hormonal urge to procreate. Bulls challenge one another with outlandish bugles (termed "roaring" on other continents where other members of this species are found), pawing the ground and raking nearby trees and brush with their antlers. Seemingly looking for a fight, bulls tend to move a lot. And they will attempt to wrest cow elk away from any other suitor. After breeding season, which takes place primarily in September, the bulls return to a life of seclusion.

Photo by Durwood Hollis

When you're an elk hunter, this is what home away from home looks like.

Photo by *Nosler*®

The .35 Whelen is more than enough gun for elk, especially when loaded with the 225-grain, Nosler® Ballistic Tip® bullets.

Here they rest and recuperate in preparation for the fall migration to favored areas where refuge can be found from winter.

Rut hunts for elk are not available in all areas where the animals are found. Where hunts are scheduled during the rut, most will take place in backcountry locales. It's easier to find a bull during this period and it gives bowhunters, blackpowder shooters and those willing to get deep into the elk country a chance before the general rifle season. Calling elk, or bugling, is a proven approach to putting elk venison in the freezer. However, bugling isn't a sure-fire method. Sometimes a bull will come to a call all pumped for a fight. Most likely, he'll gather up his harem and silently sneak away.

Smart elk hunters eschew bugling and use a cow call. Bulls aren't threatened by cow calling. When they hear the soft call of a cow, they're just as likely to stay put as come looking for love. Should a bull hold where he is and continually bugle in response to cow calling, a hunter can close the gap and hopefully get a shot. If he comes searching for the origin of the call, then the opportunity for a shot may be manifest. Young raghorn elk, will generally respond to cow calling like a moth to a flame. Older, more mature bulls are less enthusiastic

Photo by Winchester Ammunition

The Nosler® Partition® Gold bullet, loaded by Winchester in their Supreme ammunition line, is a great choice for work on elk.

Whatever caliber you select for elk, the most important thing is to sight-in so you can hit the target all the way out to 300 yards, or father.

about a lone cow. If you were a bull elk, would you leave a group of fine cows for some unseen lonely old gal in the brush? I wouldn't!

Most general elk seasons are conducted in October and early November. At this time, bulls are seldom found with herds of cows, but they will be somewhere in the general vicinity. Bulls may respond vocally to calling, but most likely they won't come to the caller. During this period, you'll really have to hunt hard and cover a lot of ground to find a bull. Hunting in the general elk season can be tough. In spite of competition from other hunters, if you know where to go and how to hunt, putting a bull in your sights is just a matter of time.

When the snow begins to fly, it can trigger the winter migration. Cows, calves and immature bulls will be the first to start the trek out of the backcountry. The big bulls will be the last to make the trip. If you can time your hunt just right, then shooting a bull may just be a matter of waiting until the right one crosses in front of you. Should you try your luck late, weather can be the real kicker. Snow and freezing conditions might put elk on the move, but it can also impact your ability to

negotiate roads in elk country. Late-season elk hunting depends on how the dice roll. You take turns and try your luck. Sometimes it's seven-come-eleven. All too often, however, you find yourself with nothing but a pair of snake eyes. For most elk hunters, antlers on the wall and elk meat in the freezer are worth taking a chance on every roll of the dice.

Elk calibers: Even when shot in the boiler room, a bull elk can carry a bullet a long way. I can remember shooting a bull with a .30-caliber, 180-grain, Winchester Fail-Safe® bullet. The distance, from the muzzle of my .300 Win. Mag. boltgun to the elk, was about 160 paces. The projectile struck low and right behind the point of the shoulder. During the subsequent field dressing procedure, I learned that the bullet tore up the top of the heart and scrambled both lungs. At the shot, the bull jumped straight up into air and took off at full tilt. Covering about 100 yards, he fell and landed with all four feet in the air. Amazingly, he got to his feet and covered another 80 yards before expiring. Like I said, elk are tough!

Serious elk medicine centers more on bullet weight and construction, than it does on specific calibers.

Many outdoor scribes have commented in print that the .270 Winchester, firing a 150-grain bullet, is the absolute minimum elk cartridge. While there is a certain amount of validity in that statement, personally I don't think that particular chambering is the right choice in all venues. No doubt, with a well-placed bullet, you can drop a bull in its tracks. Countless elk have fallen to the .270 Winchester and many more will continue to do so. Even so, experience has convinced me that there are too many other better caliber choices. For this reason, I find little to recommend about the .270 Winchester as an elk round.

A suitable elk caliber must be able to put a bullet from any target presentation angle into the heart-lung region of the animal. To accomplish this, one must shoot heavy bullets, preferably weighing 175 grains, or more. This would put the minimum elk caliber at 7mm, with no absolute maximum. Certainly, the 7mm Rem. Mag. is a satisfactory elk chambering when used with the right bullet. With 140-, 150- or 160-grain projectiles, however, bullet placement must be precise. The .30-06 Spfd., .300 Win. Mag., and all the rest of the .30-caliber magnums are right at home in elk country. The uses of 180-, 200- and 220-grain projectiles, at appropriate shooting distances, are the bullet weights of choice for this assignment. The premier elk cartridge (my own personal choice) is the .338 Win. Magnum. This chambering can drive a relatively heavy bullet through an elk from brisket to tail, even at the ragged edge of meaningful performance. Of course, any of the other .338-caliber whiz-bang magnums are just more of the same thing. Other good elk calibers are the 8mm Rem. Mag., .35 Whelen, .350 Rem. Mag.

With the right load, in a modern in-line rifle, blackpowder hunters can handle an elk out to 125 yards, or even a tad farther.

Photo by Durwood Hollis

*Prompt field dressing is important
keep the elk venison from spoiling.*

Photo by Durwood Hollis

HANTA VIRUS

Hanta viruses infect rodents, particularly field mice, worldwide. Several species of the virus have been known to infect humans with varying severity. The pulmonary syndrome of this disease was responsible for a 1993 epidemic in the Southwest. Since that date, several cases of the disease have been reported in many other Western states, some Eastern states and Canada.

The major carriers of this disease are deer mice, but disease antibodies have also been detected in pack rats, chipmunks and other rodent species. The disease is transmitted through inhalation of fine particles (dust) of rodent scat.

The disease is characterized by fever, muscle pain and intestine complaints. Unchecked, this illness can progress to severe respiratory failure and shock. Hunters are cautioned to be careful where they camp. Sweeping the floor of an old cabin or outbuilding, or stirring up dust from areas that are inhabited by field mice can present a real danger.

and the reliable .375 Holland & Holland Magnum. Similarly, the .356 Win. and the .358 Win. are both fine elk rounds in the timber and mixed cover. When you're up close and personal with a bull, the .444 Marlin, .450 Marlin Magnum and the venerable .45-70 Gov't will punch a sizeable hole in an elk's hide, as well as delivering a healthy dose of energy.

No matter what caliber you choose, shot placement is everything. Take out a single lung and a bull can go for miles. Likewise, let your point-of-aim drift too far back (read that as a gut shot) and you might never find the animal. The preferred shot placement is behind the shoulder, through both lungs and out the opposite side. Avoid targeting the front shoulder. You'll probably break the shoulder, but your bullet might only make it a short distance into the chest cavity. A bull with a broken front leg and one lung out of commission means a blood trail forever. You'll need a stout heart, good legs and lots of determination to finally put that bull on the ground for keeps.

Blackpowder shooters seem to prefer .54 caliber, or larger, frontloaders for use on elk. I've used a .50 caliber smokepole without having any problems, but heavy bullets are my choice. A .54-caliber rifle offers enhanced frontal impact, but with bullets of the same weight .50-caliber has better sectional density for enhanced penetration. Take your choice, but never take a chance on fringe shots. About 100 yards is a good maximum shooting range for blackpowder elk hunters. I've never been on an elk hunt when it didn't rain, or snow, or both. Since blackpowder and Pydrodex are both sensitive to ambient moisture, cover the muzzle of your rifle with a thin piece of tape and weatherproof the ignition cap. There's nothing worse than taking aim at the trophy of a lifetime and then experiencing powder ignition failure. Believe me, it happens (Been there, done that!).

Bowhunters will want to use carbon or graphite arrows for maximum penetration. Two-bladed broadheads are my choice for elk, but some guys do well with other blade configurations. The cutting edges of your broadhead must be absolutely razor-sharp. When placed correctly, most elk won't go any farther when hit with a broadhead, than they will when hit with a bullet. The trick is putting your arrow where it counts. Avoid taking any shot at an elk head on. There isn't a very good target when the bull is facing you. You're better off letting the elk pass by and placing your arrow right behind the nearside shoulder. Then, the broadhead is more likely to compromise arteries within both lungs and possibly the top of the heart. Death will come within minutes. And if you're sure of your shot, avoid pushing the elk. Elk are tough (I've said that more than once). Wait for the broadhead to do its job. Calm down, take lots of deep breaths, have something to eat and then take up the trail. When you find the bull, if he's still on his feet, or has his head up, put another arrow in him.

Field care: Even promptly gutted, with snow on the ground and cold weather, elk carcass spoilage can occur. If you're alone, field dressing an elk can be a real chore. Even turning a bull over to get at the

Photo by Durwood Hollis

When you have to transport an animal as large as an elk, pack stock is the only way to go.

There are lots of opportunities for elk throughout the West. This bull was taken in eastern Oregon.

Photo by Bob Robb

underside may be difficult for a lone hunter. Remember, an elk is a big animal. Wrestling all of that dead weight can be impossible in some situations. Whatever you do, don't leave the kill site without removing all of the internal viscera, including the heart and lungs. If you have to leave to find help, then do so, but don't be gone too long. The key to prime elk steaks on the table rests in prompt field care.

Once the elk is gutted, use something to prop open the abdominal cavity. Furthermore, get the carcass off of the ground by sliding several large diameter branches underneath. The containment of body heat over a period of time can result in spoilage. The secret to lowering the internal temperature of the carcass is air circulation. Another good idea is to pull the gut pile some distance away. Any marauding predators, including birds, will most likely focus their feeding efforts on the viscera first, rather than going directly to the car-

cass. You wouldn't believe what a couple of ravens, or a mob of crows can do to an elk carcass (they tend to peck at the eyes, tearing out pieces of the surrounding hide in the process) in a short period of time.

If you quarter the carcass on the spot, make sure to hang the meat off of the ground. Not only will this allow for better cooling, it keeps it away from hungry black bears. Most game departments provide printed flyers about where and how to hang game meat. Read the advisory carefully and follow it to the letter. If you don't, then don't complain when a bear makes off with all of your meat.

Meat transport: After you gut an elk, you're still left with the problem of getting it back to camp, from there to your vehicle and then to the butcher. Elk quarters will weigh about 150 to 175 pounds each. It's a rare individual that can pack an entire elk quarter uphill and down over any distance. Split the same weight between two guys and the task just became doable. Even then, it will take four separate trips between the kill site and camp to accomplish the job. A fifth trip will also be necessary to retrieve the cape, antlers and any meat trimmings that have been left behind. Just how far you have to backpack the meat will dictate how much time it takes to get the job done. Believe me when I say, packing elk quarters is lots of hard work.

The use of pack stock transport is the most practical way to bring meat out of many wilderness locations. Elk are often hunted a considerable distance from any roadhead. One of the last bulls I took fell some 27 miles from anything that resembled a vehicle track. The two in previous consecutive seasons were taken some 30 miles into the backcountry. Just try backpacking more than 400-pounds of meat, cape and antlers any of those distances. In such locales, horses and mules are the only meat retrieval mechanisms (short of a helicopter) that make any sense.

Western movies will not a horseman make. I've ridden horses for years and consider myself reasonably competent in the saddle. That said, I've also been bitten, stepped on, kicked and worse in the process. I once rode a very difficult seven hours with a dislocated shoulder after being thrown from a horse. Years later, my shoulder still aches at times. Unless you have enough equine experience to feel comfortable with saddle and pack stock, I wouldn't advise riding off into the elk woods alone trailing a couple of pack animals. The best approach is to hire a packer, or hunt with an outfitting service. If a horseback hunt is in your future, make sure you acquire a saddle scabbard that fits your rifle or bow. Since most guys who hunt elk on horse do it over and over again, you'll find a set of saddlebags another good investment. And rain is always possible in elk country, so a waxed-cotton riding duster is an absolute "must have" piece of gear when horses are in the picture.

Some guys have tried to use llamas for pack stock, but these animals fall short in that department. You can't ride a llama, so they must be led on foot. Furthermore, you can only pack about 50 pounds on each animal. Llamas are easy to handle, and demand little in the way of care when they are in camp. And while they spit, they seem to like humans (one will probably try to crawl into your tent at night). However, you just can't leave a string of llamas out grazing, even hobbled or staked, while you're hunting. Some of the best elk country is also bear and mountain lion country. While these predators will seldom bother horses or mules, they wouldn't hesitate when it comes to making a meal out of a llama. While llamas might work as pack animals on a deer hunt, they are out of their league when it comes elk hunting.

Of course, you can use a game cart. Most of these contraptions are homemade, but a few models are factory-produced. I've used a game cart upon occasion; both by myself and with some assistance, to move freshly killed meat over significant distances. It can be difficult to maneuver a cart in heavy timber, across areas of blow-down, through brush and in really rough country. When rolled along an established trail, one of these ingenious man-powered vehicles is just right for the job. It should be noted, that it isn't legal to use a game cart in a designated Wilderness Area. If you had plans about wheeling a load of elk venison out of the backcountry this coming season, first make sure there are no mandated constraints about its use in your hunting area.

Tips on where to go: Most elk hunters head for northern Idaho, western Colorado, western Montana and northwestern Wyoming since all four states can boast of huge numbers of Rocky Mountain Elk. Both British Columbia and Alberta, Canada also receive their fair share of elk hunters. There are some great bulls to be found here, but it's best to book your hunt with a reliable outfitter. Likewise, Washington and Oregon are on the short list of states where good elk hunting can be found. Roosevelt elk can be found in the west and Rocky Mountain elk in the east in both Pacific Northwest states. While elk can be found throughout the west, the best license availability and hunting opportunities will be found in the six states listed below:

My advice is to try hunting Roosevelt elk along the Oregon coast. Tags can generally be purchased across the counter before the season begins. There's plenty of public land and easily accessible timber holdings. The downside is extremely tough hunting terrain and jungle-thick cover.

There are so many elk in some regions of Wyoming that they are becoming a plague. The hunting won't be easy (when is elk hunting ever easy?), but seasons are liberal. Many of the desert and cedar country herds north of Rock Springs and east of Thermopolis remains under-hunted. And there are always the hunts for both bulls and cows on the National Elk Refuge and Grand Teton National Park. My favorite Wyoming elk haunt is just south of the southeast corner of Yellowstone Park. You'll need a guide if you're a nonresident, but that's the way it works in the Cowboy State.

Utah also has a burgeoning population of elk. Many of the hunting units in the southeast region are at or over game department elk management objectives. The best hunting here will be on private ground or with limited-entry permits. In northern Utah, the South Slope area usually has permits for both bulls and cows available. This area is probably the best bet for elk in the Beehive State.

Idaho is kind of a mixed bag when comes to elk hunting. In my experience, it's either feast or famine. The middle fork of the Salmon River is great elk country and I've seen lots of animals there. You'll have to struggle through heavy timber and be in good enough physical shape to handle the straight up and down terrain, but the hunting can be awesome. Most of this country is really wild, so hunting with a guide can tilt the odds in your favor.

Colorado is a favored destination for many, but you're going to have to put in some serious research to find the hot spots. The elk tag situation changes from year to year, so lots of preparation will be in order if you want to hunt this state. The San Juan Basin in the southwest has been good for the last few years, but you'll burn up plenty of calories to score on a bull. The northwest corner of the state gets a lot of hunting pressure, but there are plenty of elk there. And east of Denver, the towns of Craig, Rifle, Grand Junction and Montrose bracket some peerless elk country. If you do your homework (telephone, maps and personal contact) and are willing to go beyond the crowds, I can almost guarantee you a bull in any of these areas.

Montana has been a real hunting bug-a-boo for me, but there are lots of big bull elk in that state. Elk numbers have really been exploding in the last few years. The best areas are in the southwest, south-central and central regions of the state. Hopefully, you'll have better luck there than I have had.

There are some record elk herds to be found in Arizona, New Mexico and California (this state has Roosevelt, Rocky Mountain and tule elk). Unfortunately, it's tough to draw a tag in any of these states. New Mexico has some land-owner permits that can be had, but expect to dig deep in your wallet. The biggest elk I've ever seen were in east-central Arizona, but don't hold your breath expecting to draw a tag. California's Tejon Ranch, located just an hour's drive north of Los Angeles, produced a bull in 2000 that scored more than 420 Boone & Crockett points. There are only five permits issued on this ranch every season and they are expensive, but if it's a "book elk" you want, then get on the waiting list.

What about the future? Prior to European contact, elk herds on this continent ranged from the Atlantic to the Pacific, and from Canada all the way down into the American southwest. An estimated 10 million elk roamed throughout much of North American. As an easy source of food for settlers, without hunting seasons or bag limits, the animals were shot indiscriminately. Of the six elk subspecies found at the time of discovery, only four remained by the mid-19th century. At the beginning of the 20th century, only a fraction of the Manitoba elk population remained. While Rocky Mountain elk persisted in the Yellowstone-Jackson Hole area, their numbers, too, were on the verge of collapse. And the tule elk, which once numbered more than 500,000 animals, barely escaped extinction.

Today, the total North American elk population numbers more than 1 million animals. Without the vision of many early naturalists, conservationists and hunters, this tremendous comeback wouldn't have been possible. Aggressive game management, the protection of traditional winter grounds, the creation of National Parks and Wilderness Areas, the beneficence of private land holders and even forest fires have all been part of the reemergence of elk from the sunset of history.

Just 25 years ago, there were only about 500,000 elk. These numbers have doubled and are continuing to rise. Much of the credit for this accelerated population growth goes to the Rocky Mountain Elk Foundation (RMEF), whose tireless effort in acquiring and enhancing elk habitats, as well as funding scientific studies and transplanting elk into suitable areas, is without parallel.

With the elk population booming, there are more hunting opportunities than you can imagine. You'll most likely have to participate in a license lottery, but that's just part of the overall management plan. With the addition of special archery and blackpowder elk seasons, most usually scheduled during the rut, your chances at scoring on a bull are better than ever. A set of elk antlers will never grace your wall, nor will a mouth-watering elk roast get anywhere near your dinner table if you don't make the effort to get into the game. It will take planning, preparation and just a little luck for everything to come together, but the time to begin is right now! Good luck.

Photo by Durwood Hollis

Heavily loaded pack stock means antlers on the wall and meat in the freezer. You can experience this kind of success, but only if you start to plan next season's elk hunt now!

Fleet of hoof and possessing uncanny eyesight, the pronghorn antelope is truly the "Prince of the Prairie."

PRINCE OF THE PRAIRIE: PRONGHORN ANTELOPE

The last of its kind, the pronghorn antelope has made a remarkable comeback from near extinction.

The barking noise came from somewhere on the far ridge. Sounding like a dog with a sore throat, the sharp wheezing sound was the first real evidence of what I'd searched for the past two days. With the naked eye, only an ocean of sage and a scattering of rocky outcroppings were evident. Clearly, the optical search for the origin of the strange sound would take more than just a casual glance. Finding a comfortable place to sit down on the side of a rocky hillside was a challenge, but necessary if any amount of time was to be spent in

Photo by Durwood Hollis

Binocular work, and lots of it, is the key to finding antelope.

Photo by Durwood Hollis

The typical pronghorn herd includes a dominate buck (seen here in the rear making a strategic retreat) and several does.

visual scrutiny. Using my binoculars in a consistent manner—left-to-right, right-to-left, then dropping down to each subsequent level—I was able to discern every scrap of perceivable visual information.

Even though the strange barking was heard several more times, the gusting wind prevented me from pinpointing the origin. What finally put all the pieces of the puzzle together was a slight flicker of movement on the opposite ridge. Confirmation came when the images of two pronghorn antelope became manifest in my field of view. A doe and buck stood just below the top of the ridge, easily blending in with the chest-high sage. The barking came from the buck, which used the vocalization to alert others of his kind, or as a warning threat. Not being another pronghorn, I wasn't quite sure with certainty what the sound meant.

Both antelope stood completely still and watched me. Even at nearly 500 yards, the pronghorns were aware of an alien presence in their environment. Apparently, the distance was adequate enough to provide a measure of security for the antelope. Of course, even with a solid rest any shooting attempt on my part was out of the question. Slipping behind some rocks, I dropped over the back edge of one ridge and made for the other. Keeping low and out of sight, I planned on making my way in behind the pronghorns. Once in position, the shooting distance would be optimal. Like

so many other antelopes stalks, the entire operation fell apart at the most critical moment.

Crawling the last few feet, I moved in next to a low rock outcropping. Not taking the time to look for the antelope (they had to be where I last saw them), I slipped off my pack and pushed it in front of me for a rifle rest. Removing my hat, so as to minimize my outline, I slowly eased into shooting position. Surprisingly, the antelope had vanished! Thinking that they had only moved a short distance, I brought the binoculars into play. The animals weren't hard to find. Four ridges away, both antelope were quickly disappearing over the horizon. What tipped my hand? Who knows? It could have been an undetectable breeze that carried fragments of my scent in the wrong direction. More likely, the pronghorn caught sight of some suspicious movement and decided to head for the next county. If there's one asset that antelope have in generous supply it's keen eyesight.

A family affair: Pronghorn antelope, or *Antilocapra americana* as they are known taxonomically, is the last survivor of a group of animals that became extinct at the end of the last ice age (about 11,000 years ago). In addition to the pronghorn, paleontologists have discovered two other related species in the fossil record. The larger of the two was a four-horned rock-hopping antelope that lived in the mountains. The smaller species wasn't much larger than a jackrabbit. This tiny antelope also had four-horns and made its home on the plains. The pronghorn is thought to be a distant relative of some Asian antelope. However, without any direct genetic connection to other living mammals, it stands alone as the quintessential American big game animal—a monotype.

Since pronghorn populations vary slightly geographically, there are currently five recognizable subspecies: the American pronghorn, *Antilocapra americana*; the Oregon pronghorn, *A. a. oregona*; the Mexican pronghorn, *A. a. mexicana merriam*; the Baja California Peninsular pronghorn, *A. a. peninsularis nelson*; and the northern Mexican Sonoran pronghorn, *A. a. sonoriensis goldman*. Quite frankly, to the untrained eye, all pronghorn antelope look surprisingly alike. While there are slight dissimilarities between each subspecies, taken as a whole these variations may be nothing more than simple environmental adaptation.

Prairie dwellers: While many explorers and mountain men encountered pronghorns, the Lewis and Clark exploration (1804-1806) was the first to name the animals and collect scientific specimens. Historical accounts indicated that these animals were only found on the prairie land east of the Rocky Mountains. However, pronghorns also reportedly lived in California's Central Valley and throughout southern California wherever adequate habitat could be found. Today, these animals are well-entrenched in southwestern Oregon, southern Idaho, Nevada, Texas, Montana, Wyoming, Colorado, California, Arizona, New Mexico, the Dakotas, parts of Kansas, Nebraska and Oklahoma, northern Mexico, Baja California and the Canadian prairie provinces of Alberta and Saskatchewan.

Ravage and recovery: It is estimated by some researchers that the total number of antelope prior to the exploration and settlement of the West exceeded that of buffalo. Conservative estimates (who was there at the time to count?) put the pronghorn population of that time ranging from 35 to 50 million animals. Toward the end of the Ice Age, antelope numbers began to exhibit an abrupt decline. No doubt climatic and habitat changes were initial factors. Of course, the arrival of man on the North American continent also played a role in the downward spiral of the pronghorn in both total population and variety of species. In recent times, early settlers with their fences, rifles and pursuit dogs quickly decimated the remaining pronghorn. Range conversion from a prairie of mixed forbs, sage and grass that feed both the antelope and the buffalo, to ungrazed grassland after the killing off of the buffalo herds that smothered the tender buds that pronghorn

The white hair on a pronghorn's rump can be raised quickly, signaling danger to other antelope over a wide area.

Photo by Durwood Hollis

Here's what you're looking for— good prongs with lots of curve.

Photo by Durwood Hollis

relish, was another important factor in an overall reduction of antelope numbers. Likewise, market hunters also took their share.

At the beginning of the 20th Century, less than 5,000 antelope remained. Thanks to efforts by a few concerned pioneering individuals like Gifford Pinchot, Theodore Roosevelt and others, the pronghorn antelope has made serious recovery throughout much of its historic range. This recovery is not one entirely dependent on protective laws. Active wildlife management, including the trapping and reintroduction of the pronghorn to areas where they once flourished, has helped immensely. Current population estimates place the total number of these animals in excess of a million.

The look: A mature American pronghorn buck will stand approximately 35 to 42 inches at the shoulder and weigh 90 to 120 pounds on the hoof. Does are

about 20 pounds smaller in size. Both sexes have apricot-tan, hollow body hair, with sharply contrasting white rumps, underbellies, chests and facial patches. While both sexes are similarly colored, bucks have distinctive dark brown or black facial masks and similarly colored cheek patches just below each ear. Pronghorns have brittle, hollow hair, with a sparse undercoat of finer textured hair. A short mane runs along the top of the neck, from between the ears to the top of the shoulders. This pelage can be raised or lowered for ventilation or heat retention. The white hair on the caudal disk (rump) can be quickly raised (flashed) and seen from a long distance. This serves as a danger signal to other herd members, as well as other herds at large.

Visual acuity: The eyes of a pronghorn are quite large, allowing the animals to see both laterally and vertically. This ability serves as an early warning mechanism to alert the antelope to ground-based pursuit predators (mountain lions, wolves, coyotes and bobcats), as well as airborne attack (eagles, condors, and hawks). Furthermore, the eye itself is heavily pigmented for protection against the glare so often encountered in a cloudless sky, or from the glare off of a carpet of snow. Additionally, long, black eyelashes are effective shades from direct sunlight. Pronghorns reportedly have visual acuity more than eight-times greater than man. The scientific determination of this remains to be seen, but suffice it to say that these animals definitely have superior distance vision.

Specialization: Pronghorns have a large heart and windpipe. While these animals are about the size of a sheep, their heart is twice as large. The windpipe is more than two times larger in circumference than that of a human. Furthermore, an antelope can move four times the volume of air in a single breath than is humanly possible. These cardiac and respiratory enhancements allow the pronghorn to run 35 to 40 miles per hour over broken ground, with bursts of more than 60 miles per hour possible. Reportedly, a doe antelope can run slightly faster than a buck. The pronghorn antelope's ability to outdistance human predators likely accounts for the scarcity of fossil evidence in connection with prehistoric butchering sites. And a pronghorn has far less fat than deer, elk, or mountain sheep. Since indigenous peoples sought out the fattest and most easily accessible food resource, antelope was not their first choice.

Antelope can't jump? Research has established that a mature pronghorn antelope can leap across a span of 27 feet in one bound. Even more amazing, these animals possess the ability to jump a distance of 8 feet straight up into the air. Unlike deer, which can link both horizontal and vertical movement together, antelope usually can't seem to duplicate such a feat. And while they have been known (on rare occasions) to jump barriers, they usually don't even try to clear a raggedy barbed-wire fence sagging less than 24 inches in height. No sir. Pronghorn would rather slide under, go around, or pile against a fence than jump over it.

Prongs and cutters: Antelope horn is made up of fused hair over a bony core. This imparts a fibrous, furrowed, rough texture to these manifestations of masculinity. The term "pronghorn" is derived from the sharp point at the terminus of each horn. Tiny supplementary projections (burrs) can also be present at any place along the length of the horn. The horn tip is curved and

Photo by Durwood Hollis

Female antelope also have horns, but they are short and insignificant.

Having survived the winter, this young buck is easily identified by his curved horns, dark facial mask and cheek patches.

Photo by Jim Matthews

provides a purchase point for combat wrestling between two bucks. While antelope do occasionally inflict puncture wounds with their horns, most fights center around pushing, shoving and chasing. A prominent fork (cutter) extends forward and out from the main shaft. With the exception of the white tip, the rest of the horn is completely black in color. Horns are fully grown by July, or at the latest, September. A representative mature pronghorn antelope buck will wear horns measuring at least 14 inches in length (measured around the outside curve). Any set of horns in excess of 15 inches in total overall length, with substantial cutters, is a fine trophy. Horn length can be difficult to judge under field conditions. Pronghorn ears are about 6 inches in length. Any horn that is greater than double the length of an ear starts to get interesting.

Female antelope also have horns. These adornments are short and unbranched. Instead of being firmly connected to a solid core, horns on does can easily be lifted off of their attachment points. All antelope horns, buck and doe alike, are shed annually. Horn shedding begins shortly after the conclusion of the September rut period and continues on through the middle part of November. Even though pronghorns shed their horns, the bony inner core remains in place. Only the outer sheath is cast off. I once shot a buck in late October and at bullet contact one of his horn sheaths simply "popped" up into the air. Horn loss is one of the problems that last season antelope hunters must face. And it's easy to loose a horn sheath in the sage. Once the horns are

Photo by Durwood Hollis

Even handgunners can find a keeper. Hunter Algird Kavalauskas proudly poses with a fine buck.

shed, both bucks and doe look very much alike. This allows the normal solitary or bachelor herd buck to blend in with the large predominately female winter "super" herds as a protective device.

Birth and death: Once successful mating has taken place, the gestation period is approximately eight months (250 days). Most pronghorn does give birth to twins, which are quickly imprinted on their mother and follow her everywhere. Shortly after birth, the doe consumes the byproducts of the birthing process and licks the tiny fawns clean. This eliminates any scent that may attract predators. Furthermore, fawns can lie out flat next to natural objects in the environment (rocks, brush, cow droppings, etc.) and easily vanish from sight. Once the fawns are safely out-of-sight, the doe allows the predator to chase after her. Easily outdistancing any pursuer, when the danger has passed the doe returns to her offspring. Even with superior camouflage and predator avoidance mechanisms, only one fawn generally lives to maturity. Most fawn mortality can be attributed to coyotes. However, bobcats are also responsible for some predation. And in rimrock country, golden eagles are another pronghorn predator.

Pronghorns are well adapted to handle adverse weather conditions. During a storm, antelope will lay down with their backs to the wind. The hollow hair is held flat to the body for maximum heat retention, even in below zero conditions. Pronghorns are built to handle such extremes. As long as the snow depth doesn't prevent movement and access to food sources, most pronghorns will survive. Nevertheless, winter is hard on both the young and the old. The greatest herd mortality will occur during this time of the year. Subject to the vicissitudes of nature, few older antelope survive the first tough winter. In captivity, pronghorn may live more than 20 years. In the wild, however, an 8-year-old pronghorn is a senior citizen.

I can recall watching pronghorn rebound from a particularly tough winter, only to have the entire population crash during a late spring storm. Each subsequent hunting season after that horrible winter of deep snow and subzero temperatures, larger and larger animals were taken. Those hunters who managed to draw a license reported sightings of near-record class bucks. The upcoming hunting season had real promise. That is, until a late spring snowstorm swept across the plains devastating the antelope in that region. Come hunting season, there wasn't a buck with horns longer than 12 inches to be found. Such unanticipated occurrences are just part of the overall picture of pronghorn hunting.

Cud chewers: Even though pronghorns are predominately found in areas of vast grasslands, unlike

After several attempts, the author finally scored on this nice buck using the burlap sack trick described in this chapter.

Photo by Durwood Hollis

An accurate rifle chambered in a flat-shooting caliber is a pronghorn prerequisite.

Photo by Durwood Hollis

the buffalo, domestic cattle and sheep, they are browsers and not grazers. Antelope prefer newly sprouted buds, forbs and sedges, with grasses accounting for only a small portion of pronghorn fodder. On the prairie, sage makes up much of their diet. And they will consume agricultural crops, with a strong preference for alfalfa and winter wheat. Pronghorns are true ruminants (cud chewers). Bacterial fermentation takes place in the large rumen, just ahead of the true stomach. This process occurs again in the intestinal sac at the terminus of the small intestine. The internal workings of rumination, in conjunction with the liver and kidneys, serve to remove poisons from plant materials ingested by the animals.

While they are often active throughout the day, at some point in the late morning or early afternoon pronghorns will often lay down. During these rest periods is when the cud is masticated. Antelope are never completely unguarded. Even at rest, these animals are still on the lookout for danger. Let a coyote get too close and the herd will be up on its feet in an instant. Likewise, the appearance of a hunter in the distance can be cause for alarm. Despite their ever-cautious nature, I've found it easier to stalk prong-

horns when they are bedded down for an afternoon of cud chewing.

Find a keeper: One good thing about antelope hunting is that you don't have to get up early in the morning to be successful. Pronghorn are creatures of the open prairies and can be found feeding nearly all day long. For the most part, you can encounter antelope without much trouble. While finding an antelope isn't difficult, getting within rifle range of a trophy buck can be almost impossible. There are places— Wyoming's Red Desert for example—that are as flat as a slate pool table. Even worse, there isn't enough cover to hide a prairie dog, let alone a hunter. In this county, you can find some of the largest antelope anywhere. Putting your license on one is another story altogether! Carefully devised hunting tactics, familiarity with pronghorn movement patterns, and a flat-shooting rifle are important. And if it were my license, I'd try to catch the animals during the rut. Then the buck you're after is more likely to have his thoughts on sex, rather than survival. And this is just the edge you'll need. Hunting in these areas can be frustrating, but a determined hunter who can handle extreme target presentations can pull it off.

Another place to find a trophy buck is in the foothills after opening day. Any buck that's outlived four hunting seasons hasn't done so without using his brains. At the first shot, many of those old boys, along with a scattering of does, come to their senses really quickly. Most would-be antelope hunters roar around the flatland in their four-wheel-drive vehicles searching for pronghorn. At such times, the older bucks generally move to the roadless foothills nearby. Since the average pronghorn hunter wouldn't think of getting too far away from a vehicle, the truly big bucks usually escape detection.

Hunting the foothills for pronghorn isn't something that came to me naturally. After two days of looking for a trophy buck in the flats, the only animals I had encountered were does and smallish bucks. Quite frankly, I was ready to give up and try another area. A set of foothills lay adjacent to where I had been hunt-

ing. Now, these weren't gentle rolling knolls. No sir. What I am talking about is an expansive set of sage-covered, seriously steep near-mountains. Lacing my boots tight, I began my ascent. About halfway to the crest, I ran into antelope tracks. A short distance farther the first pronghorn came into view. As I expected, it was a solitary buck. After that it was only a matter of finding the right animal. The rugged foothills provided a refuge from hunter harassment and allowed the pronghorn to hide in plain view.

Burlap sack bingo: Another pronghorn hunting tip that I picked up had its origin on the plains of southern Africa. The behavior of the African springbok and our pronghorn antelope is quite similar. While the springbok can jump, like the pronghorn it prefers to go under, rather than over any fence it encounters. In springbok country traditional fence-crossing points are clearly defined by well-used game trails that run under the bot-

Special blackpowder hunting seasons can give the frontloader a real edge.

Photo by Matt Foster

Photo by Durwood Hollis

A Wyoming game department wildlife biologist records hunter success data as part of an overall pronghorn management plan.

tom strand of wire. The best way to hunt these animals is to ambush them at one of these crossing points. Knowledgeable hunters channel the springbok to a specific point by draping a burlap sack over the fence at every crossing. The burlap sacks tend to frighten the springbok and they avoid going under the fence at that point. This tactic is used to funnel the animals to a specific crossing where there is a waiting hunter and no burlap sack.

Returning from Africa, I couldn't wait to try the burlap sack trick on North American pronghorn. In one area of southwestern Wyoming a trophy buck had eluded me for several seasons. The region was absolutely flat, which made stalking completely impossible. And the pronghorn knew enough about hunters and rifles to stay well beyond shooting range. Any time a vehicle or person came into view, the buck and his band of merry followers headed for the barbed wire fence that ran right through the middle of his territory. Furthermore, they never crossed under the fence at the same location twice.

Well before daylight, I hiked into the area with an armful of potato bags. At every antelope crossing along the fence, I draped a sack over the top stand of barbed wire. When I was finished, there was a sack at every point where pronghorn crossed. Everywhere, that is, except one location. It was there I made my stand, hidden under some discreetly positioned tumbleweed. Just after dawn, my hunting partner made his move. Making no attempt to conceal himself, my buddy made straight for the resident band of antelope. Right on cue, the black-horned buck and his followers started trotting toward the fence. Sure enough, the antelope shied away from every crossing point guarded by a burlap sack. Like a pull toy on a string, the buck and his lovely ladies were on a direct course for my position. A big doe was in the lead. Following her in single-file were several other does, fawns and a couple of run-of-the-mill bucks. The big buck was dead last. Pausing only to duck down and slide under the lowest strand of barbed wire, one-by-one the antelope quickly made it to the other side of the fence. When my old nemesis started to follow the rest of his clan, it was time for action. Finding the buck in my scope, a practiced trigger squeeze and an appropriately placed bullet settled the matter.

Pronghorn guns and calibers: With few exceptions, most antelope hunters will use a bolt-action rifle.

For the money, this design offers peerless accuracy and reliable functioning. There are a few that enjoy the special challenge that comes with the choice of a single-shot rifle. Since the first shot at an antelope is your best and often only opportunity, a single-shot rifle isn't much of a hindrance. Pumps, autoloaders and lever-action rifles are subject jamming-up when used on the high plains. All of the wind-blown dirt, dust and sand, so often encountered in typical antelope country can gum-up the best of these repeaters. Furthermore, the level of accuracy demanded by pronghorn pursuit is difficult to achieve with these firearm designs.

Antelope hunting is characterized by somewhat longer shots than the average deer hunter is used to making. This being true, then the selection of the flattest-shooting calibers possible is a prerequisite to success. To wring the best out of any high-intensity chambering, a relatively high-magnification riflescope is another necessity. Veteran speed goat hunters have long depended on the .257 Roberts, .25-06 Rem., .270 Win. and the venerable .30-06 Spfd. for much of their hunting. Since pronghorn aren't all that tough to kill, my preference tends to move in the direction of the .243 Win., 6mm Rem., and the .264 Win. Magnum.

The 100-grain loads in any of these calibers will provide sensational results. The 6mm Weatherby and Lazzeroni magnum chamberings offer enhanced ballistic potential, but pronghorn hunting is about trophy selection and projectile placement. Those critical elements are your responsibility alone.

Smoke and mirrors: Even with a scope mounted on the frontstuffer of your choice (permissible in some areas), it's challenging to launch a blackpowder-driven projectile any distance with complete assurance of hitting where you're aiming. The maximum distance most frontloading affectionados are able to shoot is about 125 yards. Any seasoned pronghorn hunter knows that such shots at antelope are usually the exception, rather than the rule. While you can certainly be successful with a primitive firearm by employing the same tactics as a bowhunter, I recently observed something new in this arena.

Watching a herd of antelope with my binoculars as they fed across a distant sage-covered plateau, I tried to devise a course that would intersect the direction of their movement. While I mentally plotted out my strategy, a puff of smoke followed by a loud boom erupted from the sage. All of the pronghorn, with the exception

Pronghorns are suckers for decoys. This is one weakness that bowhunters can use to their advantage.

Photo by Jim Matthews

Trophy pronghorn don't come easy. Putting a buck in the record book means that you're going to have to do lots of looking.

of a buck, started running. Within seconds, the buck keeled over. Just then, I noticed a hunter materialize out of the sage. It should be noted that whatever sage was present on that plain wasn't any more than a few inches in height. In my binoculars, I could see that the hunter hadn't climbed out of a pit blind. In fact, I couldn't really determine where he came from.

Curious about what had happened. I made my way over to where my camouflage competition was field dressing a nice pronghorn buck. Nearby, a blackpowder rifle lay over his hat. As I subsequently learned, he had used a folding box made out of reflective plastic as a blind. The external surfaces of this hideout mirrored the surroundings in which it sat. And longitudinal slits near the top allowed a view of approaching game. Unless you were really close, the box was virtually undetectable. As it turned out, the guy designed office interiors for a living. He had simply used some of the materials from his trade to fabricate a mirrored blind.

When hunting pronghorn, blackpowder hunters need an edge. There are times when stalking just won't work. Setting up a blind at a waterhole, fence crossing

or other suitable location is one answer. A blackpowder hunter must do whatever it takes to get into position for a manageable shot. It isn't all that difficult. Creativity is the name of this game. And the interior designer's unique blind certainly fell within that paradigm.

Bow and arrows: If you want a shot at pronghorn in states like California, Arizona or New Mexico, where a limited number of licenses are allotted, try your hand at bowhunting. Usually the drawing odds for bowhunting licenses are much more favorable than putting in for a rifle permit. Like blackpowder pronghorn hunters, archers are faced with the problem of getting close enough to put an arrow into a buck's boiler room. You can stalk pronghorn successfully if the hunting terrain possesses enough irregularities to provide adequate concealment. A blind will work, but only when the animals are used to seeing it. If they are not, they will shy away from it.

The best pronghorn bowhunting approach I've used is a decoy. When the rut is on, a dominant buck will drive off every perceived competitor. And he'll go out of his way to pick a fight. A bowhunter can exploit this antelope behavior easily with a decoy. To get the buck to come to you, prop a pronghorn decoy in front of your position. A silhouette decoy that folds for easy carrying is just the ticket for this performance. Stalk close, position the decoy where it's visible and wait for the action to start. An antelope call can also be incorporated with the decoy to draw the buck's attention. Whatever else you do, be ready to shoot. With a decoy, things can develop rather rapidly.

Where to go: From Oklahoma to Oregon 17 states play host to antelope. While there are a number of trophy-caliber pronghorn bucks in nearly every area, those looking to put a head in the record books will be best served by concentrating their efforts in those states with the greatest potential. Arizona, California (residents only) and Nevada are three top trophy pronghorn

states. You'll have to fight long odds to draw a tag, but that's just part of the game.

Some years back a friend of mine obtained a license the first time he entered his application in the California antelope tag drawing. On opening day he shot an incredible buck that easily made the record book. While he was involved in field dressing chores, however, he watched wide-eyed as another antelope with significantly larger horns trotted by. And before he was able to pack his trophy back to the truck, he saw two more equally as fine pronghorns. The reason for all of this was an antelope management plan that limited the number of available licenses.

New Mexico: This is another state with sizeable numbers of trophy bucks. The best antelope habitat is on private land, but that isn't necessarily a drawback.

The best way to preserve the delicate flavor of pronghorn venison is to field dress your buck immediately and get the carcass into the shade as soon as possible.

Photo by Craig Boddington

Mapping out a plan for pronghorn success takes some serious strategy and a little luck.

Photo by Durwood Hollis

Landowners are issued private land permits to use as they deem necessary. Outfitters specializing in trophy antelope hunts can simply make arrangements with a rancher for one of these licenses. With a season of only a few days and limited hunting pressure, the potential for a trophy buck is incredible. These hunts aren't cheap, but what did you expect? If you're serious about putting a set of horns in the book, then New Mexico is definitely one place that I'd consider.

Utah: A real sleeper when it comes to record-book antelope heads, the animals are scattered in small herds all over the western half and they go unnoticed. Just finding antelope in Utah can be tough. If you draw a license, then it's time to get on the telephone with local game biologists. In my experience, these seasoned professionals can put you in the right spot.

Colorado: This is another antelope state that's often overlooked. Like everywhere else, you'll have to draw for a license. Most antelope found in Colorado live on private land, so count on shelling out a trespass fee. In spite of all of this, there are still some fine bucks to be had in this state.

Wyoming and Montana: Both of these states are the best prospects for finding antelope on public land. Just because they are popular pronghorn destinations, doesn't mean that they don't have record book bucks—they do! You're just going to have to invest in some serious boot leather to find a nice specimen. Put enough distance between yourself and the nearest road access, then your chances at finding a trophy buck will significantly improve.

The largest pronghorn buck I ever laid eyes on made his home in central Wyoming. There in some rugged little hills between Shoshoni and Riverton, I encountered what must have been a new world-record pronghorn. That particular buck was a loner and his horns were two and one-half times the length of his ears in height, with incredible forward cutters (prongs) and a curve that traveled halfway down and then jutted straight back. A conservative estimate would have put the length of a single horn at somewhere near 21 inches. If that isn't a world record, then I don't know what is. Unfortunately, I was hunting sage grouse and not pronghorn. I kept in contact with the rancher where I saw the animal, and as far as he knew that huge buck never fell to a bullet or arrow. Yes, there are still big antelope out there and in the most unlikely places.

On the table: Despite all of the great things about pronghorn hunting, the meat does have somewhat of a checkered reputation on the table. No matter what kind of big game you hunt, if you push an animal hard, massive amounts of adrenaline will be released into the body. Furthermore, during the rut, male animals spend most of their time chasing females, copulating and driving off rivals. All of these activities involve the production of vast quantities of adrenaline, testosterone and other hormones. A neck roast taken from an elk (some of the best venison of all) during the height of the rut isn't fit for man—or the family dog. Any delay eviscerating and cooling a carcass during warm weather will also impart a pungent taste to game meat. Combine all of this and the result can be some raunchy tasting pronghorn venison.

Personally, I've never had a bad piece of pronghorn venison. This is probably true because chasing the animals from hell to breakfast with a four-wheel vehicle isn't part of my hunting methodology. Since most pronghorn pursuit takes place during warm weather, I also make every effort to immediately field dress, skin and remove the meat off of the skeletal structure. You wouldn't believe the number antelope that have not yet been gutted that end-up at game meat processing operations. Even those carcasses that have been field dressed are often left to hang in the sun, thrown in the back of a pickup bed and carried around all day long—or worse. Given such poor primary field care, nobody should be surprised if antelope venison isn't up to par.

Even with every precaution, antelope taken early in the season may be difficult to deal with. Combine rutting activities with hot weather and you can have some gamy tasting meat on your hands. My suggestion is to field dress and cool the carcass without delay. And rather than taking a chance with fresh venison chops and ground meat, have your antelope made into smoked sausage and salami. The spices and smoking process usually overpower any residual funky game taste. I've always believed if you're not going to eat it, then why kill it? This axiom holds true with pronghorns, just like it does for any other game.

The final word: At the beginning of the last century, the pronghorn nearly joined the buffalo in a march toward the shadows of existence. Presently, herd numbers now exceed more than 1,000,000 individual animals. And the remarkable prairie prince can be found throughout western North America. Obviously, pronghorn antelope are a very real testimony to what game recovery and management are all about. These animals are survivors. This is a proven fact. The next time you take to the field in pursuit of the last member of the *Antilocapra* family, remember the pronghorn antelope stands alone as a reminder of what once was and can never be again.

Photo by Bob Robb

Moose and water are usually found in close proximity to one another. This makes canoe transport a practical way of getting into and out of the best hunting country.

THE GREAT ONE: MOOSE

Enigma: Something hard to understand or explain.
These words describe the very essence of what moose hunting is all about.

When Sir Winston Churchill, in a 1939 radio speech during the dark days leading up to World War II, said of Russia, "I cannot forecast to you the action of Russia. It is a riddle wrapped in a mystery inside of an enigma," he may well have been speaking of *Alces alces*, the North American moose. Indeed, the bull moose is an enigmatic animal. Hunt during the height of the rut and you'll find a red-eyed, belligerent, swaggering beast. Driven by a hormonal urge to breed, the males of this species are your basic street thugs that will fearlessly attack a locomotive or recklessly charge toward a hunter's calling attempts. Outside of the rut, however, these massive animals are as shy as a small child. Moose will often react to a careless hunter by holding tight in thick cover like a ruffed grouse. At other times, they may disappear like a wisp of fog, or gallop off across the tundra like a herd of wild horses. The unpredictability of these actions will depend entirely on the circumstances and mood of the moose. Like I said, these overly large deer are enigmas.

Moose hunting is one of the most challenging and exciting adventures you'll ever tackle. As the largest antlered animal on earth, the moose's massive body and gigantic headgear are guaranteed to raise blood pressure and heart rates, as well as produce sweaty palms. In most cases, moose hunting involves a trip to some of the world's most incredible wilderness, covered with virgin forests and dotted with lakes, rivers and streams filled with the purest water, set against a backdrop of spectacular mountains. Just being in such country is health food for the soul.

Photo by Joe Herring

The Shiras moose is the smallest of the subspecies. Even so, a mature bull can weigh more than a 1,000 pounds.

However, a moose hunt is not to be taken lightly. Unless you're in top physical condition and have lots of wilderness hunting experience, undertaking such an activity isn't recommended. On-your-own moose hunts are incredibly difficult—and that's without considering the mind-boggling meat-packing job! Just the neck meat alone can weigh nearly 100-pounds. And a single hindquarter can exceed the field-dressed weight of the largest whitetail deer. The foremost consideration of any moose hunt is always meat care.

Meet the North American moose: North America is home to two subspecies of moose. From the smallest to the largest, they are the Shiras (*Alces alces shirasi*) and the Canada moose (*Alces alces americana*). For big game record-keeping purposes, the Boone & Crockett Club recognizes moose taken from across Canada (except the Yukon and Northwest Territories), Vermont, Maine, Minnesota, North Dakota and New Hampshire as Canada moose. Moose coming from Alaska, the Yukon, the Northwest Territories are classified as Alaskan-Yukon moose. And those coming from Colorado, Idaho, Montana, Washington, Utah and Wyoming are classified as Shiras moose.

Moose are actually the largest member of the deer family. Even a small moose is as large as a horse. These animals have long legs, high humped shoulders, a stubby tail and a large dewlap under the chin. They also have a huge, pendulous muzzle and overly large ears. Furthermore, there is a size difference between bulls and cows, with the bulls considerably larger. A mature Alaskan-Yukon moose can weigh nearly a ton and stand 7-1/2 feet tall at the shoulder. Canada moose are somewhat smaller, weighing between 1,200 and 1,400 pounds. While the Shiras moose is the smallest member of this family, nevertheless, a large bull can go 1,000 pounds on the hoof and stand 6 feet at the shoulders.

The tracks put down by these large antlered animals are 5 to 6 inches long and 4 to 5 inches wide, which

If you want to find a bull moose, the best tactic is to climb high and glass for bulls on the move.

Talk about a righteous rack, these antlers are enormous.

makes them easy to identify in the field. Moose scat (droppings) is also oversize, resembling a large olive. During the rut, bulls will rub trees and brush with their antlers, often destroying vegetation in their frenzy. Also, bulls will make rutting "pits" that are similar to whitetail deer scrapes, only larger. They scour out large areas of earth in which they urinate and wait for the cows to catch wind of the aroma and come for a visit (the love-making process is really interesting).

Despite an appearance of clumsiness, moose are quite agile and able to cover ground at an amazing speed. Also, they are excellent swimmers. In the summer, moose are solitary animals living high on mountain slopes. As fall approaches, the animals migrate to lower elevations. The rut occurs in mid-September and continues through October. Onc, and sometimes two, calves are born after an eight-month gestation period. The calf is weaned at about six months of age. After that, the young moose is able to fend for itself. While some young moose hang close to their mothers for an extended period of time, most are run off just about the time the cow is ready to give birth again. In the wild, moose can live up to 20 years.

Righteous racks: Moose antlers are incredible in size. Weighing up to 90 pounds, they can be a chore to

pack out of the backcountry. Antler growth starts in April, when a bull approaches the completion of his first year of life. Like deer, newly sprouted antlers are covered with velvet. The antlers harden-up in late August and September, when the velvet covering dries and is shed. The continual rubbing against trees and brush gives the white bone of the antler a dark color. The fact that a bull can produce a huge set of antlers in just four months seems to be an extraordinary feat of nature.

Moose antlers have two basic parts—the palms and the shovels. The palms are the most massive part of the antlers and they sweep out and back. The shovels, which extend to the front, are also quite impressive. Both the palms and shovels have a number of points jutting out from them. As the bull grows, his rack will also increase in mass. When the animal reaches its prime, about 6 to 7 years of age, his antlers will have developed to their genetic potential. The best antlers come from bulls between 6 to 12 years of age. After a bull reaches his prime, the antlers tend to decrease in mass. While they may continue to have extremely long beam length, the antlers will have fewer points and weigh less. Near the end of life, moose antlers exhibit a reduction in both palmation and tines. A set of big

Photo by Bob Robb

When bulls are on the prowl for cows they are constantly on the move. During the rut, if you find a cow, most likely a bull won't be far behind.

moose antlers is one of the most impressive of all North American big game trophies. A prize generally hard earned and one to be proud of.

When to hunt: No matter which subspecies of moose it is, or where it lives, the best time to hunt is during the rut. This is when all bulls—especially the largest bulls—are most vulnerable. That's not to say that you cannot find a good bull at other times. However, outside of the rut it's much more difficult to find them.

For example, in August the weather is warm and the days are long. During this time of the year the bulls are usually holed-up in the thickest, nastiest stuff they can find and moving very little. They are also isolated, living a solitary bachelor's life. In mid-October or November, after breeding season, bulls often retreat back to the high country. Here, they try to recover from the rigors of the rut and prepare for the coming winter. Once again, they tend to live in the thick stuff most of

Photo by Bob Robb

Since a Far North moose hunt is usually a once-in-a-lifetime event, hunting with a quality outfitter will provide a better chance at a memorable trophy.

the time, moving only when necessary. Add to these facts that in most areas a high moose density might be three animals per square mile and you begin to visualize just how difficult moose hunting can be.

Guided vs. unguided hunting: Both guided and unguided hunts can be good things, however, for entirely two different reasons. Where legal, unguided hunts will allow you to hunt with a companion or two (you'll need lots of help). If you draw a moose permit in the lower 48, unguided hunting is often made easier by the greater access to backcountry areas when compared with the Far North. Unguided moose hunts are substantially less expensive. You can charter an Alaskan bush pilot to drop you off in prime moose country for $1,000 to $3,000, depending on actual flying time. However, a fully-guided Alaskan or Yukon moose hunt will set you back $7,000 to $11,000. The cost of a guided Canada moose hunt can vary depending on the locale. In Newfoundland, you may only spend $3,000 for a "meat" bull. In other areas, the cost can be two or threes time that. Guided Shiras moose hunts can set you back $1,500 to $5,000, depending on where you go and whom you go with.

There are three reasons for saving your nickels and hiring the best moose outfitter you can find. First, for most folks a moose hunt is a once-in-a-lifetime adventure. Your chances of both success and a crack at a trophy-size bull are exponentially better on a hunt with a quality outfitter. Second, you have to find a bull before

Photo by Bob Robb

Hunting outside of the rut can mean covering lots of ground and using binoculars constantly.

Photo by Bob Robb

A motorized canoe will allow greater access to more hunting country. And when you find a recently used moose bed and fresh droppings, it's time to get busy.

The traditional funnel-shaped moose call is used to magnify the sound of your own voice imitating the grunting of a rut-crazed bull moose.

you can shoot one. Trust me, finding a bull isn't an easy task. Finally, there are all of the problems associated with meat care. Hundreds of pounds of meat and wilderness terrain with few, if any, roads equal bad news. It's that simple!

The reality of a moose hunt: Outdoor writer Bob Robb has hunted moose every season for the past decade that he has lived in the Far North country. His retelling of a guided moose hunt in Manitoba, Canada will give the reader the flavor of hunting these big animals.

"I took my first moose on a guided hunt in the northern reaches of Manitoba. Choosing to hunt there with an experienced bush pilot and guide was a blessing in several ways. For one, it enabled me to hunt an area that I would not have otherwise ever been able to see. We flew in a DeHaviland Beaver floatplane from Winnipeg to a remote river that drained to the Hudson Bay. The guide had a camp all set up and canoes for river transport. During the course of the hunt, we canoed the river for several days, glassed and called for moose. During slack periods, we tried our hand at fishing and caught a pile of big walleyes and northern pike. The guides in camp were all well experienced at their game and I learned a lot about moose hunting.

"After a few days of canoeing, we spotted a cow swimming the river with a nice bull hot on her tail. As we paddled for all we were worth to catch up to the moose, another bull joined the action. This was a real dandy of a bull. While the first two moose swam across the river and disappeared into the thick stuff, we were able to beach the canoe not 50 yards from where they were last seen. It didn't take a rocket scientist to figure out that the big bull would follow the other two on the same trail. I waited for the bull to plant both front feet on the shore before shooting. A 220-grain Winchester Power-Point bullet out of my .30-06 Spfd. was all that was needed to put the bull down and not 75 yards from the riverbank. This early moose hunting lesson—as well as skills learned on other guided moose hunts—have served me well in later years. This became apparent when I began hunting the animals on my own with friends."

Regardless of the way you decide to hunt, research everything carefully. Call the game biologist in the region you are planning to hunt and ask about specific areas that offer the best prospects. Make sure that you don't forget to inquire about any potential meat salvage problems. Take the time to contact several different guides and outfitters, ask about costs, services, success rates and so on. Be sure to get a complete list of the past year's clients (including those that didn't score on a moose) and call each one.

How to find a moose: There are really two separate moose seasons—the rut and everything else. Before the rut, moose hunting is a glassing game. This is made even more difficult because the animals don't move much and you'll have lots of vegetation to deal with. When the leaves are still on the trees, you'd be surprised just how difficult it can be to find a moose, even a big bull. Most hunters climb high and spend hours upon hours scouring the thickets for a bull. Even in a valley filled with moose, it can seem like a wasteland when the animals are bedded in heavy cover. After the first week in September, bulls shed their velvet and the bright white antlers glow like a beacon in the night. This makes glassing a bit easier, but it's still tedious business.

In contrast, hunting rutting moose can quickly become exciting. Make no mistake, it's still hard work, but at least the bulls are up and moving. Hunters still get high whenever possible and use binoculars in search of both cows and bulls. Float hunting along rivers, stopping to hunt open parks and along pond and lake edges can also be productive. In both instances, calling in hopes of drawing a bull into the open—or right in your lap—is very effective.

There is no real secret to call a lovesick moose. I've seen them come to the sound of an ax chopping wood. Even beating a stick against a tree trunk will work sometimes. Using an old scapula bone from last year's bull to scrape and bang against brush can work wonders. The traditional funnel-shaped moose call—which does nothing more than magnify your own voice imitating the grunt of a bull or the moan of a cow—can also do the job. Likewise, pouring water from the call into a lake or stream, which imitates a moose urinating (don't laugh), can produce action. Goofy sounding? Well, that's a moose for you!

After the rut, the bulls head high into the mountain timber stringers (if there are mountains nearby, contrary to popular belief, moose are really not bottomland animals). It is easier to find them now, than in August. The leaves are gone from the trees and bone-

Photo by Bob Robb

The best way to pack moose meat is on a horse or a mule. Otherwise, it's backpack and boot leather.

white antlers are a dead give away. However, the bulls are solitary and they can be extremely difficult to hunt on foot.

No matter when or where you hunt them, never forget that a moose's natural senses are well tuned to the environment. Their hearing and sense of smell are first-rate and they can easily see movement or out-of-place shapes, as well as shiny hands and faces.

Arm yourself: Despite their enormous size, moose are not all that tough to kill cleanly. Cartridges such as the .30-06 Spfd. or 7mm Rem. Mag. are good minimums. While you can go as big as you like, you really don't need anything larger than a .338 Win. Magnum. The trick is to use well-constructed bullets.

Bowhunters should use a bow-and-arrow setup that generates a minimum of 60 foot-pounds of kinetic energy. Both razor-sharp broadheads and moderately heavy aluminum or carbon fiber shafts are recommended.

Blackpowder hunters should use a rifle of .50 caliber or larger, with the nod going to .54 caliber. Conical bullets of at least 300 grains, seated on top of 100 grains of black powder or the equivalent charge of Pyrodex are also in order. In the frontloading game, more is better. Make no mistake; a heavy projectile and a stout powder charge are important considerations when it comes to moose hunting.

Regardless of the power, the placement of your bullet or broadhead is critical. Put either through both lungs and even the largest bull will hit the ground. A

bad hit can be a nightmare. Whatever you do, pay attention to where your bull is standing before you shoot. The last thing you want is 1,500-pounds of dead moose in the middle of a river or pond. Let them step out of, and away from, the water before you shoot. You'll be glad you did.

All that meat: As mentioned at the outset of this chapter, a moose is one big animal that will yield several hundred pounds of edible meat. When hunting these animals, your first consideration is how to take care of the meat. How you do so depends on where you are, how you hunt and how many hands you'll have to help.

First off, anyone who takes off moose hunting alone could be judged legally insane! If you happen to shoot a big bull and he dies in a river, lake or pond, or tumbles into a depression, or ends up expiring in a nasty, brush-filled hole, one person isn't going to be able to even roll the animal over for basic field dressing. Read what Bob Robb once told me about a big Alaskan bull he took a few years ago.

"Things started out nicely on an open tundra meadow. However, before the moose was down, he ended up running off and dying in a 6-foot-deep hole on a spruce-choked hillside. Thankfully, I had a companion, but even field-dressing the animal was an unbelievable chore. We had to start from the rear end of the animal. First, the hide was split down the center of the back. Then, we removed the back straps, half of the neck, one hindquarter and one front shoulder. After lots

The use of a floatplane for hunting transportation is commonplace in Alaska and Canada.

Photo by Bob Robb

If you call in a bull, you better be prepared to deal with lots of fresh moose venison.

Photo by Bob Robb

of tugging and pushing, we were able to roll the carcass over far enough to allow us to work on the other side. It was a real mess, but that's what moose hunting often turns out to be.

"On another occasion I took a bull in Alaska with my bow during late September. My friend, Mike Davis, and I were huddled around a small fire at midday, questioning our sanity when a bull came along trolling for a cow in heat. Quickly grabbing our gear, we slogged off through thigh-deep snow in pursuit. When he came by in range, I arrowed him through both lungs. We were able to quickly quarter the bull without even being

involved in basic field dressing. The pack horses were loaded and we headed back to camp. The next day, when we rode past the remains of the moose on our way back to civilization, I stopped and opened the visceral cavity to see exactly what damage the broadhead had done (hunters tend to do things like that). At the first incision, a blast of hot steam shot forth. Though the nighttime temperature had been 30 degrees below zero, amazingly the internal organs were still quite warm. Had we left the bull out overnight without being field-dressed, chances are that lots of meat would have been spoiled. Because of their immense size and heavy,

Photo by Dan Herring

Taxidermist, Dan Herring (left) took this extremely nice Shiras bull near Big Piney, Wyoming.

thick hides, caring for a downed moose promptly is all-important. Otherwise, the retained body heat will begin to rot the meat from the inside out."

Whatever else you do, when you hunt moose you must be prepared to care for the meat. If you're hunting areas where it is feasible, a chain saw is the best moose-butchering tool ever invented. Oil the blade with vegetable oil and you'll quarter your moose in no time flat (be sure to wear a full rain suit and eye protection to keep flying meat and bone chips off of your clothes and out of your eyes). If this isn't practical, a large meat saw or a sturdy and sharp hatchet will be needed to split the brisket, the pelvis and to remove the antlers from the skull. A couple of sharp knives, including both a standard hunting knife and boning knife (a filet knife works just as well) will be needed to take the animal apart. You'll also need some rope or lots of strong nylon cord for tying off legs and antlers while you work. If you can bring one along, a small hoist will make it easier to hang the quarters on a meat pole or in a convenient tree.

Yes, caring for a moose isn't a picnic, but believe me it's worth it. Moose meat is some of the leanest and tastiest of all wild venison. Furthermore, the meat is high in protein and low in fat and cholesterol. And a set of big moose antlers is an awesome addition to any hunter's trophy collection. However, a freezer full of prime moose meat is worth the price of admission in and of itself.

Where to go: You don't have to spend lots of money and travel outside of the lower 48 to hunt these animals—if you can beat the long odds of drawing a moose permit in one of the 11 states that allow moose hunting. Canada moose hunting is allowed in Maine, Minnesota, North Dakota, New Hampshire and Vermont. And you can hunt Shiras moose in Colorado, Idaho, Montana, Utah, Washington and Wyoming. Here's how to get in on the game:

Colorado: The moose population totals about 1,000 animals. Though most hunts are for residents only, nonresidents can hunt in selected areas. It takes the maximum of three preference points to draw (don't ask, just submit your application).

Idaho: A booming moose population here has opened hunting opportunities for nonresidents—albeit only to those who hold a lifetime hunting license. Success rates are high, with the north-central area of the state the best bet.

Maine: Both resident and nonresident can buy up to six chances at one of the 3,000 moose tags issued annually. An estimated 29,000 moose can be found in Maine, with excellent hunting opportunities and an astonishing success rate.

Minnesota: The resident-only season wasn't held in 2000 due to a lack of funding, but the 2001 season saw 182 tags issued in the northeast portion of the state. Hunters must apply in parties of 2 to 4 individuals (that makes sense) and success rates are very high.

Montana: Nonresidents are allowed up to 10 percent of the available moose tags. The state's northwest corner has the highest animal densities, with trophy quality and success rates quite good.

North Dakota: Another residents-only hunt, with the state issuing both general tags and a limited number of

Photo by Joe Herring

You don't have to spend a fortune or travel far to shoot a good moose. Joe Herring took this Shiras bull not far from his home in central Wyoming.

landowner permits. The northern part of the state has the highest moose numbers.

Utah: The draw here is tough for nonresidents (in 2000, nonresidents were allowed only four permits out of the 79 available). However, if your finances are solid enough, you can purchase one of the 30 to 40 landowner permits issued each year.

Vermont: This state has a four-day season and 200 permits, but success rates are high. With more than 8,500 resident and nonresidents applications, it's tough to draw a permit. Most of the moose are found in the state's northeastern region and along the Green Mountains.

Washington: A limited number of tags make it tough for both residents and nonresident to obtain a moose permit. If you're one of the lucky ones, you'll find the best hunting in the Selkirk Mountains.

Wyoming: With 14,000 moose, this state is the king of western lower 48 hunting opportunities. Each year, about 1000 to 1200 resident and nonresident permits are issued through a random drawing.

Let's go: The moose is the Rodney Dangerfield of big game animals, never getting the respect it deserves! To my mind, they are magnificent creatures, worthy of the time and effort it takes to hunt them. Every moose hunt is a guaranteed adventure. In later years, as you sit and gaze at that gigantic set of antlers, you'll remember the inspiring country and what it took to put those mammoth cranial protrusions on the wall. I promise the memories alone will bring a smile to your face.

Photo by Dan Herring

Too old to go moose hunting? Noel Collins didn't let the 80 years under his belt stop him. He shot this Shiras bull in Wyoming and used an ATV to bring out the meat.

Photo by Corel

The central barren ground caribou, like this one in the Northwest Territories, are the largest of all caribou species.

THE WANDERERS: CARIBOU

Here today, gone tomorrow; the always-on-the-move caribou provides hunters with fun, incredible success and oversized antlers.

There's a special charm about being in caribou country in the fall. As the season progresses from August to September and on into October, the tundra begins shifting colors, deepening to orange, red and purple as it starts to enter a dormant phase just before winter. Even the low-growing scrubs are changing with the promise of the long winter to come. Most characteristically, the ptarmigan are beginning their annual transformation from brown to white. You'll see these northern grouse, clothed in both colors, flushing noisily as you hike about.

If you climb a high knob (should there be such a thing in the bleak tundra), the landscape can seem as barren as the moon. However, the caribou must be out there, somewhere, perhaps hidden by a seam in the terrain or by a line of tall brush. If you're very lucky, on the distant horizon, as if by magic, a great herd of these animals will appear. Driven by instinct, the caribou will

Photo by John Higley

A couple of tents on the tundra may not seem very spacious, but to this group of caribou hunters it's home.

Photo by Bob Robb

Does it get any better than this? Bob Robb took this record-book bull with his bow while hunting in Alaska.

be marching along the same migration route that their ancestors have followed since time began.

At this juncture, I must emphasize the "very lucky" comment made in the preceding paragraph. One of the great myths about caribou hunting is that all you have to do is show up!

Once you're there (wherever "there" might be), the great herds will appear, right on schedule. I am sorry; it just doesn't happen that way. The fact of this matter is, that while caribou will appear along their known movement route at some point in time, the chance of you arriving at that point at the same time isn't all that great.

Caribou are herd animals, more so than other cervids of this continent. Where you find one animal, you're likely to find many more. The trouble is, the animals roam vast tracts of the Far North and are prone to change their exact migration patterns unexpectedly. Change in caribou movement can be brought on by a variety of reasons, including weather, food availability, vexing insects, human intrusion and who knows what else. Regardless, caribou are always surrounded by a lot more country than the actual ground they occupy, which makes the hunting sometimes quite problematic.

Simply put, caribou hunting can be one of the continent's great feast-or-famine hunts. Either the animals are there, or they're not. If they are there, the hunting can be unbelievable. You can glass bull, after bull, after bull, for days on end and hold out for a real whopper. If the animals are conspicuous by their absence, you can literally spend days waiting for them to appear and find absolutely nothing.

Generally, if your hunting camp is located somewhere near historic migration routes, you'll see caribou. However, the animals you find won't be in the huge migratory herds that are often depicted in film and on television. More commonly, hunting caribou necessitates lots of work with your binoculars. What you'll find is a small bunch of animals here, a small group there, but not in overwhelming numbers. You must evaluate any potential trophy animal optically first, then take it from there. This involves lots of hiking and the physical ability to pack a load of meat, cape and antlers a considerable distance over broken ground.

Divide them up: Caribou are well distributed in the Far North from the Pacific to the Atlantic coasts. In reality, there is only one caribou species, scientifically known as *Rangifer tarandus*. Like with many other species of game, there are those who are "lumpers" and others who are "splitters." To be sure, genetic isolation and slight differences in habitat have resulted in a certain level of caribou subspeciation. The problem is that scientists, game departments and record keeping organizations are not in agreement with one another as to how the species should be subspeciated. Most hunters are "lumpers." As an old Alaskan sourdough once told me, "they're all caribou, so what's the big deal." Game departments and record keeping organizations like the Boone & Crockett Club and Safari Club International are definitely "splitters." The reason for splitting caribou into separate groupings has to do more with size and antler configuration, than anything else.

For those interested in such things, the Boone & Crockett's *Records of North American Big Game, 10th Edition*, splits these animals into five different categories: Mountain caribou (*Rangifer tarandus*), Woodland caribou (*Rangifer tarandus caribou*), Barren Ground caribou (*Rangifer tarandus grandi*), Central Barren Ground caribou (*Rangifer tarandus groenlandicus*) and the Quebec-Laborador caribou (also *Rangifer tarandus caribou*).

Mountain caribou (believed by taxonomists to be a variety of the Woodland caribou) are found in British Columbia, Alberta, southern Yukon and the Macken-zie Mountains of the Northwest Territories. The boundary begins at the intersection of the Yukon River with the boundary between the Yukon Territory and the state of Alaska. It then runs southeasterly following the Yukon River upstream to Dawson, then easterly and southerly along the Klondike Highway to Stewart Crossing, then easterly following the road to Mayo, then northeasterly following the road to McQuestern Lake, then easterly following the south shore of McQuestern Lake, then upstream following the main drainage to the divide leading to Scougale Creek to its confluence with the Beaver River, then south following the Beaver River downstream to its confluence with the Rackla River, then southeasterly following the Rackla River downstream to its confluence with the Stewart River, then northeasterly following the Stewart River upstream to its confluence with the North Stewart River to the boundary between the Yukon Territory and the Northwest Territories. North of this line the caribou are considered to be Barren Ground caribou, while the animals south of this line are considered Mountain caribou.

Taken by Joe Herring, this central barren ground caribou has great antlers and is a fine trophy.

Photo by Dan Herring

Photo by Bob Robb

Floatplanes are common in caribou country.

Woodland caribou are eligible for record book entry from Nova Scotia, Newfoundland and New Brunswick. Though Woodland caribou occur sparingly all across Canada to southern British Columbia and elsewhere, only those from the aforementioned three Canadian provinces qualify as Boone & Crockett record book entries.

Barren Ground caribou are the largest of all of these animals. The Barren Ground species is found in Alaska, northern Yukon Territory, Saskatchewan, Manitoba and Ontario. Central Barren Ground caribou come from Baffin Island and the mainland of the Northwest Territories, east of the Mackenzie River and west of Hudson's Bay.

As the name implies, only those caribou taken in Quebec and Labrador are considered to be Quebec-Labrador caribou. Of course, the individual groupings of caribou understand all of the borders of their territories and would never cross those established lines. And one subspecies of caribou would never initiate a love affair with one outside of the designated regional borders. If you believe all of that, then you're in for a big surprise. This is why I hate record book delineations. The points of demarcation only exist in the minds of the biologists, game depart-

ments and record keepers and not the animal in question. All too often such parameters are arbitrary and subject to change politically. And when did politics ever have anything to do with subspeciations? Absent some type of genetic correlation, the matter of subspeciation can be more of a problem than a reality. The bottom line is: a caribou is a caribou and that is the sum total of the matter.

It's all in the looks: A caribou looks like it was put together by committee. Depending on subspecies under consideration, a mature bull will weigh 300 to 350-pounds. Cow caribou are somewhat smaller, although not a lot. The animals have a distinctive hump at the shoulders, not unlike a grizzly bear. The shoulders, back and sides are brownish in color, with the chest and rump white. The lower legs, the tops of ears and the sides of the face are dark brown. The rather bulbous nose resembles a miniature moose. And the antlers are just overwhelming in size. The hooves are long and well designed to support the animal on the spongy tundra. When caribou run you can actually hear the hooves make a "clicking" sound. A friend of mine once said that caribou are "so ugly that they are beautiful."

Headgear heaven: No matter where you stand on caribou subspeciation, everyone can agree on one

Horseback caribou hunts are commonplace in parts of Alaska, British Columbia, Yukon Territory and the Northwest Territories.

Scoring on a mixed-bag hunt isn't a sure thing, but it can be done. This bull is proof of that.

*Packing set of caribou antlers and a
cape can be a real chore.*

Photo by John Higley

thing about these animals—the antlers. When you
compare the actual size of a caribou with the mass of
its antlers, that headgear is the largest of any member
of the deer family. Interestingly, caribou cows also
grow antlers, albeit, short and thin in size. Basically,
caribou antlers have three components—the shovel(s),
the bez and the crown. The shovel, or shovels (a single
shovel is more common than double shovels) rise from
the main antler beam and project forward over the
nose. A good shovel(s) will be broad with a number of
short tines. The bez makes its appearance about one-
third of the way up the main beam and like the shovel
projects forward. Lots of tines and plenty of length in
the bez add to the overall trophy potential. Finally, the
crown or top points are where the true trophy potential

is manifest. The top points are found at the terminus of
the antlers and curve forward and out. A real big set of
caribou antlers will have it all, with good mass and lots
and lots of tines.

Hunting caribou: Most caribou hunts fall somewhere in between the full-blown migration and a tundra devoid of animals. It is pure folly to depend on the
migration for success. Sometimes the animals show
up right on time and sometimes they never come at
all. There are periods when the caribou are as reliable
as clockwork, moving past the same traditional hunting grounds as they have for decades. At times like
this the hunting is uncomplicated. The guides get
spoiled and the clients come with expectations of easy
pickings, big bulls and 100 percent success with little

effort. One year, or another, things will change and the caribou might not show up on time—or at all. What animals are found will be few and far between. Only those hunters who are willing to get out and get after it will be rewarded.

In the air: Many of those after caribou get to the hunting area by small airplane. The most common aircraft are the DeHaviland Beaver, Cessna 206 on floats or a Super Cub on floats or tundra tires. Flying provides the opportunity to locate the animals before choosing the exact spot to land. If your destination is a fixed camp, you'll leave the bulk of your gear in a cabin or wall tent, then fly out to a smaller spike camp near the herd.

It's quite common for caribou to stop for a day or two along their migration route. This is true for both the large herds of Barren Ground caribou that move hundreds of miles, as well as the Woodland Mountain subspecies that travel only a few miles. An aerial evaluation of herd migration is really the best way to hunt these animals. Since they are often "here today, gone tomorrow," looking the area over by air first can save miles of fruitless hiking.

Another common way that caribou are hunted is by horseback. In the western part of their range, including parts of Alaska, British Columbia, Yukon Territory and the Northwest Territories, many outfitters use horses. Often, these hunts are centered around a comfortable wall tent camp, though old cabins are also used for this purpose. Hunters and guides ride out of camp each day, covering as much ground as possible, pausing only to glass the countryside from atop high points. Guides will often bring another horse along to serve as a pack animal if you connect. This saves making an extra trip out to the kill site and also keeps the meat out of the clutches of hungry grizzlies and scavenging birds.

How to be successful: All too often, caribou hunting sounds too easy. Some folks think that you only have to book a hunt with a good outfitter in a traditionally hot caribou area, show up and shoot straight. Often, that's the way it is, but only if you go there specifically to hunt caribou. There is a big misconception in the mind of the hunting public that caribou can easily be added to other species on a mixed-bag hunt. Furthermore, it is also believed that collecting a

Photo by Bob Robb

Wind, fog and rain can wreak havoc with most firearms. A stainless steel rifle with a synthetic stock is the way to go.

nice caribou while hunting something else is fairly routine—wrong!

In the Far North, it is rare that one area is a hotbed of hunting for more than one species of animal at any given time. Adding a caribou to the hunt package isn't always a slam-dunk. Oh sure, you can pay more money, but you're likely to go home empty-handed. Some outfitters combine moose and caribou in the same package, but rarely do both species live in the same area at the same time. Thinking that a caribou can be an easy addition to your hunt package is a big mistake. Most hunters who have repeatedly booked mixed-bag hunts have piles of unused caribou tags. And who wants to deal with a caribou, when sheep or moose is the main item on the hunt agenda? Sure, you might get lucky and take a caribou, but don't count on it.

If you're really serious about taking a trophy caribou bull, then concentrate your effort in that direction and no other. Naturally, you'll have to be in the right place at the right time. This is where a topnotch outfitter and mobility—via horse, boat or airplane—play a big role. Knowing where the animals are at any given moment, then being able to intersect them is the key to taking a big bull. If one place doesn't pan out then you can have another chance. With ready transport you can move and start over again.

Removing a caribou cape takes patience and a sharp knife.

Photo by John Higley

Photo by Bob Robb

Bill Woodin took this nice bull in a valley near the headwaters of Alaska's Mulchatna River.

What it takes: Serious caribou hunters need to be in fairly good physical condition. In many instances, no matter how you're hunting, packing the meat, cape and antlers back to camp will have to be accomplished on your back. Also, it's commonplace to find caribou high up in the mountains. The animals go high to escape the clouds of bothersome flies that often plague them on the tundra. Caribou are just as likely to be found up high, as they are down low.

Mountain hunting can certainly sap your energy, but hiking on the tundra is just as bad. Tundra looks really flat, but looks are deceiving. This boggy terrain is punctuated by a series of ups and downs, as well as spongy tussocks that can break an ankle instantly. Furthermore, this country is sliced up by waist-deep streams and covered with miles of impenetrable brush. Mix in a little hot weather and more bugs than you can imagine, or freezing rain and a dose of snow, and you'll soon discover that hunting on the tundra is a labor of love, to be sure, but a labor nonetheless.

The best way to hunt: Simply put, the best way to hunt caribou is to be in an area that holds animals. Then, climb high, sit down, get comfortable and put your optics to good use. The flat tundra that, at first glance, seems like a tabletop, is generally pockmarked with cuts and folds that can easily hide hundreds of caribou. You can glass for hours and see nothing. Then, as if by magic, animals appear out of some mysterious hiding place.

Caribou are, by their very nature, curious. These creatures do not exhibit the same immediate terror as other game animals do at the sight of a human. That said, you cannot just walk up to them and start shooting. If they smell you, the animals will disappear as quickly as they appeared. The same is true if they hear man noise like loud talking or metal-on-metal sounds. They may spook wildly at the sight of a man, or they may not according to their mood at the moment. No matter what species of caribou, or where they live, the animals usually like to have a "wolf cushion" around them. You might be able to get within 80 to 100 yards of them, but any closer will necessitate keeping downwind and out of sight. While this isn't a big deal for riflemen, for a bowhunter it can be more frustrating than trying to wring a straight answer out of a politician.

When stalking caribou, get the wind right and use available terrain features for cover. Move to within a couple of hundred yards of the animals and use your optics to look them over. Should you find a bull that meets your trophy criteria, it's time to get busy. Centerfire riflemen should try to get within 100 to 150 yards before shooting. This way, you'll be sure of precise target acquisition. It's no fun trying to track a wounded caribou over hill and dale, especially on the boggy tundra. Blackpowder hunters will have to be especially careful about bullet placement. Caribou aren't all that tough, but they can take some lead. The closer you are before you touch off a round from your blunderbuss, the better. If you're bowhunting, at 100 yards the game has only just began. Since caribou are herd animals, you'll have to contend with lots of eyes, ears and noses.

Caribou calibers: Any caliber from .25-06 Rem. to .257 Wby. and up through the various .300 Magnums are quite capable of cleanly taking a bull. Keep in mind that wind is almost always a consideration in caribou country. On long shots, wind drift can present a problem when shooting light bullets. Knowledgeable caribou hunters will use chamberings in the .270 Win. to .30-06 Spfd. range, with bullets weighing 150 to180 grains. Blackpowder hunters will be well served with muzzleloaders in either .50 or .54 caliber. And most bowhunters use the same rig that works for deer or elk.

When it's all over, your reward will be a load of fresh caribou venison and a set of outsize antlers.

Photo by Bob Robb

Slip a bullet or a broadhead into a caribou's engine room, and shortly thereafter you'll find yourself elbow-deep in field dressing chores. Make target contact too far back and that same animal can cover a lot of ground before it drops.

Gear and gadgets: Just like any other Far North country hunting, you'll need the best rain gear possible. A lightweight Gore-Tex rain suit is by far the best choice. And make sure you pack some warm gloves (make mine neoprene) and a hat that can protect you from inclement weather.

Depending on where you're hunting, you'll need waterproof hiking boots and ankle-fit hip boots to negotiate creeks. On hunts that depend on human muscle power to care for the meat, you'll also need a large capacity pack frame and bag.

The best cutlery kit I've ever used for caribou field dressing, skinning, butchering and trophy work is made by Knives of Alaska. Included in the Cordura® nylon cover wrap is a hatchet and three knives. Made to easily slip into your pack, this set up can handle any game care situation, including those that occur on the tundra or in the mountains.

In the treeless terrain, a Global Positioning System can be quite valuable, especially if it takes more than one trip to pack out all of the meat, cape and antlers. Fluorescent flagging is another item that will be useful to mark the path to the carcass location. And a small pad of paper and a pen will be of assistance in writing down any details.

A real hunt: Caribou hunting is addictive. Friend and outdoor writer, Bob Robb, has been in the field after these animals for nearly every year of the last decade that he has lived in the Far North. His words convey the reality of the hunt better than my own. Read on.

"One rainy afternoon in the fall of 2001, my friend Bill Woodin and I loaded up his DeHaviland Beaver and headed for an area near the headwaters of Alaska's Mulchatna River. The caribou had not yet begun their southern migration in earnest. And when Bill slid his plane down through a hole in the rain-filled clouds, we could see thousands of caribou milling round in a broad valley. It was a caribou hunter's Mecca.

"Both of us know a good thing when we see it. Despite the huge numbers of animals making up this particular herd, finding a couple of trophy bulls in a ball of thousands isn't all that easy. Bill found a nearby lake where he could land and take off, set the plane the down easy and we tied it up securely. Next was camp set-up and then 'look-and-drool' time (you can't fly and hunt in the same day).

"The following day broke cloudy and wet. The good news was the caribou were still where we left them on the preceding evening. Peeping out of the tent door, I spotted half-a-dozen cows and calves feeding less than 75-yards away. We both dressed as fast as possible, loaded our packs and were out after bulls.

"It quickly became apparent that the animals liked to skirt the lake shore and cross at one point. We moved to that location and set up in anticipation. Just as quickly, about 500 to 700 caribou were within 70 to 100 yards of our location. This was great for two reasons. One, we were all over them (or was it the other way around?). Second, we were moving farther away from the sow and pair of brown bear cubs we had seen less than one quarter mile from camp.

"That was just the start of things. In three days, we had quite an adventure. For one thing, each day our valley of thousands of caribou emptied out a bit more, until by the last afternoon there was hardly an animal left. For another, it never quit raining and without a tent and propane heater we would have been a couple of drowned rats by the time it was all over. Third, we were also covered up with predators. In the course of this hunt, we saw 22 different brown bears and five wolves.

"When it was all said and done, Bill and I each took dandy bulls. We also had to backpack the meat and antlers a couple miles. We worked hard, but the sight and sounds we saw and heard were like something straight out of the Discovery Channel. It was awesome, to say the least."

The sum of it all: Caribou hunting doesn't seem to get a lot of respect in the circles of serious big game hunters. Generally, these are folks who have made a caribou hunt or two and shot the first decent bull they saw, or have incidentally taken a nice bull on a mixed-bag hunt. However, actually hunting a true trophy bull with outrageous antlers can be quite a challenge. Add to that the spectacular country in which these animals live, the other game and the immense size of a caribou headgear and you have a superb game animal that's just simply fun to hunt. Most of us will never get enough of it!

Photo by Bob Robb

Guided to this Dall's ram by Striker Overly (left), Bruce Peterson (right) is thrilled with the 37-inch horn length. Oh yeah!

FULL CURL: WILD SHEEP

In sheep country make sure of your target, squeeze the trigger and then watch your step!

Sheep hunting. Those two words, taken together, have inspired North American big game hunters for decades. That is how it should be, because sheep hunting is one of the most exciting, awe-inspiring and thrilling adventures any sportsman or woman will ever undertake.

It's not just the animal, though our wild sheep are truly magnificent in their own right. The country in which they live is some of the wildest left on the continent. Mountain sheep inhabit tall peaks guarded by wild rivers and unconquered lowlands. Rocky Mountain bighorn sheep occupy rough-and-tumble country, living inside of the tree line and using the steep, nasty places as escape cover. In contrast, the desert bighorn lives in some of the most inhospitable lowland country imaginable. This is a locale where water is scarce and every plant is covered with thorns.

Wild sheep are also one of this continent's incredible conservation success stories. For decades, sheep hunting has attracted the world's wealthiest sportsmen. These individuals have demonstrated a willingness to fund research projects and re-establish sheep populations in areas where they have disappeared. Organizations like the Foundation for North American Wild, as well as Safari Club International, have been able to raise countless millions of dollars for sheep habitat, animal transplants and other restoration activities. The special "governor's tags" various state game department's allow to be auctioned at these conservation organiza-

Photo by Bob Robb

Legendary Montana hunter and booking agent, Jack Atcheson, Sr., with an Alaskan Dall's ram that measured a solid 38-inches around the curl.

tions' annual conventions often go for tens of thousands of dollars.

What does it cost? Unless you're one of the fortunate lucky few to draw the handful of bighorn sheep tags issued every year, or a resident of Alaska or Canada (which allows you to hunt sheep on your own), you'll find sheep hunting to be a rich-man's game. In most cases, the question is, do I buy a new car or hunt sheep?

Of the four species of sheep, hunts for Dall's rams are the most reasonable. Priced somewhere between $7,500 and $10,000, a Dall's sheep hunt is a real bargain. Stone sheep hunts are absolutely outrageous, going for between $14,000 and $20,000. What does it cost to hunt for the two bighorn sheep species? The best word to describe that cost is—Wow! A Rocky Mountain bighorn sheep hunt will set you back between $20,000 and $30,000. And a hunt for a desert bighorn ram is between $30,000 and $50,000. Despite the cost, I still find any sheep hunt worth every penny.

Dall's sheep: A hunt for a Dall's ram is a grand affair. The mountain country in which they live is as dramatic as any you'll ever see. It is immense country, defined by rough-edged peaks, verdant grass alpine bowls and huge glaciers. On a hunt for Dall's sheep you might also see grizzly bears, caribou, moose, black bears, wolves, small game and a variety of bird species.

Named after the Alaskan explorer, William H. Dall, in 1897, *Ovis dalli* is one of two so-called "thin-horned" sheep in North America (Stone sheep is the other). Characterized by a pure white coat and flaring yellow-brown horns, a mature ram will weigh between 150 and 250 pounds. The ram is nearly twice as large as the ewe. A full-grown ram will stand 36 to 42 inches at the shoulder and measure 54 to 60 inches in overall

Photo by Bob Robb

Mountain sheep hunting is all about glassing and climbing and glassing some more.

Photo by Bob Robb

Dark and lovely, this is what a trophy Stone's sheep looks like.

length. A ram in the trophy category will have horn bases of 12 to 15 inches in circumference. Any ram with horns over 36 inches in length is a good one. Those sporting horns in the 38- to 40-inch range are real dandies. And a 40-inch ram with heavy horn bases is truly a monster.

Dall's sheep can be found in Alaska, the Yukon Territories the extreme northwest corner of British Columbia and the very western portions of the Northwest Territories. These sheep are most numerous in Alaska, where they can be found in the Kenai, Chugach, Wrangell, Talkeetna, Alaska, White, Tanana and Brooks mountain ranges. Current game department population estimates place the total number of Dall's sheep in Alaska at between 55,000 and 65,000 animals. In British Columbia, these sheep can be found in the Skeena Mountains and number about 500 animals. In the Northwest Territories, they can be found in the Mackenzie and Richardson Mountains, where they number 20,000 and 2000, respectively. In the Yukon, Dall's sheep are scattered north to south in eight different mountain ranges, including the Kluane, Coast, Ruby, Nisling, Dawson, Hess, Logan, Ogilvie, Wernecke, Richardson and British Mountains. The total Dall's sheep population here is about 22,000 animals.

Stone's sheep: Hunting for Stone's sheep is the very stuff of legend. The late Jack O'Connor wrote extensively about his horseback trips into British Columbia in pursuit of a Stone's ram. Those articles were published in the pages of both *Outdoor Life* magazine and his classic book, *Sheep and Sheep Hunting*. A hunt for Stone's sheep will leave you feeling like you've stepped back in time. If nothing else, a hunt for a Stone's ram is what being "wild and free" is all about. You never have to worry about hunting competition, because you'll never see another living soul in Stone's sheep country.

Stone's sheep, *Ovis stonei*, gets its name not from the dark-colored rocks or stones that cover its home range, but rather from hunter-explorer, Andrew Stone. A resident of Missoula, Montana, this adventurer was the first to bring back a fine specimen of this sheep from the headwaters of the Stikine River, in British Columbia, in 1896.

In appearance and body size, Stone's sheep look a great deal like Dall's sheep, with the exception of the color of their hair. This coloration can vary widely from area to area and even between sheep in the same band. The Stone's sheep have a very dark coat, ranging from deep blackish chocolate to a dark brown. A

Photo by Dan Herring

Dan Herring took this Rocky Mountain bighorn ram near his home in Thermopolis, Wyoming.

subspecies of Stone's sheep, the Fannin sheep is unrecognized by biologists but well known to sheep hunters. This subspecies has very little dark coloration. Stone's sheep almost always have heads that are more lightly colored than their bodies. They also have a large, white rump patch that extends well above the root of the tail. A dark stripe runs dorsally down the rump patch to the tail. And there are broad white stripes running from the rump down the rear of each hind leg. There are similar white stripes inside of both front legs.

Stone's sheep have a small home range, being found only in northern British Columbia. These animals can be found in a narrow band, extending northward up into south-central Yukon Territory. Most notably, Stone's sheep can be found in the Pelly Mountains and the Prophet/Muskwa regions. The narrow home range, along with the high demand for Stone's sheep hunts are the two factors that have driven the cost of a Stone's sheep sky-high since the mid-1980s.

Rocky Mountain big horn sheep: The Rocky Mountain bighorn, *Ovis canadensis canadensis*, is the brute of North American wild sheep. Blocky of shoulder and thick through the chest, a big ram can weigh well over 300 pounds on the hoof. These sheep are a dark brown color, with a white muzzle, rump patch, belly and trim on the back of all four legs. They generally live to about 12 to 15 years old, which is half-again more than any of the three major deer species. A slightly smaller subspecies, *Ovis canadensis californiana*, is found in California all the way north to the western half of southern British Columbia. These animals are generally a bit smaller and less blocky in appearance than their Rocky Mountain cousins. Also, the California sub-species have longer ears and legs, no doubt an adaptation to their environment. A third bighorn species, known as the badlands bighorn, *Ovis canadensis auduboni*, fell on bad times in the early part of the 20th century and has become extinct.

Photo by Bob Robb

Hunting sheep will take lots of rigorous glassing. Hunters are well advised to keep a low profile. If the sheep see you they usually take off!

The biggest of bighorn sheep can have horns that measure between 14 and 17 inches in circumference. When measured on the curl, horns can go 40 to 45 inches. What is interesting about bighorn sheep is that they carry the heavy horn base structure all the way through the curl. Dall's or Stone's sheep may have bases 13 to 14 inches in circumference, but the horns thin out along the curl (hence the designation, "thin-horned"). Furthermore, bighorn sheep horns don't flare outward like the horn of Dall's or Stone's sheep. Typically, bighorn sheep horns curl close to the head, so close that the tips often obscure a ram's vision. Bighorn rams tend to "broom" the tips of their horns off against a rock outcropping. This activity allows the animal a better side view of his surroundings. Interestingly, the horns of a mature Rocky Mountain bighorn ram can weigh somewhere between 8 and 12 percent of total body weight. This makes the horns of these animals the largest in proportion to the body weight of any ruminant in the world. A large set of horns, including the skull plate, can weigh as much as 40 pounds. Toss in the head skin cape and 100 pounds, or more, of fresh meat and you can see what a chore it is to pack a ram out of the backcountry. Quite frankly, most sheep hunters will need lots of help.

Rocky Mountain bighorns live in rugged, mountainous country. Their range extends from the Peace River in British Columbia southward through the Rocky Mountains, as well as isolated populations occurring in the Coast and Cascade ranges, the Sierra Nevada range and numerous smaller mountain ranges of the Great Basin and Plains states. As stated previously, the somewhat smaller California bighorn can be found in lower-elevation mountain ranges of southern British Columbia, eastern Washington and Oregon, southwestern Idaho and in pockets along the eastern front of California's Sierra Nevada range.

The most distinguishing characteristic of good Rocky Mountain bighorn habitats is the availability of rocky outcropping in relatively open country, with relatively open visibility. This encompasses a wide range of area, from the spectacularly high Rocky Mountains to the steep walls of Hell's Canyon along the Snake River on the Idaho-Washington-Oregon border. The rocky ridges enable sheep to both spot predators at a distance and escape from them, as well as raise lambs in relative safety.

Bighorn sheep are not territorial animals. Instead, they move between a series of seasonal home range

Photo by Bob Robb

Practice with your rifle before going sheep hunting. Sight-in about 2-1/2 to 3 inches high at 100 yards to maximize the trajectory.

Photo by Bob Robb

A horse can put you deep into sheep country without all of the effort it takes to carry everything on your back. If you're successful, then the trip out is a breeze

habitat areas. Of course, rams and ewes with lambs generally utilize different areas, except during the rut. The distance between these various ranges varies greatly depending on where the sheep live, but it can be up to 20 miles from one area to another. Sheep are also attracted to mineral licks and water seeps. Following the breeding season, which is normally the month of November, all of the sheep (regardless of gender) band together and move down to low-elevation, grassy areas. Here they remain until spring when the melting snow permits them to easily return to their higher-elevation range with its newly sprouted grasses.

Desert bighorn sheep: There are four subspecies of bighorn sheep that are considered in composite as "desert bighorn sheep." In reality, all these subspecies represent environmental adaptation of the Rocky Mountain bighorn. All desert bighorns are less stocky of body, smaller in size and have shorter and somewhat thinner horns than the Rocky Mountain species. The four desert bighorn sheep subspecies are: *Ovis canadensis nelsoni*, which can be found from Nevada and Utah down through much of California and southwestern Arizona; *Ovis canadensis mexicana*, from southern Arizona down through Sonora, Mexico; *Ovis canadensis cremnobates*, from southern California southward about two-thirds of the way down the Baja California peninsula; *Ovis canadensis weemsi*, is found only on the extreme tip of Baja California. In recent years, both New Mexico and Texas have received transplanted populations of the Nelson and Mexican bighorn subspecies.

Photo by Bob Robb

Sheep hunting isn't restricted to riflemen; bowhunters can be successful also. Here's Bob Robb showing off his first archery Dall's ram, taken in the Wrangell Mountains of Alaska.

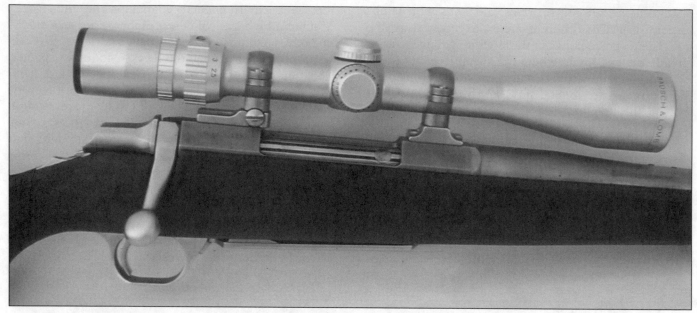

Photo by Durwood Hollis

This synthetically stocked, stainless steel Savage rifle is topped with a Bushnell 2.5-10X scope and chambered in .300 Win. Magnum. It can handle the abuse and weather that are typical of a sheep hunt.

Current estimates of desert bighorn sheep populations total about 25,000 sheep (all subspecies), with about 19,000 of them found in the United States. Arizona can boast about 6,500. Nevada has about 5,500. California has somewhere near 3,500. Utah counts about 2,500. Colorado has 500, Texas near 300 and New Mexico has about 200 sheep. The remainder of the desert bighorn population can be found in the Mexican states of Sonora and Baja California. The population in those two regions is 2,500 and 3,500 animals, respectively. Nearly everywhere, desert sheep populations are growing, albeit slowly. However, the future for these animals is promising.

When compared to a Rocky Mountain bighorn, desert bighorns are much smaller in size. And a size differential between genders is also manifest. A fully-grown desert bighorn ram might weigh 150 to 220 pounds on the hoof, while ewes will have a live weight of 75 to 130 pounds. A mature ram can sport horns as long as 40 inches, though most run 30 to 35 inches. Horn bases generally measure 13 to 15 inches in circumference. Like all bighorn sheep, the desert variety is famous for "brooming" its horns. Occasionally, an old ram will be seen with broken horns that are a result of rut-based combat activities.

Desert bighorn sheep have an extremely long breeding season, extending in some areas from July through October. These animals have a life expectancy of 12 to 14 years, but have been known to live as long as 18 years. Mortality is highest in young sheep, with upwards of 50 percent of all lambs dying within six months. Mountain lions, bobcats, coyotes and even golden eagles are among the chief predators. Beyond one year of age, sheep mortality is very low. However, mortality rates increase tenfold beyond the age of 9 years.

Desert sheep range is restricted by the availability of food and water. Amazingly, these animals have been observed to go as long as six months without ever drinking water. The moisture that they derive comes from the food they eat. When they do go to water, an individual animal may consume as much as three gallons a minute. Well adapted to their harsh, arid environment, desert bighorn sheep can withstand considerable dehydration (even more than a camel can endure) and have a body temperature that can safely reach 107 degrees.

Hunting mountain sheep: The key to hunting both Dall's and Stone's sheep is getting into the remote areas where the rams live. This means going many miles off of the beaten path and usually requires a bush plane to start the adventure. After landing on a remote mountain landing strip, you'll be met by a guide who will lead you deep into the mountains where the sheep live. In some cases, this can involve saddle and pack horse transport. In other instances, the hunt is a backpack affair. And in some selected situations, you can begin the backpack portion right from a paved highway, although this is rather uncommon. I can recall seeing a large group of sheep about 500 yards up from the end the dirt road that runs along the Shoshoni River in Wyoming. There were no large rams in the group, but they may have been close behind.

Once in sheep country, it becomes a spot-and-stalk game. Using high-magnification binoculars and a spotting scope, you scan distant mountains for sheep. Once located, trophy quality is evaluated. If the rams you've found through an optical search are to your liking, an approach is planned and executed. This sounds easy, but there is so much more to it than that. The terrain between you and the sheep is generally rugged and steep and can be difficult to negotiate. You might have to ford several waist-deep glacier streams in the process. There can be glaciers to cross, which usually requires special equipment and an ability to read the ice. Rams like to bed where they can see forever. This can make stalking without being seen quite problematic. And since sheep have excellent olfactory senses, you'll have to constantly monitor the wind. At the first hint of human scent, the rams will simply evaporate. Most of the time, you'll never be able to find the same group of animals again.

Then there's good old Mother Nature. She can be an evil witch on a mountain sheep hunt. One day it'll be clear and crisp with the sky so blue it's almost purple and the temperature so pleasant shirtsleeves will be fine. A few hours later, a cold wind can kick up dropping the mercury to 30 degrees. Before you know it, freezing rain or snow is blowing sideways down the collar of your jacket. Furthermore, a fog can blow in so you can't see the peaks. Climbing in this kind of weather is an exercise in futility. So you have to wait patiently for the rain and snow to stop and the fog to abate—which can take hours, or days. Sounds like fun, doesn't it?

Of course, some enjoy good weather and their hunt only lasts a few days. However, most of the time something always happens that forces you to deviate from the original game plan. But then, that's just something that makes mountain hunting for sheep in the Far North such an adventure—and so it is!

Hunting bighorn sheep: Sheep hunting is sheep hunting, no matter what the species or subspecies. The use of binoculars and a spotting scope are *de rigueur* for the sport. The secret to success is to find the sheep before they see you, and then remain out of sight while you stalk into comfortable shooting range.

Hunting Rocky Mountain bighorn sheep can involve some arduous work. This can mean hours in the saddle or miles with a pack on your back, depending on where you hunt. In Alberta, Canada, for example, bighorn hunting is often done in November when the temperature is below zero and snow covers the steep, high-altitude mountains. Sometimes it's possible to look for sheep right out of the front seat of a warm pickup truck. Likewise, in parts of Montana hunters report glassing more than 100 sheep from their vehicles late in the season. If you find a ram that you want, then it's only a matter of making a good shot, field dressing and sliding the carcass down the slope and into the bed of the truck.

Desert bighorn sheep hunters usually camp near a dirt road, then hike and glass in search of sheep. This can take them across the desert floor to many different small mountain outcrops. And upon occasion, you might just run into a ram out in the flats. Desert bighorn sheep have been known to take off across the floor of the desert bound for a distant mountain range. If you're lucky enough to encounter one of these wanderers, then count it good! No matter where they hunt, desert sheep hunters must be prepared. This means lots of water (you'll have to bring it with you) and a camp able to withstand dry, dusty and often gale force winds.

Guns and loads: A stainless steel rifle with a synthetic stock is the "cat's meow" for most sheep hunting. Your rifle is going to take considerable abuse,

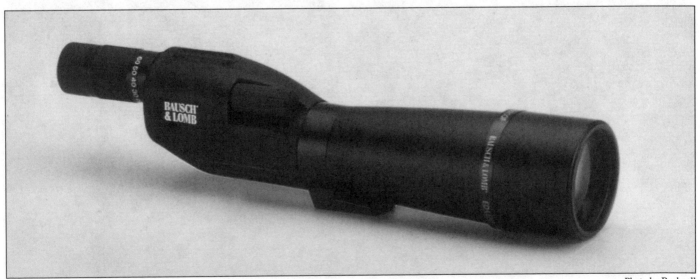

Photo by Bushnell

Featuring multi-coated optics and fully sealed against moisture with Bushnell's exclusive Rainguard® lens coating, this Bausch & Lomb spotting scope is the kind every hopeful sheep hunter needs for trophy evaluation.

both from the weather and the country. It's best if it's able to take such exposure and handling. Lightweight mountain-type rifles are welcome companions when hiking and climbing mile after mile. The best all-around sheep chamberings are the .300 Magnums, including the .300 Win. Mag., .300 Wby. Mag., .300 Rem. Ultra Magnum, .30 Rem. Short-Action Ultra Magnum and the .30 Win. Short Magnum. Other solid sheep performers include the .270 Win., 7mm Rem. Mag., and the .30-06 Springfield.

Sheep Optics: You'll need lots of glass on top of your rifle. A variable scope in the 3-9x, 2.5-10x, 4-14x and 4.5-16x class will be super. For mountain sheep hunting, especially when backpacking is involved, many guys carry compact 10x25 or 12x25 binoculars. Sure, they don't work well under low-light conditions, but sheep hunting isn't just an early morning and late evening affair. Besides, the weight and bulk of larger binoculars can be a hindrance. Most important is a spotting scope and a sturdy, light-weight tripod on which to support it. The 15-45x Bushnell Elite spotter provides excellent distance resolution for trophy evaluations. For horseback and truck-based hunts, the larger Swarovski 20-60x80

cannot be beat. Without question insure that all of your optics—riflescope, binoculars and spotting scope—are top-quality, waterproof and fog proof. So bite the bullet, spend the money, and get over it!

Clothing and gear: Sheep hunting clothing will be determined by the terrain and weather. In the mountains, wear only synthetic or wool clothing when sheep hunting (no cotton allowed). Start with some Coolmax, Thermax, or other wicking fibers for your full-length underwear. On top of that, add layers of fleece or light wool pants and shirt. Fleece or micro-fleece pants and coats laminated to either a breathable Windstopper or Gore-Tex membrane will block 100 percent of the ever-present mountain wind and moisture. And never go hunting without packing a rain suit. My rain gear is made by Whitewater Outdoors and features a water-proof, breathable Gore-Tex liner and weighs less than 2 pounds. A baseball-style cap, warm earflap hat and good gloves are other essentials. In the desert, I like tough, double-faced Carhartt trousers that can take the abrasion of rocks and help protect against thorns, stickers and cactus. In this environment you're not usually worried about hypothermia as much as you are dirt, dust and sharp pointed stuff.

Photo by Bob Robb

A quality operation, like Pioneer Outfitters, is the key to nonresident Dall's sheep success. These professionals can give you all the help you need in applying for a license.

Your guide will be fully qualified to field dress, skin and cape your ram. This is just one of the services you pay him for.

When it comes to footwear, don't wear anything other than the best mountain boots ($200-$300) from Danner, Rocky, Georgia Boot, Browning, Meindl, Cabela's, Bass Pro and other reputable manufacturers and distributors. A Gore-Tex membrane lining is essential to keep your feet dry. Socks like those made by Thorlo, SmartWool, Wigwam and similar quality manufacturers are also in order.

Whatever else you take with you in the field, make sure you include a flashlight (extra batteries and bulb), small first aid kit (bandages for cuts, scrapes and blisters), a canteen (sometimes two), and some high-energy food. You might get caught out overnight or have to make it through some wet weather (rain and snow), which means a small tarp or Space Blanket® in your pack is a sensible item to have. You can forget about matches (they blow out in the wind), instead carry a lighter. If you need to build a fire, a wad or two of steel wool is a great fire starter.

Finding an outfitter: In some instances—especially when contemplating a sheep hunt in Mexico, Alaska or Canada—the law will require nonresidents to hire an outfitter. If you draw a sheep tag in the Lower 48 you can go it alone or hire a guide. In my opinion, hiring a top outfitter is the only thing that makes sense in all cases. Here's why. Drawing a sheep tag is probably a once-in-a-lifetime event. You'll definitely want to tip the odds in your favor, both in terms of trophy quality and overall success. Most sheep guides (approach any guided hunt with caution) know the hunting area and where rams are likely to be at any given time. And you'll hunt out of a comfortable camp and eat good food. This all adds up to money well spent for a hunt you'll never forget. Of course, things can go sour. Booking a hunt without checking outfitter and guide references, including those hunters that weren't successful, is pure stupidity. You wouldn't spend that kind of money on a new truck without first checking everything out first. A few bucks spent on long-distance telephone charges can save you thousands in the long run.

You can locate a good sheep outfitter many ways. One of the best is to contact a booking agent that deals with several different sheep guides. These professionals can help you pick an outfitter and guide that offers a hunt that meets your budget, physical abilities, hunting experience and personal preferences. The game department in the state or region where you've drawn a sheep tag can also be helpful. Chances are, too, that when you take the time to do the research you'll be able to get comfortable with the thought of entrusting your dream hunt to the right folks before any money comes out of your pocket. And you can take that piece of advice to the bank!

What's it like? Most of those who have pursued sheep can tell hunting stories for days on end. This means lots of references regarding unbelievable country, ripe berries on sunny slopes, the northern lights, grizzly bears, wolves, caribou and moose too numerous to count. You'll also be treated to talk of the "death march" to the ends of the earth, hikes up steep drainages, searching for rams that were never seen, freeze-dried food and wet clothes that were pure hell to remove at night. Any sheep hunter worth his salt will tell you about being frozen, soaked-to-the-bone and

Photo by Bob Robb

Bob Robb is rightly proud of this fine Dall's ram from the Wrangell Mountains. It was taken with the help of outfitter Terry Overy of Chisana, Alaska.

downright tired beyond all imagination. And you'll listen to stories about sheep guides who make little money and give their all for their clients, just because they love the game so much.

Outdoor writer, Bob Robb, once spent more than an hour bending my ear recounting one of his recent sheep hunts in Alaska. He wrapped that adventure up with these words:

"One night in the Alaska mountains, I sat in front of my tent, all bundled up against the chill, as a light northern wind blew down off of the face of a nearby glacier. I had just completed covering perhaps 50 miles in four days, on foot, in rain so hard it was impossible to see a 100 yards ahead at times. Yet, this day the sun had come out and warmed both my body and soul. God had smiled and let me shoot a superb Dall's ram. I had caped the animal and boned-out the sweet meat, then packed it all back to my little tent just before nightfall.

"Supper had been sheep tenderloin, the finest meat in the world. I washed the entire meal down with some ice-cold water from a nearby glacial trickle. Watching the shooting stars streak across the flawless sky, I marveled at the peaks as they glowed in the light of a three-quarter moon. When the northern lights came out and danced across the sky, their performance was for me, and me alone. I felt as though I could reach up and shake hands with the angels that were most surely at the controls.

"I realized in that moment how fortunate I was to be healthy and alive and physically able to see this country. Beyond that, to experience sheep hunting and taste the joy and pain that come with testing one's own abilities were the fruit that gives meaning to life."

Win, lose or draw, sheep hunting will leave you a better person for having taken the challenge. Isn't it time you did?

Photo by Bob Robb

Outdoor writer Bob Robb poses with this fine mountain goat billy he took in Montana. Does it get any better than this?

ROCK DANCERS: THE MOUNTAIN GOAT

*Mountain goats are one of North America's most magnificent big game animals.
Why, then, do they get such little respect?*

When discussing the virtues of North Country big game animals, why is it you seldom run into exciting tales of mountain goat hunting? Grizzly and brown bears get the lion's share of the attention, of course, with no end to the number of "he almost got me" tales. Moose, with their giant antlers and oversized bodies, are both highly coveted and greatly respected. The stately caribou is revered for its almost delicate beauty and massive headgear. Dall's sheep are placed on a pedestal only slightly lower than a deity. And even the usually timid black bear draws more conversation than the mountain goat.

Grizzlies are arguably the most wonderful animals roaming North America today. If the truth is told, however, most encounters with *Ursus arctos horribilis* are fairly unremarkable. Memories of moose hunts more often are centered on the weather, instead of the animal. Stalking caribou brings to mind bugs and lots of ptarmigan, rather than immense headgear and the clicking of hooves. To be sure, Dall's sheep are tough to come by, but most hunts for rams are nothing out of the ordinary. The biggest problem involved in sheep hunting is locat-

Photo by Bob Robb

Mountain goat country is filled with beauty and the hunt is always something out of the ordinary.

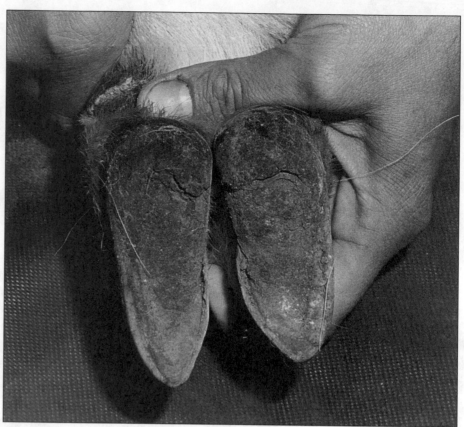

On their edges mountain goat hooves are hard as nails, but the inner portion is spongy for a sure grip on the rocks.

Photo by Bob Robb

ing animals, after that the shooting is generally unspectacular. And black bear hunting is great any way you can get it, but it's rarely anything special.

What about mountain goats? Harvesting a good billy is filled with adventure. Beating the onslaught of bad weather in the peaks is always a challenge. Likewise, negotiating treacherous terrain can get any heart beating for a couple of reasons. And anchoring a goat in place with a bullet or an arrow can be almost impossible. No, a mountain goat won't attack you, but that doesn't mean that pursuing this wonderfully beautiful animal isn't always exciting! It is, and more than that!

A mystery: The mountain goat, who carries a purely American scientific designation of *Oreamnos americanus americanus*, is something of a mystery. Interestingly, these animals are not true goats at all. The mountain goat is a member of the antelope family, which includes the European chamois, as well as the goral and scrow of Asia Minor. These creatures live where no other animal would, or for that matter, could. They can get fat and healthy in habitat where others would find slim pickings at best. And the toughness of a mountain goat is legendary, while its sagacity places it high atop many hunters' wish list of big game trophies.

Unique Appearance: Mountain goats have an unusual look, with a blunt, rather squarish body shape

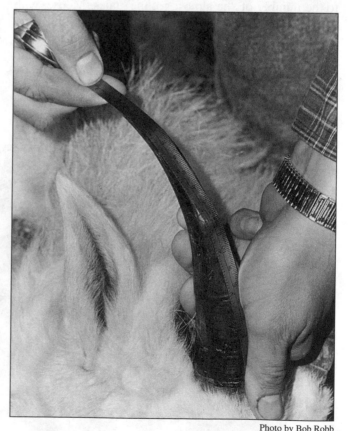

Photo by Bob Robb

Any billy goat with horns over 9 inches long is a true trophy.

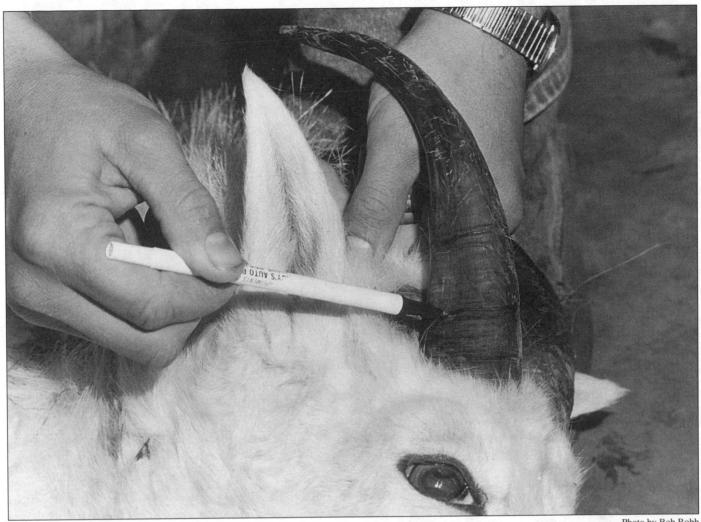

Photo by Bob Robb

Mountain goats, just like sheep, are aged by the growth rings on their horns.

and slightly humped, muscular shoulders that are almost out of proportion to the rest of the body. A narrow head features pointed ears and is culminated at the black nose. On average, a full-grown goat will stand 35 to 45 inches in height and measure 60 to 70 inches in length. The billy goat is somewhat larger than the nanny. And a fully mature male can weigh upwards of 300 pounds on the hoof.

Mountain goat horns are relatively short, slender and shiny black. Rising up off of the forehead, the horns sweep back in a graceful, parabolic curve. Both billy and nanny goats have horns, with the horns produced by the females generally longer than those worn by the males. However, nanny goat horns tend to be smaller in diameter than those on a billy of the same age. Most mature mountain goats have horns measuring 9 to 11 inches. The longest set of horns ever recorded came from a nanny goat and measured 12-1/2 inches. In terms of trophy quality, any mountain goat with relatively heavy horns (over 5 inches in circumference at

the bases) and measuring 9 inches in length is a fine animal. Goats with horns that exceed 9-1/2 inches are very good, and anything measuring more than 10 inches in length considered exceptional.

Goat horns may be tough, but they're not that tough. That's one reason you have to pick the location where you shoot a goat very carefully. Goats are famous for jumping off of ledges or rolling down steeps slopes when hit with a bullet or an arrow. A long drop down a steep rock face might leave the horns, as well as the cape, in shreds.

The all-white pelage of a mountain goat is as soft as fluff. Composed of an almost downy under layer of very fine fur, the coat also has a longer outer layer of guard hairs. Goats have a distinctive "beard" under their chins, which is really an extension of their neck guard hairs. This "beard" is more prominent on males, than it is on females and serves as a gender-distinguishing characteristic. The coat reaches its maximum length in late winter, with long luxurious guard hairs

Photo by Bob Robb

In coastal Alaska, goat hunters are often dropped from a boat onto beaches. Once on dry land it will take serious uphill hiking and climbing to reach the goats. This is definitely hard work!

Photo by Bob Robb

A white suit and head covering was used during the stalk to put the hunter within bow range of this fine goat.

and a thick undercoat. However, during the hot weather of the summer the coat is shed and hide can look like a buzz hair cut. Winter or summer, a mountain goat coat is still one of the most beautiful of all North American big game animal hides.

Dumb to approach? Many of those who don't know the ways of the mountain goat believe them to be dumb creatures that are easy to approach. Quite frankly, I don't buy it. Because the animals live in the toughest spires and peaks of the continent's steepest and tallest mountains, goats are by nature more trouble to get to than the average person can handle. For that reason, it may be years before a goat lays eyes on a person, if ever. To a goat, danger comes in the form of wolves and bears; predators with fearsome power at close range but harmless at 100 yards, or more, away. Stalking into comfortable rifle range of a mountain goat isn't all that difficult, but you must watch the wind. Furthermore, don't make any unnecessary sound; stay hidden behind rocks and down low in gullies as you approach. And whatever you do, try to stalk from the same level as the goats, or above them.

Hunters generally get into northern goat country by small airplane, horseback or boat. Once in the chosen locale the serious hiking and climbing will begin. In the Lower 48 states, goat country is accessible first by

Photo by Bob Robb

Serious mountain goat hunters will need to glass the steepest terrain possible to find animals out in the open.

road, then backpacking. Spot-and-stalk techniques work best, but you must make every effort to avoid the goat's excellent sense of smell and keen eyesight. If you have to expose yourself across an open slope, one way to fool a goat is to use the white suit trick. Most goat hunters carry a full-length white coverall, complete with hood and white facemask. Whether or not this really convinces a goat that you're "grazing," may be difficult to prove, but believe me it can work to your advantage. However, at the first whiff of four-day-old stale human stench, the goat will disappear from sight with the speed of a rocket. Don't forget to keep the wind in your face. Liberal application of scent-control products like Scent Killer can also help in this area.

The legal goat: Since they look so much alike, even up close, both nanny and billy goats are legal game. That said, when possible, most game managers encourage the taking of only mature male goats. Dis-tinguishable by their longer chin "beard" and heavier horn bases (though not always longer horns), with more curve to the horns, if you carefully scrutinize any individual goat the gender can generally be determined. Billy goats are also larger in size and have a blockier body build than nanny goats. At times the coat of a billy goat has a slightly yellowish tint that isn't seen on nanny goats. Furthermore, male goats tend to live higher on the mountain than do females and young offspring.

Goat hunts to remember: More than any other outdoor writer, Bob Robb knows mountain goats. He has stalked these animals in Far North, as well as in the Lower 48. His firsthand experience on a couple of hunts is well worth sharing. Read on!

"I vividly remember one goat hunt in British Columbia. My guide and I rode a pair of saddle horses for two days into the wilderness. There were lots of goats

Photo by Bob Robb

Much of goat country is above old-growth forest, meaning you'll have to climb up through heavy cover to get there. There are times when going through the thick of it can take all day.

Photo by Bob Robb

This goat, taken in August, had really short hair. Nevertheless, the weather was perfect and the hunting outstanding.

around and soon we found ourselves climbing after a pair of better-than-average billy goats bedded at the top of some extremely steep cliffs.

"As we worked our way up the mountain, using the vertical rocks to keep hidden, we finally were able to peek over a rim down onto where the goats were positioned. The animals were about 200 yards away, which made trophy evaluation with the naked eye nearly impossible. I belly-crawled to a small saddle and set up my spotting scope. I wanted to carefully look the goats over before deciding on whether or not to shoot.

"Unfavorable occurrences seem to happen in goat country and this was one of those times. Just as I got settled into behind the spotting scope a gust of icy wind whipped through the narrow saddle at about 40 miles per hour. The wind swirled up lots of dust and made it impossible to use any form of optical enhancement. Chilled to the bone, I curled up into a ball to conserve body heat. Unfortunately, the wind took my spotting scope clean down the mountain before I could even make an attempt to grab it. All I could do was watch my scope break into pieces 1,000 feet below. Since it was obviously beyond repair, we never even went to

look for the scope. Likewise, we never had another opportunity to get a shot at one of the goats. The wind must have chilled them, too, because they moved around the mountain to a sheltered cliff face. The terrain was so steep, that any attempt to follow the animals would have been folly.

"Another time the Alaskan weather beat up on me. What began as a beautiful week of sunshine and warm temperatures (seldom the case in Alaska, especially on a goat hunt), ended up quite badly. I had climbed more than 5,000 feet up from the beach into great goat country. The weather was so nice that it was almost unbelievable. The next morning, however, I awoke to ground fog and drizzle, which soon turned into serious rain (so much for good weather). Three days—I had only left my tent the entire time to answer the call of Mother Nature—passed before it finally stopped raining. I took advantage of that opportunity by going out and shooting a nice billy goat. By the time I returned to camp with meat, horns and a cape, the fog and rain started up again. I was stuck in my tent for two more days (thank God for pocket books) before visibility increased to the point that I felt safe about going down the mountain."

This hunter selected a synthetically stocked bolt-action rifle for his backpack mountain goat hunt.

When to hunt: For the most part, goats will be found only in the steepest, worst, toughest, highest and most spectacular country anywhere in southern Alaska, coastal British Columbia, Yukon Territory, southwestern Alberta and isolated parts of the states of Washington, Oregon, Montana, Idaho, Utah, Nevada and Colorado. However, in the winter along the southern Alaskan coast snow will push these animals down, almost to the beach. In this region, the mountain goat winters in the shelter of the trees.

In early August, goats get as high up as they can get, often well above 10,000 feet in elevation. At this time of the year, their coats are still thick, but extremely short. As the season progresses, the goats move lower and their hair grows longer until it becomes quite long in late October and early November. It is because the longer

Bow hunting mountain goats is the ultimate challenge. This will demand a steady stalk and deliberate arrow placement. There is no room for error.

Photo by Bob Robb

Your choice of gear and equipment for mountain goat hunting can make the difference between comfort or concern, success or failure. Choose wisely and leave all non-essentials behind.

hair makes for a superb trophy that most goat hunts are scheduled in late fall. While you can be rightly proud of any mature billy, the incomparable coats of late-season animals make them the much preferable trophy.

Calibers for goat hunting: A mountain goat can pack some lead. Even when shot through both lungs and dead on their feet, a goat can race another 100 yards, then leap off of a 1,000-foot cliff, completely destroying both horns and tearing the cape to tatters in the process. And don't bet on a bullet through both shoulders as an effective way of anchoring a goat. It doesn't work that way with these tenacious animals. I can recall one campfire conversation that spelled out just how tough goats really are. As the story went, an outdoor writer was using a rifle chambered in .280 Rem., firing stiffly hand-loaded 160-grain Nosler® Partition® bullets. This combination had proven effective on everything from ground squirrels to grizzlies. Lining up his crosshairs so his bullet would tear through the nearside shoulder, the scribe touched off a shot. Amazingly, the goat sprinted for the edge of a spectacular cliff as if he'd been poked with a cattle prod. A second shot broke the opposite shoulder, at which time the animal began to roll like a fuzzy white bowling ball. The goat went over the edge of the cliff into what seemed like a bottomless drop. Only good fortune prevented the horns from breaking into pieces and saved the cape from damage. The writer was lucky, but that isn't always the case. Like I said, things happen when you're goat hunting. And sometime those events are disastrous.

The first of many goat hunting rules is, quite simply, forget about shooting a goat if you haven't first considered what will happen next. Don't even think about shooting if a goat is on the edge of, or near, a vertical face. If you do, you can bet your last dollar that the animal will jump or fall off of it. This will not only destroy the horns and the cape,. it can also make recovery horribly dangerous or impossible.

Because solidly anchoring a goat with the first shot is highly desirable, some hunters are using the .338 Win. Magnum cartridge. With 220-, 225- or even 250-grain bullets, this chambering is a very dependable goat caliber. However, most rifles chambered for the

It's usually cold, wet and slippery in goat country. You'll need waterproof and well-broken-in boots with sure-grip soles.

Photo by Bob Robb

.338 Win. Mag. aren't designed for mountain hunting. Complete with scope, sling and a magazine full of ammunition, my own personal .338 Win. Mag. bolt-gun weighs a little more than 10 pounds. This is much too heavy for hauling around goat country. Even though the .338 Win. Mag. is a real powerhouse, more sensible caliber choices will be found in chamberings like the .280 Rem., 7mm Rem. Mag., the reliable .30-06 Spfd. and the .300 Winchester Magnum. The key to goat hunting success lies in the use of heavy-for-the-caliber premium bullets. I like the 160-grain and 175-grain bullets in the .280 Rem. and the 7mm Rem.

Magnum, respectively. The 180-grain pill in either the .30-06 Spfd., or the .300 Win. Mag. is also good goat medicine. A rifle with a lightweight synthetic stock, a quality variable scope in the 2-7x, 3-9x or 2.5-10x range and a sling (a very important rifle accessory), usually will come in under 8-1/2 pounds. That's a lot lighter than carrying a heavy, wood-stocked magnum with a 24- or 26-inch barrel.

The goal of your first shot at a goat is to break down at least one, or both, of the front shoulders. This is a serious assignment and only solidly constructed bullets are up to the job. The Nosler® Partition®, Winchester

No matter where you hunt, a set of fresh goat tracks is a sure sign that you're in the right place.

Photo by Bob Robb

Photo by Bob Robb

Mountain goat hunting permits are often tough to get, so ask questions and follow instructions to the letter.

Fail-Safe®, Swift A-Frame®, Barnes X-Bullet® and even the Remington Bronze-Poin®t have good reputations in this arena. And it goes without saying that you will need no-joke, waterproof, fog proof, top-of-the-line optics. It makes no sense to spend a tremendous amount of effort, time and money on a goat hunt, without also using the best optics (rifle scope, spotting scope and binoculars) and ammunition.

Muzzleloaders should leave their .45 caliber deer blasters at home. In my opinion, only a .50, or better yet, a .54 caliber frontloader is a serious goat rig. Also, consider using one of the sabot-encased conical bullets, pushed by at least 100 grains (150 grains might be better if such a combination groups well in your rifle) of black powder or Pyrodex. Since inclement weather is always part of the goat hunting game, special care should be taken to keep your powder (granular or pelletized) dry. This includes protecting both the cap and the open muzzle from moisture.

Bowhunting for goats is great fun and a real challenge. Most veteran goat hunters use for their goat rig the same bow and arrow setup that works with elk and bear. Bows that have a pull weight of 60 to 70 pounds are about the minimum for this game. Carbon arrow shafts tend to penetrate deeper than aluminum, which is what you want. Tough broadheads, ones that won't shatter on impact, are essential. Whatever type of broadhead you select, it must be absolutely razor-sharp. The whole idea is to blow that arrow in one side and out the other, slicing and dicing everything in between. A laser rangefinder is a great asset and gives you the edge when it is time to shoot. Finally, make sure you can shoot accurately out to 50 yards. Forget about launching arrows at a target on a hay bale. Spend the money and get a full-size foam goat target, then shoot a few arrows at it every day. When you finally stalk into range of a trophy animal, you'll have developed the shooting confidence necessary to make the shot a given.

Weather and terrain can be your worst nightmares: When you're goat hunting, it can rain buckets, snow like it'll never stop and fog up so thick that you can't see. Hypothermia is a real concern in this kind of weather, which is one reason to dress in layers (clothing made out of synthetic fibers won't hold water) and use proven rain gear.

Photo by Bob Robb

Goat hunting will put you in some of the most spectacular country imaginable. If you find success, you'll feel it deep down in your soul.

Furthermore, the wet, cold and icy weather can make hiking and climbing interesting, to say the least. Crossing a slippery shale slide almost always leads to a bone-jarring slip. When that happens, you must take care not to slide over a cliff edge. And jumping on top of a boulder as big as a battleship can easily start an avalanche. You see, goat hunting can be interesting, even life-threatening. If the weather doesn't get you, then the unstable footing so typical of goat country will surely gain your attention.

On extremely low-visibility days there's not much you can do except stick close to camp and wait for clear weather. A couple (sometimes three or four) thick pocket books can prevent you from going stir crazy in a small tent during stretches of bad weather, even if you curse the extra weight during an arduous climb up the mountain. When confined in a tent for days on end, you'll learn a lot about your hunting companions and yourself. Believe me, it can be an enlightening experience.

Where to go: The best mountain goat hunting is found in Alaska and British Columbia. However, a few places in the Lower 48 offer excellent goat hunting, although the opportunities are limited and tightly controlled. One big difference is if you draw a goat permit in the Lower-48, you can hunt goats unguided. Here's a glance at those opportunities.

Colorado: This state offers arguably the finest goat hunting for overall success and trophy quality in all of the contiguous states. The current world record billy goat came from Colorado, and the state issues 170 to 190 tags annually. Hunter success is excellent for rifle hunters (94 percent) and astonishingly high (88 percent) for bowhunters. The best areas for trophy goats include Mt. Evans, the Gore Range and Gray's Peak.

Idaho: This state is often overlooked when thinking about mountain goats. And yet, every open goat unit in Idaho has the potential to produce billy goats with horns measuring 9 inches with bases at least 5 inches in circumference. The state issues about 50 to 60 goat permits annually, with an outstanding hunter success rate. The top units in terms of trophy potential include units 10-1, 10-2, 67-1, 59A and 18.

Montana: This state remains an excellent prospect for mountain goats. In 2000, the state had 60 hunting units open for goats, 22 of those units were open to nonresidents. The best unit for a big billy is 447-00, which is known as the Square Butte unit. Here you'll find good access with some 10-inch goats available. Other top units in terms of trophy potential include units 240-01, 325-00, 329-00 and 134-00. The downside to hunting in this state is the difficulty in drawing a permit. Your chances are about 1 in 100. Somebody has to draw those goat tags and you won't be the lucky one if you don't play the game.

Utah: The Beehive state issues about 30 goat tags each year. In 2000, two of those tags were allocated for nonresidents. The Wasatch Mountains are the place to be for top notch goat hunting in this state.

Washington: This state is another good bet, though nonresidents must purchase an expensive hunting license before they are allowed to apply for a goat permit. The state issues 50 to 70 mountain goat permits annually. Although the odds are quite long at obtaining one of the coveted licenses, a lucky permit holder has a near 100 percent chance of bagging a good goat. The better units for big billy goats include Goat Rocks (where else?), Naches Pass and Methow.

Wyoming: This state has limited goat hunting, though animal numbers are steadily growing. This should provide increased hunting opportunities down the road. In 2000, only three nonresident tags were issued for unit 1, while unit 2 (a newly-opened area) had a single nonresident tag available in that year. Hunting here is not easy. The pursuit of mountain goats in Wyoming is definitely a backpack and boot leather game.

The most important thing to remember about applying for a goat hunting permit is that the application deadlines can change annually. It's best to check with each game department where you're planning to apply to make sure you won't miss any pertinent cutoff date. Also, it's a good idea to glean as much information as possible from the various Internet sites that are maintained by each game department. Just type in the name of the state and the word "hunting" and your computer search engine should find something for you.

An extra-special animal: When the weather is nice, there's no better place in the world to be hiking than the high country in search of mountain goats. The vistas are breathtaking and the rock formations were old before the birth of Christ. In the lush meadows on the way up, you'll find moose escaping the summer heat and bugs and black bears will be there getting fat on berries. Depending on where you hunt, deer and elk can also be found. Likewise, you may run into an occasional wolf or wolverine. Marmots will cuss you out with their shrill whistling, while ptarmigan and spruce grouse skitter about. It's worth putting up with several days of bad weather for just a good day or two in this realm.

The mountain goat is more than just another big game animal; it is a symbol of the true wilderness. The tranquility of this region is more apt to be shattered by the gurgle of a pristine stream or the howl of a wolf than the vulgar sound of a ghetto-blaster or a chain saw. Certainly, the weather changes by the hour, meaning the prudent are rewarded and the careless mercilessly punished.

The sky in much of mountain goat country is often clear enough to see to the edge of the universe. The water is pure and the peaks still possess their primal innocence. If you accept the challenge of hunting in this realm, you'll feel a new warmth in your soul that's hard to experience anywhere else. Quite frankly, in those times when a hunt isn't in the offering, I miss old *Oreamnos*—the all-American mountain goat.

Photo by Bob Robb

Mountain grizzly bears have some seriously big claws. This set of nails belonged to a bear whose hide squared 7 feet, 3 inches.

TOOTH AND CLAW: GRIZZLY AND BROWN BEAR

Hunting powerful carnivores that can and will bite back is a game that demands resolve, courage and a steady aim.

There are three great bears in North America—the polar bear of the northern ice pack, the coastal brown bear of Alaska and the mountain or interior grizzly bear. With the enactment of the Marine Mammal Protection Act of 1972, the sport hunting of polar bears was virtually eliminated. The pursuit of brown and grizzly bears continues. Taxonomically, both bears are biologically the same animal—*Ursus arctos*. Over the years various subspecies have emerged, but current scientific thinking is that the differences are due to climatic conditions and diet, rather than any genetic shift. The main difference between the brown bear and the grizzly has to do with where they live and what they eat. Coastal brown bears live in areas rich with summer runs of salmon, providing several months of an all-you-can-eat, high-calorie and protein-enhanced food source. They also reside in regions where winters, as well as the time they spend in dens, are a month or two shorter than those experienced by the mountain or interior grizzly bears. The added time allows brown bears to gorge, adding to their overall growth potential. Biologists who attribute the enhanced size of the brown bear to these factors have confirmed this.

The line of demarcation between coastal brown and the grizzly is really an invention of the game record keeping organizations. Both the Boone & Crockett and Pope & Young clubs draw a line that runs roughly 75-miles from the coastline. Any bears taken on the ocean side of this line are brown bears, while those living on the other side are grizzlies. This is somewhat deceptive. For example, in the most northern reaches of Alaska and on the British Columbia side of the southeast Alaskan panhandle, bears are classified as grizzlies, but they live and eat the same as any brown bear. No matter, hunting either of these two magnificent game animals, wherever they reside, is perhaps the most exciting and rewarding hunt you can ever make.

The grizzly: Today Alaska is home to well over half the entire North American grizzly bear population, which has a continental total of somewhere between

Photo by Dan Herring

This grizzly came from the Northwest Territories. Martin Webb (right) led hunter Joe Herring to the bear.

60,000 and 70,000 individual animals. In the Lower 48 states, estimates of the grizzly population are between 1,000 and 1,200 bears, most of which live inside Yellowstone National Park. The remainder of this population is found in isolated areas of Idaho, Wyoming, Montana and northeastern Washington. In Canada, the estimated grizzly population in Alberta is about 800 bears, in British Columbia there are about 10,000 animals, the Yukon Territory can boast of about 7,000 grizzlies and the Northwest Territories has about 3,000 of these big bears. In Alaska, estimates generally run between 35,000 and 40,000 bears, including both the interior grizzly and the coastal brown bear.

By law, nonresidents of grizzly country (including Alaska) must hire a licensed outfitter to legally hunt these bears. The only exception to this being that you can hunt with an Alaskan resident who is a second degree of kindred relative (game officials check on the relationship of any so-called "cousin"). Outfitted grizzly hunts are expensive, costing $7,000 or more, and can go up in cost if you add on any additional species. A combination grizzly/moose, or grizzly/caribou hunt is an excellent way to hunt fall bears. This allows you to actively pursue a good bull moose or caribou, while still searching for a bear. The best time for this kind of hunt is September.

Grizzly populations in the Far North country are quite stable. The key to this stability, of course, is keeping their remote habitat uncluttered by the development of man. During the five-year period between the 1988-89 and the 1992-93 hunting seasons, Alaska sold an average of 1,269 brown and grizzly bear licenses to nonresidents. Alaskan residents purchase an average of 6,530 bear permits. An average of 1,144 bears (brown and grizzly) were taken annually during this period, with 53 percent of that take attributed to nonresidents. That's an average annual harvest of between 2.86 percent and 3.27 percent of the total bear population. Given the remote locations of the best bear hunting and strict limits on the numbers of bears a hunter is permit-

Photo by Bob Robb

Grizzly bears root for bulbs and grubs just like pigs. This torn-up piece of earth is a sure sign that a bear is somewhere nearby.

Photo by Bob Robb

Outdoor writer Bob Robb cautiously approaches a downed grizzly. You can never be too careful when dealing with a bear of this size.

ted to take (the limit is one bear every four years in the majority of Alaska), this percentage should not increase significantly in the near future.

Hunting grizzly bears has been described as 95 percent boredom and 5 percent absolute terror. That's a very fair assessment. The boredom part comes from simply trying to locate a bear suitable to stalk. This can take days, or even weeks, depending on just how much good fortune is involved in the matter. Unlike coastal brown bears, which concentrate on salmon streams in the fall making them relatively casy to find, grizzly bears of the Alaskan interior are much more nomadic. A game biologist once told me that a grizzly can have a home range of as much as 50 square miles. Furthermore, a bear can cover more than 10 miles daily in search of food. That's one heck of a lot of country for a hunter to cover.

Since finding a grizzly can be problematic, most outfitters and guides look for areas of favored bear food. In the fall, grizzlies tend to congregate on mountains that have vast expanses of berry bushes.

The bears also dig roots. In the spring they'll follow the moose and caribou herds, preying heavily on newborn calves, old and injured animals. Fresh grass shoots and flowers are a preferred spring food and the bears will graze like cattle. At times, these big animals will expend hundreds of calories trying to excavate a ground squirrel or marmot from its den. These little animals must taste like chocolate to a bear, since they certainly aren't worth all the effort it takes to dig them out. While they have their food preferences, grizzlies will eat almost anything. And this includes plastic gasoline cans left on a remote airstrip by bush pilots and even a grease stained tent. It happens that way when you're in bear country.

The name of the grizzly game is glassing. It can get boring (I already said that) when you glass for days on end and never find a bear. When the weather's good, glassing is tolerable. The country in which these animals live is stunning and there's always something to see. However, when things turn sour and the cold, wind-driven rain or sleet eats its way under your clothes, it's hard to keep on task. If you stay at it long enough, the chances are in your favor that you'll be rewarded with the sight of a grizzly working along a near mountainside.

Your first grizzly is something you'll never forget. Even if everything about the hunt goes wrong, just the sight of that bear is enough to get your adrenalin going. This is also when nagging questions begin to creep into the back of your mind. After all, a grizzly can be a cantankerous and extremely dangerous animal. The palms of your hands will get a little sweaty and breathing will come a little faster. And the pounding in your ears will be nothing more than your own heartbeat. You know that you've seen the bear and he hasn't spotted you. There's a proven rifle in your hand and you're with a guide who also carries a firearm. The wind is blowing from the bear to you and the stalk shouldn't be any different from moving in close to a deer back home. Yet, deep down inside, you know that it is different. Even the best grizzly hunt can go terribly wrong—and that's one of the reasons these big bears are so special. No doubt, you've read all of the stories about wounded bears in the alders, of bear attacks and mauling and of chance encounters won by a bear. At this point in time, most hunters will begin to doubt their shooting ability and courage.

Friend and outdoor writer Bob Robb brought this point across better than most when he recounted a grizzly encounter of the most exciting kind.

"One time while hunting Stone's sheep on horseback in the Yukon Territory, my guide and I happened into a lone grizzly. The bear was about 100 yards off and rooting along a river bottom. The bear saw us about the same time we saw him. He immediately stood up on his hind legs to have a better look at us, then dropped down to all fours, gave a gruff growl and started to trot our way. I was bow hunting and had no rifle in my possession. The guide, a grouchy old trapper by trade, carried a battered rifle chambered in .30-06 Springfield. It could have been a grenade launcher or a bazooka for all it mattered, as the guide wheeled his horse around and galloped past me in a heated rush never saying a word.

"It didn't take a rocket scientist to figure out that this particular situation was 'every man for himself.' I spun my knot-headed horse around and kicked him in the ribs, trying to hold on as we tore down a narrow, muddy trail lined with alders. The grizzly chased us for maybe a mile or so. At the time, I was completely terrorized. Look back at that incident, I think the bear was just playing with us. I'm sure he could have closed the distance between us if he had really wanted to. After that brief chase, the bear stopped and went back to rooting as if nothing ever happened. For my part, I couldn't stop shaking for days."

If you hunt grizzlies long enough, you'll end up with your own collection of stories to tell around the campfire. Unless you're a hunting guide, you probably won't have tales of tracking wounded bears in the thick stuff. This is an arena where, as the British like to say, things

Photo by Bob Robb

Hunting mountain grizzly bears is all too often a game of glassing.

Photo by Bob Robb

Is this brown bear big—or what? Taken in southeast Alaska, this bear's hide squared 9 feet, 2 inches.

can get a "bit dicey." Such an adventure is stimulating, but definitely not fun at all.

Brown bears: Hunting the huge coastal brown bear is an entirely different game. Instead of riding horses or hiking up tall mountains and glassing deep valleys, you're near the ocean and concentrating on finding a bear in one of two ways. In the spring, you'll spend your time looking on steep slopes for den sites, hoping to catch a roaming bear that has just emerged from his winter nap. At this time of year, bears are headed for the best available opportunity to fill their empty stomachs. In the fall, salmon streams are the keys to success. Bears are hunted along pure, crystal-clear streams filled with fish.

Once again, one of Bob Robb's most recent brown bear adventures is worth repeating here.

"In April 2001, I hunted coastal brown bear with my good friend Jim Boyce of Baranoff Expeditions, based in Sitka, Alaska. Midway through this hunt, we stopped overnight at Boyce's southeast hunting headquarters, Cape Ommney Lodge. The stop was made to re-supply the 38-foot boat and regroup after a few hard days of hunting. The weather had been terrible, with high winds, rough seas and a combination of icy rain and some unseasonable late snow flurries. Even so, client Allen Arrington of North Carolina had connected on his dream bear, a beautiful 8-footer taken with a single-shot from his new rifle chambered in .416 Remington Magnum. The bear had been spotted feeding on a tidal flat and we moved in and made a short stalk. It was a textbook approach and nothing went awry. However, just as we started skinning the bear a rain squall blew in and completely drenched us. Tired and soaked to the skin, after we had the animal skinned, we returned to the warm lodge.

"Now with a break in the weather—the seas outside had been running more than 12 feet, but the prediction was wind to 50 knots and seas reaching 25 feet in just two days. Boyce and one of his most experienced guides, Kurt Whitehead, and I took the boat north to explore one of his favorite "bear holes." Fortunately, it was an area protected from the impending storm, so we'd be able to hunt regardless of the weather.

"Reaching the hunting area about midday, we began doing what spring bear hunters do in this part of the world—slowly cruising the shoreline, glassing the steep mountainsides for bears on the move. This is 95 percent of your hunting and after a day or two of not seeing much, it's boredom time. After just a few hours, we were already bored! Then, just as we began putting our minds into the siege mentality necessary for days of glassing, things began to pick up. Boyce spotted a bear high on the mountain. No matter how hard we tried to put some size on him, we all finally agreed that it was a youngster out for a stroll.

"Continuing on along the shoreline, we persevered with our glassing activities. Both Jim and Kurt were looking where they were supposed to—on the steep mountainsides and along avalanche chutes. I was getting a bit lazy and concentrated on the beaches. Suddenly my binoculars were filled with a brown bear. Anchoring the boat, we were off in a tiny skiff for a closer look.

"It was a nice bear, but Jim and Kurt thought it to be a big old sow. We got the wind right and moved closer to make sure. For some reason—brown bears have a habit of doing this—the bear simply got up and shambled off into the thick brush, out of sight.

"We returned to the skiff and motored back to the boat, still hoping for a bear. In less than five minutes, out prayers were answered. On a tiny rock outcropping, next to a 20-foot vertical face was a dandy of a bear. This was one of those animals that you only have to look at for a second and you know 'this is the one.' Naturally, it wasn't going to be easy. The tide was up and there was no place to beach the skiff near the bear. Finally, we found a location about 125 yards up the shoreline. There was no beach between the bear and us and a vertical cliff dropped straight down in between into over 100 feet of water. Our only hope was to get ready and pray that the bear would move out from behind the rock face that was shielding him. If he did, then we just might have a clear shot.

"I got down into a prone position, settled in, and waited. I could see pieces of the bear as it fed on the

Outdoor writer Bob Robb and outfitter Terry Overly, pose with a big bear hide from a grizzly that Robb took in Alaska.

In many areas a backpack is essential to get to the good spots.

This 400-pound black bear came after hours of diligent glassing in coastal Alaska.

Grizzly bears always make for a tough hunt.

Outdoor writer John Higley proves that California is home to a very healthy black bear population.

Talk about tooth and claw. Here's a mountain grizzly that's all that and then some. Photo by Bob Robb .

The difference between a black bear and a grizzly is readily apparent—just look for the "hump."

Always on the alert, this mule deer senses danger.

Photo by Jim Matthews.

This is typical mule deer country, lots of rocks and low mixed cover.

Photo by Jim Matthews.

Photo by Duwane Adams.

Duwane Adams guided Russ Schulpetz to this magnificent mule deer in Arizona's Kaibab region.

Photo by John Higley.

John Higley, is a "dyed-in-the-wool" mule deer hunter.

Photo by John Higley.

Cold and snow are just what every mule deer hunter wishes for.

Photo by Durwood Hollis.

The author took this typical 4x4 mule deer in central Wyoming.

Okay. He's spotted you. Don't move a muscle or this mule deer buck will spook. Give him time to settle down.

Photo by Jim Matthews.

Photo by Dan Herring.

Not only is Dan Herring an accomplished taxidermist, he's also a top-notch big game hunter. Here he is with a fine Wyoming mule deer.

Photo by Duwane Adams.

After glassing some thick cedar country nearly all day, guide Duwane Adams put Joe Kropinak on this mule deer buck.

The blacktail deer is right at home in the deepest cover possible.

Photo by Bob Robb.

This South Fox Island deer camp, situated in the middle of Lake Michigan, has a seriously heavy meat pole.

Photo by Durwood Hollis.

The coffee's hot and the fire's warm. What else matters in hunting camp?

Photo by Durwood Hollis.

Bob Robb has taken some fantastic trophies. This caribou is just one of them.

Here is a day with clear skies (sort of) and good weather. Caribou country isn't generally like this.

Photo by Duwane Adams.

Ty Goodman (left) and Steve Willie (right) teamed up with guide Duwane Adams to take this outstanding Arizona bull elk.

Photo by Bob Robb.

Broadhead or bullet, either way a big bull elk is still an impressive trophy.

Bugling for all he's worth, this incredible bull elk is a trophy of a lifetime.

Photo by Jim Matthews.

Photo by Durwood Hollis.

The author took this bull in the sage and Juniper country near Thermopolis, Wyoming.

Roosevelt elk are seldom seen in the open. This tremendous bull was caught between dense stands of evergreens. Photo by J. Mark Higley.

Shown here in its natural environment, the tule elk loves water and bull rushes.

Photo by Durwood Hollis.

By carefully watching the wind, this bowhunter was able to stalk within scant yards of these wild hogs.

Photo by Durwood Hollis.

Photo by Charles Merritt.

Charlie Merritt took this desert tusker in southeastern Arizona late one afternoon.

Photo by Durwood Hollis.

The author used a carbine-length bolt-action rifle to score on this "tooth" hog.

This bull moose isn't much in the antler department, but if it's meat you want—he's a prime target.

Jim Matthews used a muzzleloader to take this pronghorn buck.

Here's a great pronghorn buck that came after a long stalk and an even longer shot.

Photo by Charlie Merritt.

Riding the rims is one way to hunt many regions in the vast North American West.

Photo by Durwood Hollis.

Taking a mountain goat is a real challenge, but taking one with a bow is something else entirely.

These horns, from a Dall's ram taken in Alaska's Chugach Mountains, measured 43 inches, with bases almost 14 inches around. This is one tremendous white sheep.

When the weather's nice, even Dall's sheep take a break. This ram is just dozing his way through the afternoon.

Photo by Bob Robb

Looking for a wounded bear in the thick stuff isn't for the faint of heart.

fresh herring spawn that covered the rocks. And when he finally gave me a clear, quartering-to-me view of his right shoulder, I placed the crosshairs of my .375 H&H Magnum at the juncture of the neck. At the shot, the bear roared and spun around. I shot again, this time aiming for the middle of the shoulder. The bullet kicked the bear into the ocean and he swam across the small inlet to the opposite bank. When he climbed up on the rocks and out of the water, I shot again. This time, the Nosler® Partition® bullet took him through both lungs. Though he tried to climb the rock face, he couldn't quite make it. As I reloaded, the bear went down for good, or so we thought.

"Brown bears are one of the toughest animals I've ever hunted and this one was no exception. Even after three shots, the bear managed one last little kick. This put him over the rock and into the ocean, where he started to sink like a stone. Boyce, realizing what had happened—we had all seen big bears like this one float like huge corks—jumped into the skiff and raced toward the bear. Reaching the spot where the bear was last seen, the only visible thing was a big bloody sheen on the surface. Boyce looked and saw bubbles. Reaching

below the water's surface, he was able to grab a handful of the hide. Looping a rope around the bear's head, Boyce tied the end off to the skiff. Then he slowly and carefully motored back to us. It took a lot of grunting and groaning on our part to slide the bruin onto the rocks, but we were able to pull him out of the water.

"This was a giant of a brown bear. But the fun wasn't over quite yet. The tide was coming in fast and we didn't want to leave the bear on the tiny rock shelf. Jim took the skiff back to the boat. Since the water was deep next to the rocks, Boyce was able to motor right up to Kurt and me. We passed him the rope attached to the bear and tried to muscle the carcass aboard.

"It wasn't as easy as we thought. With no swim step to make the job any easier, it took about an hour-and-a-half to get the bear on the deck. Jim ran the boat out of the sheltered cove and into the rough ocean on the outside. After about an hour of pitch and roll, we were once again in quiet waters (this all occurred in pitch darkness just for added excitement).

"Since all of us wanted photos, we had to find another cove. Then it was a repeat of the old tug and haul routine. We had to get the carcass over the side of the big boat and into the skiff without losing the bear to the ocean. More muscle, more rope and lots of hard work and into the skiff the carcass finally went. We motored ashore, found a good spot for photos, rolled the bear out onto the beach and slid him all of 10 feet up onto a nice little hump. It was here, well above the high tide mark, that we left the animal. By the time we made it back to the big boat, it was 3:00 in the morning. The next morning, we awoke to a low tide. We went ashore in the skiff, cleaned the bear up and took our photos. After skinning, the hide ended up squaring 9 feet 3 inches, which is a monster bear from anyplace on earth. Just another routine brown bear hunt in southeast Alaska."

How much gun is enough? No doubt about it. When hunting both grizzlies and coastal brown bears, you'll want to pack enough firepower. However, the most important thing is to bring a rifle you can shoot well. It's far better to carry a light caliber with which you are both familiar and can shoot accurately under field conditions, than one chambered in some cigar-sized cartridge that scares you into flinching. In this business, there are no second chances. Big bears aren't deer or elk. If you hit one poorly, you must track him down and finish what you've started. A badly hit bear usually means a wounded animal in the thick stuff, where he can and will try to turn the tables on you. Like I said before, this is where the fun stops.

That said, contrary to popular belief, you don't need a cannon to safely hunt grizzlies. Most hunters take their animals with rifles with cartridges in the .30-06 Spfd. class. However, the .300 Win. Mag. and the .338 Win. Mag. are probably better choices for every situation. Brown bears are a tad tougher than most grizzlies and demand a little more punch to put them down and out. The .338 Win. Mag. is a good minimum, with lots of room for the .375 H&H Mag. and the .416 Rem. Magnum. Of course, you'll want to use heavy-for-the-caliber premium bullets. Good choices are Nosler® Partition®, Winchester Fail-Safe®, Barnes X-Bullets®, as well as the Remington Cor-Loc® and the Speer Grand Slam®.

Are you ready? For most, a grizzly or brown bear hunt is a once-in-a-lifetime adventure. The cost of a hunt alone keeps most folks from even thinking about more than one hunt. And that's a shame, because the more you play this game, the better you get at it. I promise you, once you hunt old *Ursus arctos*, you'll want to come and do it again and again. Every moment you're in the field, even when you're not seeing bears, the knowledge that any second, just around the next bend, or over the next hill, he'll be there waiting is enough to keep your senses charged up. When you do finally spot a big bear, every hair follicle on your body will constrict and your heart will begin to race.

Photo by Bob Robb

The bear, taken by outdoor writer Bob Robb weighed an estimated 1,400 pounds! The bear was taken with a .338 Winchester Magnum at a mere 10 yards. Does it get any more exciting than that?

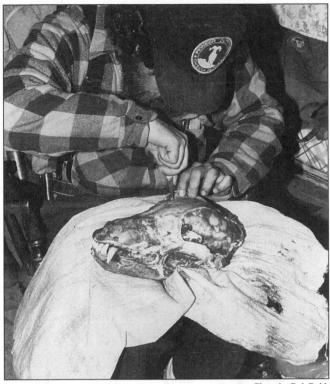

Photo by Bob Robb

A cleaned and bleached bear skull is a great trophy and one to be proud of.

Certainly, the sheer size, speed and audacity of these animals are the driving elements of the chase. The country in which they live also draws hunters. Big bears need wilderness to thrive. This is the kind of country where any real hunter feels most at home.

Once you take the challenge, you'll be addicted. And there's really no good way to withdraw from that kind of obsession.

Preventing bear trouble: Grizzly and brown bears are a fact of life in Alaskan hunting. Some areas have a lot of these bruins, others have few. All it takes is one bad-tempered bear to ruin a good thing. It's best to be prepared. Generally, grizzlies shy away from humans. However, young bears are curious and all bears are attracted to an easy meal. To prevent bear problems here are some good tips:

- Keep a clean camp. Don't leave food out and store meat downwind at least 100 yards from camp.
- Never walk through the middle of a thicket. You just might wake a sleeping bear.
- Steer clear of a sow with cubs at all costs.
- Be on the lookout for fresh bear sign. If you see a bear-kill, get away from the area immediately.
- Bears are most active at night, so try to return to camp before dark.
- Hunt with a buddy, "just in case."

If you do happen to encounter a bear, always:

- Make lots of noise and "act large." This often intimidates the bear into a non-aggressive posture.
- Always face the bear. If it tries to circle you, turn with it.
- Assume every bear is trouble.
- If you have to fire a warning shot, aim so the bullet strikes right in front of the bear's nose.
- Don't let a bear get too close.

Photo by Bob Robb

In coastal Alaska, cruising ocean bays, inlets and stream mouths in a small boat are good ways to find either a brown bear or a grizzly.

Photo by Frank Baratti

This black bear, taken in southern California by Mary Lou Baratti within sight of the Los Angeles freeway system, weighed more than 600 pounds.

BEAR TALES: BLACK BEAR

The grizzly's smaller cousin is a challenge no matter how you hunt!

It had been a long four days of fruitless black bear hunting. That's not saying we hadn't seen bears. We had. In spite of those sightings, the animals were too far away for a shot and unapproachable, or it was a matter of a sow accompanied with a set of cubs. On this last day of the hunt, my travels had taken me far up a canyon that rose from the winding course of the Salmon River.

Early on, my path crossed that of a female bear and two cubs. That old girl had been busy keeping her offspring in check and she didn't even notice my presence. Bear cubs are comical to watch, what with all of their youthful antics. When the sow finally caught a whiff of my scent, the cubs were sent up a nearby tree and she disappeared into the brush.

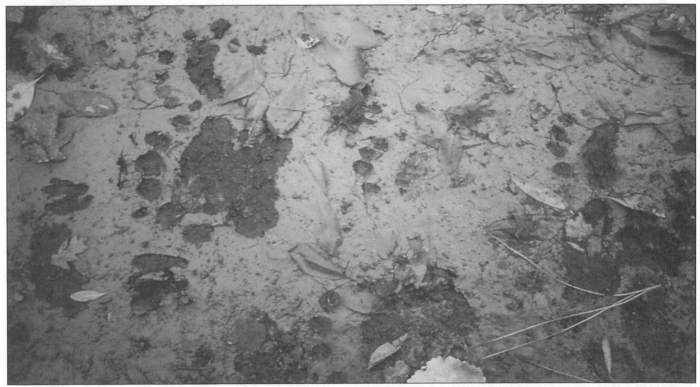

Photo by John Higley

Black bear tracks are easily seen in soft soil and mud.

The author used a Savage rifle chambered in .270 Winchester to take this black bear.

Photo by Durwood Hollis

That particular bear was the ninth that I'd run into over the last four days. Most sightings were identical to this one—a sow with cubs. Recently emerging from their winter dens, the bears were ravenously hungry. Even the little cubs, still sucklings at best, were following right along.

Two days before, my guide and I had located what looked like a solitary bear. Situated across the canyon from our position, the bear fed without interruption in a field of yellow flowers. Unfortunately, the distance was too far to chance a shot. We hoped that the bear would feed down the slope and close the gap between us. It never happened. Initially, we contemplated stalking the animal. While the bear was clearly visible from across the canyon, any attempt at stalking him from the same side of the canyon would have been impossible. The cover was too thick and there was a distinct possibility of stumbling right into the animal (not a good idea). It

seemed my one opportunity to take a black bear was only a fleeting dream.

The current day had proven to be a repeat of all of the previous days. I had glassed a single bear on the other side of the river. Without some means of getting across the raging current, the sighting was without merit. Up and up I hiked, moving deeper into the bowels of the canyon. Here and there, fresh bear tracks were visible in the muddy trail. It was one of those lines of tracks that lead to my chance encounter with the sow and her cubs.

Now, as the shadows of the afternoon lengthened, it was time to return to the riverbank and await the arrival of the jet boat. This Salmon River bear hunt had been my first experience riding in a jet boat. While maneuvering through the rapids reminded me of "Mr. Toad's Wild Ride" at Disneyland, the watercraft had proven to be an extremely practical means of transport.

Departing in the boat from the hunting lodge at daybreak, my guide and I would be dropped off at the mouth of one of the canyons that rose upward from the river. At the conclusion of the day, we would meet the boat at a designated location and return to the lodge before nightfall. In the event our hunting efforts met success, the boat would also serve to haul the bear. The boat offered easy passage to country that would have taken many hours of hard hiking to enter.

Boats and bears had been a winning combination for several spring hunts out of the Salmon River hunting camp. In my case, however, it hadn't proven to be so successful. Sure, there had been bears and the boats were reliable transportation. I just hadn't been lucky

enough to put the two factors together. But my luck was about to change.

I was tired and ready for a hot meal and a warm sleeping bag. It had been a long day of hiking and glassing. With the exception of the sow and cubs, along with a bull elk that nearly stepped on me while I napped in the middle of a game trail, no legal bear had been sighted. As I neared the riverbank, something caught the corner of my eye. Not 100 yards away a solitary black bear was scrambling up the opposite side of the canyon, headed for cover.

There was no time to think. The only thing I could do was react. Dropping to a sitting position, I found the bear in my scope and squeezed the trigger. At the shot, the animal dropped and started to roll down the

Black bears can be found nearly anywhere, including Manitoba, Canada where John Higley took this fine specimen.

Photo by John Higley

Photo by John Higley

Black bears have big paws and sizeable claws.

canyon wall. Realizing that the bear was about to tumble right into my lap, I hustled out of the way. When the black ball of fur finally came to a stop, it was obvious that the 160-grain Nosler® Partition® bullet had completed its assignment. While the flat trajectory of the 7mm Remington Magnum chambering wasn't needed to make the shot, the combination of enhanced velocity and a solidly constructed projectile had quickly put an end to the hunt.

My guide had been a few yards ahead of me on the trail and out of sight. He had run into fresh bear tracks on the trail and was kneeling down to examine them when he heard my shot. By the time he made it back to my location, the whole incident was over. What he

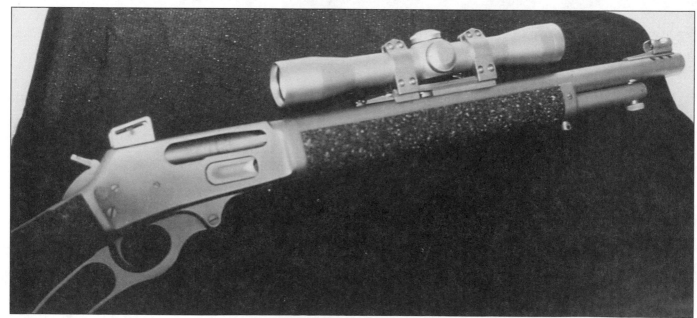

Photo by Durwood Hollis

This custom Marlin lever-action rifle is short and light enough for work in the tight confines of a blind.

Photo by Kevin Howard

The hide on this black bear, taken by Kevin Howard, is absolutely beautiful.

encountered was Yours Truly and one very dead black bear. With the boat waiting and little light left in the day (boats don't run the river at night), we quickly field-dressed the animal and carried it to the waiting craft. With a live weight of about 275 pounds, the bear was typical of a mature boar from this river drainage.

Where are they found? The black bear, or *Ursus americanus* as the scientific community knows it, is one of the best known and most widespread of North American bears. Prior to European settlement, black bears roamed over much of this continent. Found from Alaska and all across Canada in the north, to Mexico in the south and from the Pacific states in the west to the New England seaboard in the east, the black bear has the widest range of any North American big game animal. In the Southwest, black bears can be found in many desert mountain ranges across Arizona, New Mexico and old Mexico. In the west, particularly the northern Rocky Mountains, western Canada, the Canadian Territories and parts of Alaska, the range of the black bear, the grizzly and brown bear are contiguous.

"Problem" bears: Population expansion and urban development have impacted these animals, but substantial numbers can still be found in the suburbs of many major cities. Several years ago, a black bear took a liking to the hot tub in the backyard of a suburban Los Angeles county resident. Videotape of the animal, subsequently named

"Samson," taking his daily dip was shown on several television channels. Certainly, the bear's antics were entertaining. Nevertheless, the presence of a fully-grown black bear, in close proximity to a residential neighborhood, wasn't the ideal situation. The California Department of Fish & Game eventually tranquilized the animal and removed it to captivity. Since the bear had been accustomed to humankind, releasing it to the wild wasn't an option. As I recall, the animal became a popular attraction at a local zoo where it lived for many more years.

The presence of black bears in many of our National Parks, particularly Yellowstone National Park, has popularized these animals with the public. The bears are fully protected within the confines of the park and some lose their fear of man and become roadside and campsite beggars. Since they present a threat to park visitors, most of these so-called "problem" bears have been relocated. Park garbage dumps have been closed and every effort has been made place trash in "bear-proof" cans. And visitors to these areas are advised not to feed any bears they encounter. Even so, black bears continue to come into contact with man where human development and bear habitat come together, inside and outside of protected areas.

It's all in the looks: The black bear is a medium-sized animal, weighing about 150 to 350 pounds. That said, some individual bears have been taken that exceed 600 pounds. A mature black bear measures about 36

inches at the shoulders and 60 to 72 inches head-to-tail. While most are black, there are many color phases including: dark brown, reddish brown, cinnamon, blue-tinged (so-called "glacier" bears), grayish and even pure white (the Kermode bear found in British Columbia, on the offshore islands in the Queen Charlotte Island chain). A small white chevron in the middle of the chest, at the base of the throat, is also typical of this species. Regardless of the color phase of the pelage, all are black bears.

Bear life: Outside of breeding season and when offspring are still dependant on their mother, black bears are solitary animals. When they first emerge from their winter dens, however, a bear will tolerate other bears feeding in close proximity. After an initial period in the spring, when hostilities seem to take a back seat to nourishment, the bears pursue their lone existence in search of food. Only in the lushest surroundings, with an abundance of feed, will you find more than one bear.

Black bears are omnivores and will eat a variety of plant and animal foods. In the spring, newly sprouted grasses and flowers make up the major part of a bear's diet. Later on in the year, worms, insects, grubs, small animals and carrion will be added. In the late summer and early fall, berries, acorns, and other fruits come into play as preferred food. Where salmon spawn in rivers and streams, black bears can often be found along with brown bears. Since brown bears and grizzlies will kill and eat black bears, the smaller bears are cautious about not getting too close to their larger cousins.

During the winter black bears hibernate between five and seven months. However, in temperate climates, this period may be as short as two months to three months. Finding a small crevice, cave, deadfall or even under a cabin, the bear slips into a deep sleep. During this period, the heartbeat may decline by 50 percent of nor-

Outdoor writer John Higley took this bruin in California. It would appear that the "Golden State" is a great destination for black bear hunters.

Photo by John Higley

mal, the body temperature decreases and other bodily functions diminish. Pregnant females tend to go into hibernation earlier than males and if they give birth, the sows are the last to leave the den in the spring.

Black bears are able to breed between three and four years of age. This usually occurs during midsummer. The gestation period is about seven and a half months. When they are born, the tiny cubs are completely blind, deaf and nearly naked. Weighing less than one pound, the infant bear gains weight rapidly on mothers' milk. As soon as the sow is able to emerge from the den, the cubs will instinctively follow her everywhere. This bond is the wellspring from which the cubs learn how to be bears. The mother bear keeps her offspring in check by constant vocalization and an occasional swat to the rear. Like the young of any species, black bear cubs are curious and playful. By the second spring of their lives, cubs are fully mature and drift away from their mother. No doubt, the advent of breeding season and the presence of a mature boar speeds the process along.

Hunting styles: Black bears are hunted in a number of different ways, including canine pursuit, baiting, spot-and-stalk and calling. In heavy cover, like the swamps of the south or the thick chapparel of California, black bears are hunted with hounds. Usually, houndsmen travel remote back roads in their vehicle, using a "strike" dog (one that can catch bear scent on the move) leashed on the front of the vehicle. Once the dog starts to bark or howl, signaling that a bear has recently crossed the road, the tracks are located and the rest of the dog pack is released. Sometimes the chase is brief and on other occasions it can take hours to bring a bear to bay. And all too often, the bear is able to outdistance the dogs and gets away. When a bear is brought to bay, usually in a tree or thicket, the hunter approaches and makes the shot. Pursuing a bear with dogs is more about the chase, than it is the shooting. The chase itself can be overwhelmingly tough. In the process, dogs can be lost, injured or killed. And when the animal is finally at bay, it might turn out to be a sow with cubs, a mountain lion, bobcat, or who knows what (dogs aren't always scent specific).

Over bait: Baiting bears, where legal, is a good way to hunt these animals in dense cover. Most guides establish several bait stations using dog food, pastries, offal, bacon grease, burnt honey or other pungent attractants. The bait must be of sufficient quantity or securely lashed down so the bear can't consume it all or carry it off. Once the bear(s) find the bait, they tend to return repeatedly to the same location. To be effective, every bait station must be maintained on a regular schedule. Once evidence of a

Photo by Bob Robb

Bob Robb used a Remington muzzleloader to take this Alaskan black bear.

Photo by Durwood Hollis

This Winchester Angle-Eject levergun, chambered in .356 Winchester and topped with a low-power Bushnell variable-power scope, is a sensible rig for black bears.

bear's presence is found, then the hunter stakes out the bait from a tree stand (ground blinds are not advisable).

Spot-and-stalk: Spot-and-stalk black bear hunting is popular in many parts of the west. To hunt bears effectively, the environment must possess enough open areas to allow glassing. Once the bear is spotted, then the hunter stalks close enough for shot. Some of the most productive spotting locations are on the bear's path to food sources, such as fruit orchards. Other good spots to glass are south- and east-facing slopes where it's open enough to see bears feeding. Any meadow where green grass, mushrooms and grubs are plentiful is also a productive site.

Mixed bag: Many black bears are killed in conjunction with other big game hunting activities. It's quite possible to run into a black bear when you're deer or elk hunting. Should the hunting seasons overlap and you have a bear tag in your pocket, then a logical bear-hunting plan is well laid out. Even though a deer or elk hunting area may have a sizeable population of black bears, not all hunters may want to get involved with all of the effort it takes to skin a bear.

I once ran into a black bear while deer hunting. Fortunately, I had previously purchased a bear license and was prepared for such an eventuality. The bear was feeding on some acorns and was completely unaware of my presence. Getting into position for a shot wasn't difficult. When the bear winded me, he stood up on his hind legs. The confrontation with the standing bruin immediately pushed my blood pressure well above normal. Somehow, the animal didn't look like "Gentle Ben." Quickly taking aim, I touched of a round. When the bullet struck, the bear fell forward, rolled over and lay still. It was as simple as that! Two hours later, however, I was still deeply involved in skinning out the hide (the paws alone took about an hour). It took the rest of the day to finish skinning, boning the carcass and packing the meat and hide back to camp. If your primary quarry isn't black bear, then make sure you want to get involved in what it takes to put meat in the freezer and a hide on the wall before sending a bullet to the target.

Calling all bears: Hunting bears with a call is a technique that's only practiced in a few areas, particularly the southwest. In this arid country, adequate bear food is hard to find. Since they are the dominant animals, bears will try to take away food from other predators. This can include wresting a deer or elk carcass from the grip of a mountain lion, or stealing a rabbit from the clutches of a coyote. Knowledgeable guides and hunters exploit this by using a predator call to bring bears into their stand. When you're calling bears in the harsh mountain ranges of the southwest, the hunt can develop really quickly, or not at all. Callers try to cover as much country as possible, looking for fresh bear sign. When such evidence is found, the hunter sets up in an appropriate location and begins to call continually for 15 to 30 minutes, or more.

One of the best bear callers I know is Arizona big game guide, Duwane Adams. Duwane checks several areas until he finds clear evidence of recent bear activity. Once fresh tracks or scat has been discovered, he finds a stand at the top of a canyon with the wind in his favor. Duwane feels that it's important that the sound of the call be heard at a distance. He always hunts with a companion so when calling wears thin on one, the other can take over. It may take some time for the bear to come, only because the animal may have to travel a considerable distance. In this tough country a satisfying meal for a bear is hard to come by. Any bear within the sound of the cry of an injured animal will realize that the dinner bell has been sounded. When a bear comes to a call, it usually does so on the run. Hunters must be prepared for quick action.

Black bear calibers and guns: Unlike brown and grizzly bears, black bears are not known to be particu-

A blackpowder rifle in either .50 or .54-caliber will work on black bears. Most hunters use big bullets and heavy loads to ensure the bear is anchored on the spot.

Photo by Durwood Hollis

What do black bears do in the woods? Anything that pleases them. These two are relaxing in the shade of some pines.

Photo by Durwood Hollis

larly difficult to kill. Most are taken with the same rig that's used for deer hunting. While these animals are not tough to put down, a wounded a bear can be difficult to follow in heavy cover. The rather elastic hide is able to close over a bullet wound. Furthermore, fat will plug up the entry and exit holes and the heavy fur can absorb the blood flow. This will result in a scanty blood trail. Without soft soil, wet ground or snow to make tracking easy, a wounded bear can be lost in heavy cover. For these reasons, caliber adequacy is an extremely important consideration.

It is true that bears can be cleanly taken with nearly any centerfire caliber, provided that only premium bullets are used. For my part, bullet weight is more important than bullet diameter. Projectiles weighing 150-grains, or more, are the black bear bullets of choice. This eliminates most of the 6mm and .25 caliber chamberings. Certainly, the 6.5x55mm Swedish Mauser with 156- or 160-grain bullets is up to the job. Likewise any of the 7mm rounds with 160- or 175-grain bullet won't disappoint. All of the .30-caliber chamberings with bullets in the 150- to 220-grain range are more than enough. And .35-caliber numbers like the .35 Rem., .356 Win., .358 Win. and .35 Whelen, firing 200- to 250-grain bullets will provide more than satisfactory performance on black bear.

Since most black bear hunting is undertaken in close quarters—over bait, behind dogs and in heavy cover—carbine length and weight rifles are right for the job. The Remington Model Seven, Savage Sierra, Winchester carbine and similar boltguns by Sako, Weatherby and others in appropriate calibers are right at home in this assignment. I favor lever-action rifles in .307 Win., .356 Win., .348 Win., .444 Marlin, .450 Marlin Magnum and the old reliable .45-70 Government for my black bear hunting. Any of these calibers have lots of knockdown power and leverguns are easy to handle in close quarters. A black bear hit with one of these boomers won't go far and will leave a substantial blood trail. Furthermore, carrying a lightweight, short-barrel rifle won't wear you out after a day in the field.

Black bears are favored targets of blackpowder hunters. While a .45-caliber blackpowder rifle might do the job, I lean toward the .50 or .54 caliber smokepoles. My reasons behind this are the larger frontal bullet presentation and a wider range of projectile choices. Since most bears are taken at relatively close range, heavy-for-caliber bullets will give you the edge when using a frontloader on bear.

Stick, string and shaft: Bowhunters will find that whatever they use for deer will do the job on black bear. Special mention of arrow string trackers should be made. Most bowhunters don't like the idea of an arrow trailing a length of thin filaments. Sure, the tracking string will slow the flight of the arrow slightly. Over the short range at which most bears are taken with a bow, this loss of velocity is very minor. Many bowhunters have found that a string tracker will prevent the loss of a bear in the muck of swampy areas. A string tracker isn't a cure-all for poor arrow placement, but such a device might be of help in some bear hunting situations.

When and where-to-go: Of the two traditional bear hunting periods—spring and fall—a spring bear hunt is my personal choice. After emergence from hibernation bears are hungry, really hungry. Newly sprouted grass, budding flowers, and whatever else a bear comes across all goes into its stomach. The animals eat constantly. Furthermore, with plentiful food supplies in the spring, you may find more than one bear in reasonable proximity to another. I like to spot and stalk, so in comparison with a fall hunt when the animals are widely scattered, finding a bear out in the open during the spring isn't too difficult a task. Another advantage of hunting early in the year is the long, thick and luxurious quality of a spring bear hide. Within a few weeks after emerging from hibernation, bears will begin to rub their hides on any suitable object—logs, rocks or whatever. This is a mechanism to accelerate the process of removing the extra fur that has served as insulation during hibernation. A rubbed bear pelt has a patchy appearance and isn't nearly as desirable as an unrubbed hide. Therefore, the timing of a spring hunt is critical. If you go too early, the bears may still be in hibernation. Too late, and they will have already started heading for summer range and their coats are badly rubbed.

There are lots of favored locales for black bear hunting. At the top of my list is Alaska and British Columbia. I don't believe that the per-square-mile density of black bears in either area can be equaled. Hunting here will definitely guarantee you the opportunity to look at several bears during the course of a hunt. To be sure, other areas in Canada, as well as New England, and parts of the Deep South all have suitable black bear populations. Several Western states, including northern Idaho, western Montana, northwest Wyoming and northwest Colorado can also be counted as top black bear areas. While bears are few and far between in the southwest, bear guides there have taken some real monsters. The Pacific Northwest and California have burgeoning black bear numbers. Amazingly, the southern California counties of Ventura, Los Angeles and San Bernardino all have substantial numbers of black bears. Every season a few bears weighing more than 600 pounds are taken within sight of all that urban sprawl.

Black bears can be found in some unlikely places, including the Great Plains states and the Midwest. While hunting geese in Nebraska, I watched a black bear climb out of a swampy area and put a stalk on our decoys. When the bruin discovered that the geese he had been creeping up on were plastic and not flesh and blood, he tore up part of our spread. Finally, after several minutes of whacking decoys left and right, the bear left the area. That same bear and presumably others had been seen previously by my guide chasing live geese and even taking an occasional wounded bird that had gone down near the swamp. Since black bears are opportunistic omnivores, they can obtain an easy meal any way they can and cheap food is likely to bring them running (even if a spread of decoys isn't all that tasty!).

The end product: Black bear hunting is just really fun. A spring hunt will knock the winter cobwebs out of your brain and get your adrenalin pumping. Moreover, spotting bears and trying to pull off a stalk is a sure way to hone your hunting skills. And any attempt at keeping up with a pack of howling hounds as they chase a bear will wear out even the most athletic hunter. To top it all off, a couple of links of spiced bear sausage on the barbeque will make quite a meal. Isn't it about time you found out for yourself?

Photo by Bob Robb

Musk ox hunting gives an entirely new meaning to the word "cold."

THUNDER HOOVES: MUSK OX AND BISON

Hunting musk oxen and bison is a step back in time.

If you're a hunter who thinks that cold weather is a little "frost on the pumpkin" early in the morning, then the memory of your first breath in musk ox country will stay with you a long, long time. Just stepping out of the heated comfort of a Northwest Territories Air jet into the below zero Arctic weather is something that must be experienced to truly be appreciated. The cold is deceptive, able to freeze unprotected flesh almost before you know it. It is also tremendously exhilarating. And once you realize that you can take it, that you're prepared and it isn't really as bad as you thought it would be, it excites you.

What is a musk ox? Scientifically, the musk ox is known as *Ovibos moschatus*. A longhaired, dark-brown ruminant, the musk ox is related to both goats and sheep. Weighing from 600 to 800 pounds (females are smaller than the males), these animals stand approximately 4 to 5 feet in height. Both sexes have a dense undercoat or qiviut that has the texture of cashmere and is shed during the summer. This undercoat, or wool, is highly prized for yarn that is used in the knitting of warm, soft sweaters and blankets. Even if you're only going to have a shoulder mount of your trophy, remember to bring home the

Photo by Bob Robb

Hunters leaving the plane are greeted by the stark reality of the Far North.

Photo by Bob Robb

Riding in a snow machine is thought by some to be enjoyable. For musk ox hunters, it's pure torture.

rear portion of the cape to have it tanned for a throw rug. This might seem like a lot of trouble, but believe me you'll be glad you did later on. In addition to the undercoat, long ankle-length outer hair covers the animals and gives them a shaggy, rough appearance. Together, both the under and outer hair is able to keep the animals warm in subzero temperatures.

Following the late summer/early fall rut, most calves are born in late spring (April and May). However, in warmer climates, some calves may come as late as August. Immediately following birth, the mother uses her tongue to lick the afterbirth from her offspring. The tiny calf, weighing about 20 pounds, quickly joins the herd and by the end of its first week is already nibbling grass. Calves are fully weaned by nine or 10 months.

Musk oxen will consume grasses, bushes and willow branches readily. In fact, these animals will eat any kind of vegetation. In the Far North, there is little that grows on the tundra. While they prefer areas of low snow fall, musk oxen will use their hooves and horns to dig down through deep snow to reach favored food stuffs.

Trophy quality: Both bulls and cows have downward-curving horns, with sharp, upturned tips. The horns grow out of a cranial boss that resembles that of an African Cape buffalo. The bulls are easily distinguished from the cows by both their greater body mass and substantially larger horns. Musk ox horns are tough to judge in the field. Wide, heavy bosses, with a small gap between both horns will score quite well in the trophy books. Total horn length around the curve is important, as well as the horn circumference. While tip-to-tip horn spread is a great asset to the look of any set of musk ox horns, neither Boone & Crockett or Pope & Young count it toward the final trophy score. Because few hunters have any experience judging horn trophy quality, when in doubt take the word of your guide as the final evaluation of horn quality.

It's all in the name: Interestingly, the name "musk ox" comes from the musky smell that is emitted from both the pre-orbital scent glands. When nervous, oxen will rub these glands on their foreleg, which releases a strong odor thought to have a role in predator repellant. Like bull elk urine, during the rut the urine from a musk ox bull also gives off a heavy odor that can be detected from some distance.

Where it all began: Some 90,000 years ago, when the Bering Straits were dry land, musk oxen first crossed to North America from Siberia. When the last glacier covered North America, the animals survived in ice-free areas, or "glacial refugia," in the northern Arctic islands and Greenland. As the great ice sheets slowly retreated, musk oxen spread out through northern Canada and Greenland, eventually making their way to Alaska.

Canadian musk ox: Today, the range of the musk ox is much smaller than it once was. Of the total population of musk oxen found in Canada, most live on the Arctic islands of Banks, Ellesmere, Melville and Victoria. They are also found in substantial numbers on the mainland north of Great Bear Lake, up to the Arctic coast and in the Queen Maud Gulf region.

Prior to the early 1880s, it is believed that these animals played only a minor role as a food source for native Canadians. By the dawn of the 1880s, native Inuit people, European explorers and whalers were killing thousands of these animals for meat and hides. The hides became quite fashionable in Europe as sleigh robes. By the early 1900s, the demand for musk ox venison and the hides, together with the introduction of repeating centerfire rifles had led to a serious decline in population numbers. Realizing that

the animals were on the brink of extermination, the Canadian government in 1917 prohibited trading in musk ox hides. Shortly thereafter, the animals were completely protected.

By the mid-1960s, musk ox populations had so significantly increased that a quota hunting system was allowed in several native Inuit communities. In 1990, the community quotas had risen to about 3,500. A portion of the quota permits—which is controlled by local Inuit tribal hunters' and trappers' associations and regulated by the Northwest Territories Department of Renewable Resources—are used by sport hunters.

Alaskan musk ox: The story of the musk ox in Alaska is one that eventually led to the total exterminated of these animals. The very same musk oxen that made their way into Canada also established healthy populations on the North Slope of Alaska's Brooks Range. Relentlessly hunted for meat and hides, the Alaskan musk ox was nothing more than a memory by the mid-1880s.

In 1935 and 1936, musk oxen were reintroduced to Alaska's Nunivak Island. The transplants were animals brought to Alaska from Greenland herds. This effort was used as the basis to evaluate future trans-

Photo by Bob Robb

Sometimes it can be difficult to approach musk ox, but this time the stalk worked.

Camp may not be much, but it's better than being outside in the bitter cold.

plants for study and recreational purposes. Certainly, the semi-isolated nature of Nunivak Island was ideal for these purposes.

By 1968, the Alaskan musk ox population had grown to about 750 animals. A management plan, which involved sport hunting, was approved at this time. Surplus animals were moved to Nelson Island, as well as several northwestern and Arctic areas in Alaska. Political opposition delayed sport hunting until 1975 when the first season was held. Today, hunters can pursue musk oxen on Nunivak Island and the North Slope. Subsistence-only hunts also are conducted on the Seward Peninsula. While all of the hunting permits are issued through a special drawing, the hunting and trophy quality of the animals is superb.

Hunting musk ox: Generally, musk ox hunts are conducted in the spring. While the North Country is always cold, the ambient daytime weather can range from sunny and bright to total blizzard conditions. Since the days are longer in the spring, this provides enhanced hunting opportunities. Additionally, musk ox hair is lush and long during this season, making for excellent hides.

Since the time when musk oxen had to defend themselves against prehistoric predators, these animals have formed a defensive circle when confronted by danger. The mature bulls and cows form a circle, with the younger animals kept to the center of the living enclosure. Any predator must attack the entire herd to get at one of the more vulnerable members. While this was an effective defensive mechanism against wolves and bears, it offered no protection against men with rifles. Like the buffalo hunters of the American Great Plains, Arctic sharp shooters were able to wipe out entire herds of musk oxen in a single stand.

Nothing about hunting these great beasts has changed. The animals of today are still circling-up when threatened, which allows the hunter to approach within reasonable shooting distance. With a centerfire or blackpowder rifle, shooting a musk ox isn't all that difficult. Hunting musk oxen with archery tackle, however, is an entirely new dimension of hunting experience. A noted outdoor writer, Bob Robb, shares with us his bow hunt for the legendary Oomingmak.

"It was a bright, sunny day when our hunting party arrived in Kugluktuk (also known as Coppermine) on the frozen shores of Coronation Gulf, in the northernmost reaches of mainland Northwest Territories. Outfitter, Fred Webb and his partner and son, Martin, greeted us at the Kugluktuk airport. Once the handshakes were over and the baggage collected, we drove into town and went directly to the office of the Northwest Territories Fish and Game. Here, a game department officer issued musk ox licenses to everyone in our hunting party. When all of the official paperwork was completed, we sorted through our gear and packed-up for the trip to the hunting area. Less than three hours after we stepped from the airplane, all six hunters and their gear were loaded into wooden sleds that were hooked behind snow machines. Wasting no time in getting the hunt underway, hunters and guides headed out across the frozen tundra to hunting camp. Traveling 70 miles from Kugluktuk on a snow machine in featureless terrain can be somewhat unsettling for those new to the region. However, our Inuit guide felt right at home. The day was relatively sunny and calm, though the wind hitting our faces gave a new meaning to what cold was all about.

"Interestingly, the Inuit guides used hand-held Global Positioning System (GPS) units to navigate across the tundra. Given that the home range of a herd of animals is relatively small at any given time of the year, the GPS technology would prove to be invaluable when looking for the animals. In fact, just as we approached the campsite, the first herd of musk oxen was silhouetted atop a small snow-covered hill in the distance. To be sure, everyone in the hunting party was fired-up about this early sighting of animals even before we arrived at camp.

"The next few hours were involved in pitching camp, which consisted of three small wall tents. I had packed a foam block to use as a practice archery target. Once we had camp settled, I was able to shoot a few arrows into the foam in preparation for the next day. As the sun dropped behind the low hills, so also did the temperature. Fred Webb provides special, extra-thick sleeping bags for his clients. Lying atop a series of warm, soft, well-tanned caribou hides, the entire crew snuggled into their bags and slept like logs.

"At dawn, the unpredictable weather had turned sour. Although it was still clear, the wind had picked

Photo by Bob Robb

Outdoor writer Bob Robb took this impressive musk ox bull with his bow.

This synthetically-stocked, Remington Model 700 bolt-action rifle, chambered in .35 Whelen and fitted with a Bushnell Elite variable-power scope, is more than adequate for musk ox.

up. It was easy to see that a major storm was brewing. In this frozen wasteland where wind-whipped white-outs are usual fare, we hoped that the hunt would be over before the weather worsened.

"Fred Gonzales and I hunted together that first morning with our Inuit guides. The other hunters in our party and their guides had snow-machined off earlier in other directions. As luck would have it, we ran into a herd of about 50 musk oxen not more than 15 minutes out of camp. There was one great bull in the bunch, so Fred and his guide began a careful stalk. The animals were atop a small boulder-covered hill, which gave Fred limited cover as he moved closer for a shot. The wind was really starting to howl. Arrow placement is always tough. The ever-growing wind was going to make it even more difficult. Fred, an accomplished bowhunter, compensated for the blustering weather and arrowed an excellent bull.

"After caping and butchering the animal—musk ox meat is delicious and never wasted—the hunt was on again. A few hours later, we came upon a bachelor group of about a dozen bulls. A pair of real trophy animals was in the lead, but the group was reluctant to do the old stand-in-a-circle routine. It was my turn to try my hand at arrow placement, so my guide and I began moving into position for a shot.

"Every time we came within 40 or 50-yards of the animals, they would get nervous and bolt off for some unknown part of the tundra. We'd retreat to the snow machine and follow as best we could. When the musk ox settled down, another attempt at stalking was initiated. Again and again the animals spooked and ran. Since the wind was whipping about at an estimated 30 to 40 miles per hour, trying to place an arrow on target any farther than about 30 yards was out of the question. Under such conditions, the closer we could get to the musk ox, the better.

"After three-hours of frozen-hand and frosty-beard stalking, I finally was able to sneak into position for a broadside 30-yard shot. While my guide and I had gotten close on several previous stalks, the bull I wanted was never clear from the herd. During one of our stalking attempts, the herd had run us off the edge of a small hill. It was funny sight, the two of us sliding down the hill like a couple of land otters. While musk oxen are thought of as docile in nature, they have been known to get a bit nasty when pressed. Outfitter, Fred Webb, likes to illustrate this point with the story of one of his clients who had refused to pay attention to the warnings of his guide. That particular hunter ended up getting stomped so badly that he spent some time in the hospital.

"When I finally was able to get a clean shot at my bull of choice, I was very glad for the extra weight of the broadhead-tipped carbon arrow. Launched from a frost-covered compound bow, the arrow flew true despite the wind. Striking just behind the nearside shoulder, the arrow passed through both lungs and exited the opposite side. The bull was only able to run a few steps before dying.

"While I wasn't hunting to put a bull in the record book, nevertheless, that particular animal scored well enough to place him in the top 30 ever taken with a bow. He also exceeded the Boone & Crockett Club's minimum musk ox trophy score. Obviously, I was thrilled with the results of my hunt.

"The wind continued to rage all the way back to camp. Upon our arrival, a flattened sleeping tent that was completely filled with blown snow greeted us. Before we could even get comfortable, the tent had to be cleaned out and reset. Once camp was put back into order, we were able to crawl into the comfort of a warm shelter and enjoy a sundown dinner of musk ox back straps and potatoes.

"If the weather in the North Country is anything, it's unpredictable. When we crawled out of our sleeping bags the next morning, the wind was dead calm and the sky so bright that it hurt my eyes. After loading up our gear, along with the musk ox meat and hides, we started on the long snow machine trek back to Kugluktuk. That night we showered and shaved like teenagers before their first prom night. And one of the surprisingly nice hotels in town became the site of a fine meal and lots of laughter.

"It should be noted that most musk ox hunts have high success rates. Fred Webb's hunts for musk ox are all generally successful. Even so, such hunts are mostly

Photo by Matt Foster

Matt Foster (right) took his musk ox bull with a Marlin lever gun chambered in .45-70 Government. When this photo was taken, the thermometer read 40 degrees below zero (note the steam rising from the animal).

one-time affairs. Rarely do hunters go back for a second time. And that's just how I felt the day we left Kugluktuk. A few months later, however, I found myself filling out an application for one of the limited musk ox permits issued in my home state of Alaska."

"Given the opportunity, I'll return again some day to the land of the prehistoric musk ox. I guess wild place and wild things have gotten into my inner being. And there are few places left on earth that can equal the savage wilderness of the home of Oomingmak."

Hunting gear: Bob Robb's words certainly capture the mystique of musk ox hunting. Not everyone is up to the challenge of the frigid North Country, but it offers a genuine hunting experience. One thing is for sure, hunting musk oxen is an adventure that calls for some specialized gear. The best advice I can give is purchase the best quality clothing. This will be critical to your comfort and safety. Your outfitter can supply some articles of clothing, but the rest will be up to you. When in doubt, consult with the outfitter for a list of clothing and gear. Long underwear and woolen outerwear are definitely de rigueur for this kind of hunt. You'll need earflaps on your hat and a full-face mask to protect your nose. Also, ski or snow-machine goggles are essential pieces of equipment.

You'll also require solidly-built, aircraft-approved hard cases for firearm transportation from home to camp (a good idea for bowhunting gear also). Likewise, small chemical hand warmers, like *Hot Hands*, are worth their weight in gold. This is true for both keeping your hands flexible, as well as keeping rangefinder and camera batteries warm and juiced-up.

Keep your gear and clothing to a minimum. You won't be able to change clothes in hunting camp (too cold), so don't bring a lot of extras. A spare hat (thermal knit cap), gloves (two pairs, just in case you loose a glove, or leave them somewhere) and extra socks (wool or fleece) are more than enough. Don't forget to slip a tube of lip balm ("cold weather" type found in some surplus store is the best choice) into your pocket. If you don't protect your lips, they'll dry out and crack in a matter of a few hours. For your hands, visit your local feed and tack store and purchase a small container of *Bag Balm*. This product is specially formulated to keep the part of a milk cow the farmer manipulates by hand soft and pliable. Believe me. It works well as a protective hand cream in cold weather. No sleeping bag or pad is needed, since the outfitter will supply these important items. One duffle bag of hunting clothing and an extra oversize duffle bag for horns and hide are all you'll need. Your outfitter will provide a packing list, so when in doubt consult the list.

Musk ox calibers: Personally, I consider a .30-06 Spfd, firing 180-grain solidly constructed bullets about the minimum for musk ox hunting. The .300 Win.

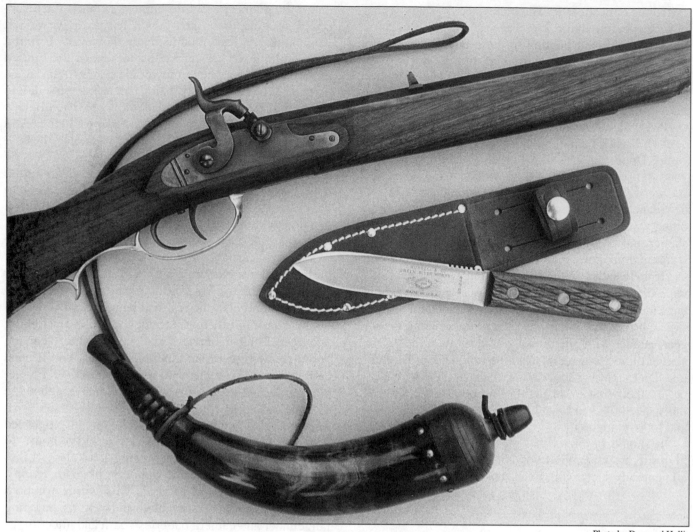

Hunting bison with the right tools—a muzzleloading rifle, powder horn and a traditional Russell-Harrington knife—can give the hunter a taste of history.

Mag., 8mm Rem. Mag., and .338 Win. Mag. are all fine musk ox rounds, but the rifles they are chambered in tend to be big and heavy. Since your shots probably won't be long, chamberings like the .444 Marlin, .450 Marlin Magnum and the .45-70 Gov't are just about right for musk ox hunting. Furthermore, these boomers are chambered in short, lightweight lever guns that are easy to pack along on a snow machine. Whatever you select, heavy-for-caliber bullets are the projectiles of choice for this game.

The extreme cold will congeal any oil or grease and your rifle will be out of commission. Prior to leaving on your hunt, take the time to degrease and remove any oil from your rifle. This activity should include disassembling the bolt completely, then using solvent to eliminate any traces of lubricant. When you're finished, graphite should be used to slick-up your rifle mechanism. If you do things right, the action will work without hesitation.

Scopes in the 4x, 2-7x, or 3-9x are all good choices, as long as they are of high quality. A fixed-power scope is probably the best choice for the Arctic, since the grease used to lubricate the variable power adjustment ring may congeal in sub-zero temperature. When you're hunting, don't blow on the lenses of any optics, since the moisture in your breath will immediately freeze to the glass. Mid-size, roof prism binoculars in the 7x35, 8x40 or 10x40 range will be needed for trophy evaluation, but spend enough to get the very best. Cheap optics will most certainly be of no use in the cold Arctic North Country. A laser rangefinder is another optical accessory that can be a big help in judging distance over the deceptively flat, white tundra. Both the Bushnell *Yardage Pro* and the Brunton *Laser 70* have given good service under conditions you'll encounter in this arena.

Don't forget: Prior to your departure, register all firearms with the United States Customs before going to Canada. No handguns are permitted, so don't even try to bring one along. Most riflemen and bowhunters will use their standard deer and elk-hunting rigs. Be prepared for high winds and learn to shoot while wearing heavy Arctic clothing. Believe me. The clothing alone will make for a different bow-shooting experience. And a padded soft case will be essential for a rifle or a bow when traveling by snow machine.

The meaning of cold: A business associate, Matt Foster of Gerber Legendary Blades, is a real fan of musk ox hunting (don't ask me why). I ran into him recently after he had just returned from a spring hunt for the shaggy beasts. Some of his comments can offer a deeper understanding of what it's like in musk ox country.

"On the very first day of the hunt, we had to travel nearly 100 miles by snow machine. No one, but someone who has been to the Arctic, can imagine what it's like traveling across the snow and ice at near breakneck speeds. The word 'cold' falls far short as a definition. On the first night in camp, a thick fog (evaporation from our bodies) hung in the tent about 6-inches above the sleeping bags. It was so cold that a bottle of whiskey froze solid. And any thought of venturing outside in the darkness to take care of personal plumbing issues was unimaginable. When I did shoot a musk ox, there was only a shallow window of about 15-minutes to accomplish game care chores. After that, the carcass was frozen stiff."

Another wild shaggy North American beast: The plains bison (*Bison bison bison*) and wood bison (*Bison bison athabascae*) are about twice the size of a musk ox, but both the musk and the bison have some similarity in appearance. Less than 200 years ago, an estimated 60 million bison, or "buffalo" as they are commonly called, could be found in North America. Since bison are neither difficult to find, nor hard to approach, the animals were easily hunted by even the most unskilled greenhorn. Market hunting, as well as a government-approved program to remove the Native American food supply from the plains, reduced the great herds to almost nothing. The demise of the bison didn't take long. By the late 1880s, only a few stragglers could be found in the foothills of the Rocky Mountains and the dark timber of Canada. At the beginning of the 20th Century, less than 1,000 bison were left on this continent.

Today, relic populations of bison have been preserved, both in the United States and Canada. Most bison hunting activities are restricted to either animals held in private ownership, herds found on Native American reservations, or a few public-drawing hunts for surplus animals in selected areas. Alaska, Arizona, South Dakota, Utah and Wyoming all have bison, but the hunting licenses are hard to come by. There are bison in other states, as well as Canada, but once again hunting (where it occurs) is closely managed. Two private operations that conduct "classic" bison hunts for animals that range free over several thousand acres are the Hawes Ranch Outfitters in Kansas and Sandhills Ranch Properties in Nebraska.

Most bison herds are fenced, but in some instances vast acreage is encompassed within the enclosure. Even so, it's no trick to clamor over a bison habitat in a 4x4 vehicle, locate a group of animals, pick out the bull you want and shoot it with a modern scope-mounted rifle. Although, if you approach the same activity by camping out, finding the bison on horseback and shoot with an open-sighted blackpowder rifle in your hands, you'll catch the spirit of what it was to once hunt these shaggy beasts in a bygone era.

Recently I visited with Stever Garber, President of Ballard Rifle & Cartridge Company (113 W. Yellowstone, Cody, WY 82414, 303/587-4914) in Cody, Wyoming. Steve told me about an upcoming bison hunt he had booked. Apparently, he and a handful of other hunters were going after the buffalo in "the old way." This, he explained, included sleeping in tents, using horse transport and shooting only blackpowder rifles. Since the Ballard rifle was one of the single-shot rifles preferred by 19th century buffalo hunter, Steve planned to use one of the several models his company produces on the upcoming hunt. A buffalo hunt may not be what it once was, but for Steve Garber, just the thought of stalking a remnant of the once great herds was something he could hardly wait to undertake.

Is it for you? Most of us will probably never venture north into the frigid Arctic for musk ox. Likewise, a bison hunt is probably not on anyone's personal hunting radar scope. Just knowing that the animals are still part of this continent's hunting scene is enough. And that knowledge alone will preserve the delicate balance of the plains and forests until nothing remains to drive the spirit of the hunter.

Photo by Durwood Hollis

The wild boar is one tough customer. Boars can cover ground like a racehorse, jump over a downed log like a kangaroo and take a bullet in stride. Here, the author carefully approaches a big "tooth" hog.

TUSKERS: WILD BOAR

After a century of residence in North America, the wild boar has become a naturalized citizen.

The narrow mouth of a broad canyon loomed before us. Scarcely wider than two men abreast, the opening was bounded by steep walls that rose more than 200 feet before they splayed out to the canyon proper. It was here, at first light, the hunt would begin.

Almost before we stepped off, my hunting companion, Don Pine, knelt down and carefully examined something in the soft earth. "Look here. The edges of these tracks are slowly crumbling in," he said. "The

hog that made them was probably spooked by the sound of the truck when we rounded the last curve in the dirt road."

The wild boar track held within its imprint the promise of what would come. More significantly, a musky porcine scent still lingered heavily at the mouth of the canyon. While the presence of our quarry had been made known, it was our part in this deadly game to seek him out. Boot laces were tied securely, shells

Photo by Durwood Hollis

A wild hog sow and her piglet are deep into a barley field. More hogs are sure to follow.

Big boars are hard to put on the ground with a single shot. Even a huge piece of lead out of a shotgun isn't all that reliable when it comes to wild hog hunting.

Photo by Durwood Hollis

pressed down into rifle magazines and packframes shouldered. The promise of a long day lay ahead.

The tracks were close together, with tiny pieces of clumped dirt scattered along their margins. Obviously, the hog had bolted through the narrow opening and was headed for the protection of the broader reaches of the canyon. While I gazed at the impressions in the soft dirt, Don took off after the spoor.

Abandoning my futile attempt at unraveling the mystery of the boar tracks, I followed my companion's lead. Momentarily, something drew my attention upward. The dark shape of a wild pig emerged the chaparral about 75 yards up the canyon wall. The animal slowly trotted along a narrow game trail, stopping

directly above me. Peering downward, the hog seemed to be trying to figure out what this two-legged creature was doing in his environment.

The shot wasn't long, but the target was straight uphill. My line-of-sight would have to be low enough to compensate for the extreme angle. Finding the hog in my scope only took a couple of seconds. Black as the bowels of the earth, the boar's gaze was malevolent and piercing. Even more notable, prominent tusks gleamed menacingly in the early morning light as they curved upward from the dark snout.

The trigger squeeze was instinctive and the report thundered off the canyon walls. When the bullet struck, the hog took a step forward, then pitched off the narrow trail into the air. For a few seconds time slowed as the boar gracefully pirouetted in midair. The realization of what was about to happen hit me about the same time the hog hit the ground at my feet. Instantly, the animal was up on his front quarters, teeth popping like castanets. The hog's intentions were obvious and my retreat was hasty.

The narrow confines provided little room for escape from those ivory tusks. Taking a step backwards, I found myself up against the steep canyon wall. Once again, slow motion held time in its grasp. Without conscious thought, I pulled the trigger and a second bullet found its mark. The boar slumped to the ground just inches from my feet.

Obviously such a tenacious animal is not to be underestimated. To do so would be foolhardy.

"It looks like you've been thoroughly baptized into the fraternity of boar hunters," Pine exclaimed when he viewed where the boar and I had our final moments together. If that experience was baptism into an elite group, then I hated to think what full-fledged membership had in store for me.

Fantasy and fact: The story of wild pigs in North American is wrapped in legend, fable and plain fabrication. Trying to uncover the kernels of truth is like husking an ear of corn. It takes lots of effort to get to the real stuff. Even then, the line between truth and fiction can be elusive. My research, however, has established some consistent facts.

At the time of European colonization pigs were not part of this continent's fauna. Christopher Columbus, as well as many of those that shortly followed him to North America, brought domestic swine along as cargo. While Columbus never set a foot on the North American continent, certainly Hernando de Soto did. With de Soto's exploration party in 1539 was a number of domestic swine. These animals were herded along as the group moved through Florida and what would become the American South. Apparently, it is not in the porcine nature to be moved like cattle. In short order, dissenting members of the herd took to the woods like criminal escapees. Nature being what it is, it didn't take too long for the animals to revert from domestic to feral. Over the years that followed, subsequent importation of domestic swine continued to augment the already established feral population in the region.

Boar beginnings: Since there has always been a certain fascination about hunting wild boar, it was only a matter of time before some well-heeled sportsman imported the surly brutes from Europe for that purpose.

Photo by Durwood Hollis

Dogs and hogs—can be a winning combination. The author took this wild pig with a handgun after a pack of mixed-breed hounds brought it to bay.

The author discovered this "hog hotel" in some dense cover. Wild pigs will root out comfortable beds in which to rest during the heat of the day.

In 1890, Austin Corbin, was just that a person. Flamboyantly rich, having made his mark in banking, real estate and the railroad, Corbin brought wild European boar to the tiny town of Croydon, New Hampshire. There are some historians who have said Corbin was a conservationist, since the 28,000-acre tract of land he purchased from local area farmers became an animal "asylum" of sorts. Conservationist, or not, Corbin was the first when it comes to the importation of wild boar to the continent. Surrounded by a tall fence and staffed with a number of full-time employees, the initial game transplanted into Corbin's property included bison, deer, elk, moose and, of course, wild boar.

When any species is moved from one habitat to another, things don't always work out. The mountainous region of Corbin's holding was a rather uncharitable environment for some of his imports. But the boars thrived. From an original importation of 14 hogs, in less than a score of years the population grew to more than 500.

Unfortunately, Corbin didn't live long enough to really enjoy his New Hampshire sanctuary. In 1896, he was killed in a carriage accident. His holdings were acquired by a group of wealthy East Coast investors, whose interests lay in the hunt. Today, the property is owned by the Blue Mountain Forest Association (Corbin's land was located in the Blue Mountains of New Hampshire) and maintained as an exclusive (there are less than three dozen members, who are said to pay an exorbitant sum to gain access to the association) hunting preserve. Reportedly, somewhere near 1,000 wild boars can still be found within the confines of this fenced holding. While the management of the association boasts that their hogs are pure blood European boar, escapees (there were most certainly several that met that criteria over the years) interbred with whatever domestic swine they encountered. Nonetheless, the dominance of wild genetic material assures that any crossbred offspring are able to fend for themselves in the wild.

The Hopper's Bald affair: While a couple of other importations of European wild boars took place farther south in New York state during the first few years of the 20th century, those animals reportedly all disappeared. It wasn't until George Gordon Moore, an American (some have mistakenly identified him as English), imported a number of wild boars in 1912 (some say he brought nine hogs, others have reported that it was 14) to property in the Snowbird Mountains of western North Carolina.

Moore's project came to fruition through his association with two Englishmen, brothers Frank and W.S. Whiting. These men desired to acquire an expansive tract of land from the Great Smoky Mountain Land and Timber Company. George Gordon Moore was called upon to serve as a financial advisor and negotiator. After the property came into the hands of the Whiting brothers, they allowed Moore to construct a private hunting preserve on 1,600 acres in the area surrounding what was called "Hooper's Bald."

Beginning in 1909, Moore had a road constructed up the mountain to the property. Workmen were hired, materials hauled up the narrow thoroughfare and several cabins, as well as a main lodge were built. In the process, two fenced enclosures were also constructed. The largest of these containment areas was a 1,500-acre lot that was designated to hold buffalo, elk, mule deer and bear. A smaller fenced section was Moore's "boar lot" and into it he released his shipment of wild Russian boars (supposedly, the hogs had been captured in Russia's Ural Mountains and shipped to North Carolina through an agent in Berlin, Germany).

Moore hired a local as his property manager, actually a "gamekeeper," by the name of Garland "Cotton" McGuire. However, like many of those who dabble with investments, George Gordon Moore lost interest in his game preserve. It is reported that he visited the location on occasion, even bringing friends along, but apparently the funding grew thin. As a result, Moore and his gamekeeper worked out a deal that resulted in ownership of Hooper's Bald being transferred to McGuire.

Just how the hogs got out of the "boar lot" isn't well documented. Some sources have reported that a full-dress, horse-mounted, pick-sticking hunt with lances was undertaken. As the story goes, the end result was a trampled fence and hogs scattered from "hell to breakfast." Who knows for sure? The facts of the matter might have been that McGuire just wanted to get rid of the beasts and simply opened the gate. What is not in question is that several "good old boys" from the surrounding area were invited by McGuire to help push the "critters" out of their enclosure. Apparently, the men were free to shoot whatever hogs they could in the process.

Photo by Durwood Hollis

<u>Guns & Ammo</u> *Executive Editor, Payton Miller, took this mammoth hog with a Thompson Contender pistol.*

Anywhere wild pigs cross under a barbed wire fence, pieces of their stiff hair can get caught. This is sure evidence that hogs are using this travel path.

When hunters, hounds and hogs all got together in that 500-acre enclosure, complete pandemonium broke out. In short order, every living thing that counted itself a wild boar departed for "parts unknown." This singular event ushered in a new era in the Great Smoky Mountains. The would-be hog hunters returned home, McGuire subsequently sold off the rest of the animals on the preserve and the wild boar were free to range wherever it suited their fancy.

There is no question that George Gordon Moore's wild boar crossed with the feral hogs that already were present (thanks to the early Spanish explorers) in the southern Appalachian Mountains. Today, wild boar can be found from Florida in the east to Louisiana and Texas in the west, and as far north as North Carolina, West Virginia, Virginia and Kentucky.

"Golden State" hogs: The story doesn't stop with Austin Corbin and George Gordon Moore. In the mid-

Green barley is like candy to a wild hog. Guide, Doug Roth (right), put his client on a nice pig right in the middle of a huge grain field.

1920s, a number of hogs from Hopper's Bald were shipped to the San Francisquio Ranch in California's Carmel Valley. Free to roam, the boar simply made friends with every domestic and feral pig they ran into. It took a few years for wild boar genetic material to spread up and down the Golden State, but today wild hybrid pigs can be found in at least 45 counties within California, with the largest concentrations located along the central California coast. The animals become so numerous that in the mid-1980s the California Department of Fish & Game estimated that hunters took more wild pigs than they did deer.

The entire picture of wild pigs in California has greater depth than just the importation of wild boar from North Carolina. In the 1700s, when Spanish explorers and Russian fur traders came into California they brought domestic swine along. The same thing happened when other settlers entered state during the famous "Gold Rush" period. As was common in that era, pigs were released from confinement in the spring and rounded up in the fall. This was done to use the readily available natural forage, especially acorns in the foothills, as food for the animals. To be sure, some hogs resisted this program and went their own way.

Like the situation in the south, an established population of wild pigs already existed in California by the time of the wild boar release in the 1925.

Swine science: Both the European wild boar and the domestic pig belong to the same scientific genus and species—*Sus scrofa*. The wild boar is native to Europe, North Africa and parts of Asia. In addition to being imported into North America, wild boars were transplanted to South America, New Zealand and some of the Pacific Islands (Hawaii included). Interestingly, all breeds of domestic swine possess 38 DNA chromosomes, but only 36 such chromosomes are found in purebred wild European boars. Interbreeding between the two groups of hogs can produce a litter from a single sow that has 36, 37 or even 38 chromosomes in its piglet DNA.

While they may be the same genus and species, the domestic pig and the wild boar don't look alike. Typically, a domestic hog has a uniformly thick body with both forequarters and hindquarters of similar size. These animals also have sparse body hair, short snouts and large, floppy ears. And all of the offspring are the same uniform hue as the parents. Conversely, a wild pig is lean, with large, high front shoulders and small,

As unusual as it may seem, wild pigs will hollow-out the underside of dried cattle droppings in search of grubs, maggots, worms and insect life.

Photo by Durwood Hollis

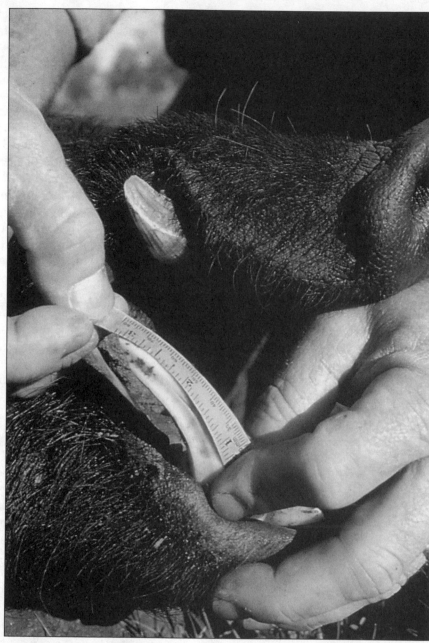

The overall length of the lower tusk determines the trophy status of a wild boar. Anything measuring over 2 inches above the gum line qualifies as a "trophy" hog.

Photo by Durwood Hollis

narrow hindquarters. Wild hogs are covered with long, straight and coarse body hair. Their snouts are elongated and flatten, with sizeable, curving and sharp upper and lower tusks protruding. Newborn wild piglets can be a variety of colors, with many manifesting horizontal stripes that disappear with age. The bottom line is that a wild pig, or boar as they are referred to, looks "wild," even primitive in appearance.

Furthermore, unlike the domestic hog that will only barely shuffle along, a wild pig can travel across broken ground at speeds up to 35 miles per hour. I've seen boars leap over fallen logs and other obstacles that were more than 3 feet high. Most domestic swine can't jump more than a few inches. Another defining feature is the keratin

sheath that lies just under the hide of wild boars, running from behind the shoulder to the neck. It is found only in male hogs. This is a secondary sexual characteristic that protects the boar from the tusk thrusts and slashes during combat over territory, feed or a sow in heat. Domestic swine have no such protective covering. Of course, the most prominent features are the tusks. In wild boars these incisor teeth can grow to considerable length. The trophy status of a wild hog is determined by the length of the lower tusks. Any boar with 2 inches or more of tusk exposed above the gum is thought to be of this category. Tusks of that length are only seen in male boars that have attained at least 4 years of age. While domestic pigs can also have tusks, they are short and thin.

Stories of fabled 500-pound wild pigs have been floating around most hog hunting locales for years. I've shot well more than 100 of the beasts and viewed countless more in the field, none of which was even close to that mark. In truth, a 250-pound wild pig is a huge hog. Given the fact that most hogs aren't ever put on a scale, a weight estimate is just that—a guess! Even in Australia, Europe, Turkey and North Africa, which have consistently produced some really big boars, an animal larger than 300 pounds is a rarity. Most full-grown wild pigs will weigh 150 to 225 pounds on the hoof. Those of us who like to eat wild pork hunt for smaller, younger animals and walk away from big old boars. If you're looking for trophy tusks, a hog in the 200- to 250-pound range is where your interests should lie. Even then, you'll have to look carefully to make sure that the tusks aren't broken. I've shot some big boars that had nothing more than stumps left in their mouths.

It's hard to keep a *good thing* contained: Wild pig sows are ready to mate even before they're a year old. Given that sows can give birth to two, or even three litters of up to a dozen or more offspring a year, these animals can quickly expand their range in a very short time. Recently, I spoke with Don Givet, game manager on the Tejon Ranch in California. He told me that the first wild pigs were seen on that property sometime in the late 1980s. As the story goes, a neighboring ranch had brought in boar for hunting purposes (where have we heard that story before?). That ranch was well fenced, but some of the pigs got out anyway (the Tejon Ranch also received Rocky Mountain elk in a similar fashion during the early 1960s).

"At first, the hogs were seen in Tejon Canyon near where they first escaped from the neighbors. Now they're all over the place," said Givet. "Some hog sightings have even been reported outside of our Kern

Matt Foster took this 200-pound boar on the famed Tejon Ranch, located just an hour's drive north of Los Angeles, California.

Photo by Durwood Hollis

A sharp broadhead accounted for this huge hog. Just look at the lower tusk on this big boy!

County property in nearby Los Angeles County. While the boar have been a boon for our hunting program, it's tough to keep the numbers in check. We have to take close to 1,000 pigs a year to just keep up with the reproductive cycle. Our hunting program has been able to stay on top of things, but we have to constantly work at it."

This is the same scenario that occurred when wild boar, feral pigs and domestic swine all got together in California in the years before World War II. The hybrid wild pigs spread into the environmental niche vacated by the extinction of the grizzly bear and the ruination of the indigenous Indian population. In the Coastal and Inner Coastal Mountains, as well as the western foothill of the Sierra Mountains, pigs found a wealth of food and cover. Add to that the agricultural crops (particularly barley, sugar beets and nuts) in the adjoining valleys and the stage was set for a boar explosion. While no reliable information is available about the number of wild hogs taken before the mid-1950s, beginning in 1960 some information on the annual harvest of these animals was recorded. In that decade, hunters took nearly 9,000 wild pigs. In the 10-year period from 1970 to 1979, more than

22,000 were harvested. During the 1980s, more than 40,000 hogs were taken. And in the period of 1990-94, 32,580 wild pigs were hunted and killed. And these numbers are continuing to climb.

Our southern states and California aren't the only ones with wild hogs. Wild boar are also present on hunting preserves in Colorado, several Plains states, the Midwest and at least one Canadian Province. Given the history of escape from confinement, it's only a matter of time before these alien intruders become naturalized citizens, whether or not many game departments like it. In truth, wild pigs do some environmental damage and compete with other game, particularly deer. California's answer to their wild pig problem was the complete removal of all hunting season and limit restrictions on the animals. While hunters must purchase pig tags, the cost is extremely low (even for non-residents) and you can buy as many as you want over the counter (when have you ever heard of that happening in the West?).

Hunting wild boar: There are three primary methods of boar pursuit—spot-and-stalk, jump hoggin' and hunting with hounds. In those areas where open terrain permits spotting wild pigs at a distance, they can be easily stalked. Hogs have very poor eyesight and it's possible to get with 50 yards, or even closer, without the animals noticing the hunter. Since pigs are gregarious feeders, they will tolerate more ambient noise than most other game, which is a plus for stalkers. The best defense boars have is an extremely sophisticated and well-developed sense of smell. I've seen wild pigs pick up traces of human scent at more than 400 yards and bolt like their hooves were on fire. The cardinal rule when stalking these cantankerous critters is to always keep the wind in your face. You may also want to apply cover scents or a scent elimination product, like Scent Killer from Wildlife Research Center. If you're not careful, a pig will be gone after one whiff of man stink.

Jump hoggin' is something that a few tenacious individuals try from time to time. This technique necessitates finding evidence of where hogs are bedded during midday. Usually, the animals like to lay-up in the toughest, thickest cover they can find. Using a combination of drivers and standers, the pigs are pushed out of their beds. When they exit the cover, it's time to lock, load and pull the trigger. Jumping boars out of their beds isn't always successful. The pigs may not go where you think they will. Furthermore, you might just run into a pig with a bad attitude that instead of running away, runs at you (not a good thing). Believe me. I've been there, done that! But in the heat of the day, with no other hunting options available, jump hoggin' can be an effective way to hunt.

Running boars with hounds is a time-honored tradition. This became a sport way back when man first domesticated dogs. Records of such boar hunts can be seen in cave paintings, in the south of France, that date back 40,000 years. All of the ancient civilizations—Assyrian, Egyptian, Greek and Roman—

It's extremely important to field dress and skin a wild hog as soon as possible. Most knowledgeable hunters carry all the right gear—rope, gambrel, saw, knife and game bag—for the job.

Photo by Durwood Hollis

Wild hogs are tough to skin. Several hands can make the task go easier.

Photo by Durwood Hollis

hunted boars with dogs. Even medieval Europeans chased wild boar with pack hounds. Sure, the weapon of choice was generally a spear, but the dogs were the ones that brought the boar to bay. The tradition continues today on this continent. Houndsmen use gritty little Catahoulas, plott hounds and other mixed-breed curs to pursue these animals.

A boar cannot bend its body enough to attack an adversary that goes for its rear end. This being true, smart hog hounds learn to avoid the business end of a wild pig. If they don't, a boar will tear any canine within reach to shreds. Houndsmen buckle thick leather protective shields on their "catch" dogs to prevent such injuries, but hogs are quick and strong. Even though a hound may have a solid hold on an ear, a boar can

shake the dog loose and then turn deadly instantly. An enraged wild pig isn't anything to mess around with. Any houndsman who runs his dogs on hogs is liable to be the best customer a veterinarian ever had. All of the suturing and antibiotics that sometimes have to be administered after a boar race can be costly.

How to find boars: Since wild pigs are only found in specific areas, locating them means finding fresh sign. Most veteran hog hunters cover lots of ground looking for recent tracks, droppings and other evidence of boar presence. Pig tracks are almost completely square, with short, blunt tips and are not easily mistaken for the prints of any other cloven-hoofed animal. Tracks of mixed sizes indicate the presence of sows, piglets and possibly a few young boars. A single set of large pig tracks usually indicates a male hog. Sows and their young are almost always found in association with food, water and cover. Boars, on the other hand, are known to wander over huge tracts of land in search of the essentials of life and breeding partners.

Unlike deer and elk, which tend to move rather aimlessly, wild boars establish well-used trails that are traveled daily. These movement paths can be found between food, water and bedding areas. Hogs are very focused in their activities and their trails are equally as straightforward. Along these "hog highways" you can find strands of hair caught in barbed wire fences where the hogs crossed under. Of course, sharp hoof imprints, droplets of wet mud and moist scat along any trail should stimulate hunter interest in following up on such discoveries.

Wild pig scat resembles thick, segmented sausages. Often, it's possible to determine where hogs are feeding by the content of their manure. Some food material can pass through the rumen and out the other end in recognizable pieces. This can be a clue to where hogs are concentrating their feeding efforts. Of course, boar scat has its own characteristic smell, with a fragrance easily identifiable as pig aroma.

Wallowing in mud is one of a pig's most cherished activities. Since boars have no external sweat glands, the cooling effect of a fresh coating of wet mud serves as a portable air condition system. Once the mud dries, pigs ease up to a rock, tree trunk or other projection and expend considerable energy rubbing. All of this exercise serves to clean the boar's hide. External parasites (lice, fleas, etc.) that have become covered with wet mud are trapped when it dries. When the boar rubs up against something, mud and a host of bothersome little critters are all removed at the same time. Mud also makes an excellent protective covering over lacerations sustained during fights. All of the rubbing activity leaves behind large grayish streaks that are readily seen. The condition of the mud (still wet, damp or completely dry) is a solid indicator of how long ago pigs were in the area. Fresh rubbings mean hogs have wallowed in that location recently. While pigs usually wallow in stock ponds, along the margins of lakes, in springs and under standing stock troughs, this endeavor can take place anywhere water or mud is available. I've come upon pig wallows right in the middle of a trail, a dirt road or where standing water from recent rain remains.

Where wild pigs and cattle share the same range, hogs will often turn over dried "cow pies" (piles of manure) in search of worms, grubs or insects that find the dark, damp and warm covering to their liking. Not only will the pigs root under the cattle dropping, they will also scrape out the undersides with their front teeth to gain access to any wiggly critters that they can find. Linear tooth marks on the underside of cattle scat is a sure sign that pigs are exploiting this particular food source. The swine will even trample the dried droppings with their hooves in an effort break them up and loosen whatever they can smell inside. While it sounds disgusting, nevertheless, I've taken many a wild hog while it worked over cow pies.

If you come across areas that look like someone turned up the earth with a Rototiller, then it's a sure sign that wild pigs have been there. Rooting can be quite extensive, especially under oak trees and near the base of earthen dams. Since acorns are a favored food, pigs will go to great length to find them. Acorns on the ground are scooped up like candy. Once the supply of easy acorns has been exhausted, the animals will root around to find any that they have missed. Where water leaks out from a stock pond, wild boars will tear up the earth in their search for worms. The conditions of the soil and associated vegetation are both clues too just how recently the rooting took place. Dark, damp soil and fresh plant material means that the rooting maybe minutes or just a few hours old. When you find fresh rooting in hog country, that's the place to start hunting in earnest.

Photo by Durwood Hollis

When you go after wild boar in the backcountry, a pack frame and a stout back are both essential elements of the hunt.

Boar calibers: Wild hogs are tough, really tough. Short of the big bears and an adrenalin-pumped bull elk, a mature boar is one of the most difficult big game animals to put on the ground with a body shot. Even hit through both lungs, a big hog can carry a bullet or broadhead a long way. Complicating the matter is the fact that often there is little, if any, blood sign. The wound can get plugged with fat and the thick hair absorbs most of the blood flow.

Once, while hunting with guides Craig Rossier and Doug Roth of Camp 5 Outfitters, on some of the property they control on the central California coast, I shot a big boar with a Brenneke shotgun slug at a distance of about 60 yards. The projectile hit the pig just behind the front shoulder. The animal sagged in the middle and I thought it was going down. No such luck. The boar pulled himself together and took off like a shot,

heading for the nearest patch of brush. Before I could shuck another shell into the chamber of the Browning pumpgun, the wounded brute was out of range. Craig settled the matter with his centerfire boltgun before the boar slipped out of sight nearly 200 yards away.

After we field dressed and skinned the hog, I discovered that the shotgun slug had entered just behind the shoulder shield, traversed through the middle of the nearside lung and out the top the far lung, coming to rest just under the skin near the neck. The projectile, complete with a series of wads that were screwed into its base, must have weighed well more than 500 grains. The penetration damage the slug inflicted was considerable. Nonetheless, the boar still-covered lots of ground before a 150-grain, .270 Winchester bullet from Craig's rifle stopped his forward progress. Like I said, hogs are tough—and then some!

The author (left) and his eldest son, Dustin (right), teamed up to take this tusker. This pig weighed well more than 200 pounds on the hoof.

Photo by Durwood Hollis

Photo by Durwood Hollis

Wild pigs in the barley will mean pork chops for dinner tonight!

Certainly, any medium caliber that works on deer can do the job on a hog. Even though I've taken a number of wild pigs with a .243 Winchester, most guides don't advocate the use of small centerfire calibers on boar. Bullet diameter, weight and construction are all important considerations. The more bullet you can shoot, the better. My own personal boar caliber preference is one of the .35-caliber chamberings. The larger bullet diameter offers greater frontal impact and the heavier projectile weight penetrates hide, shield, bones and muscle tissues a lot better. Chamberings like the old .348 Win. (a near .35-caliber), .35 Rem., .356 Win., .35 Whelen and .350 Rem. Magnum are all top choices for use on wild pigs.

Most boars are shot at relatively short range, so you don't need all of the earth-shattering velocity of most of the sizzling magnums. Still, bullet placement is critical. Veteran hog hunters like to get close enough so they can slip a bullet in right behind the nearest ear. A shot to the brain or spine will drop a pig like a sack of concrete. The same bullet sent into the heart-lung region isn't nearly as effective. Where you target your quarry and how far that hog is from the nearest cover

should always be considered before pulling the trigger. If you come upon a big boar, near heavy brush in the late afternoon, unless you can drop him on the spot with a shot to the brain, it's best to walk away. He'll probably be in the same area the next morning when there's plenty of daylight to work things out right.

Blackpowder shooters should also use care when hunting boar. Use the largest bullets possible and pack your smokepole with lots of propellant. Stalk as close as possible and take only high-percentage shots. I've had lots of success on boars with my frontloader using 444-grain Black Belt bullets, packed on top of three .50-grain (150 grains total) Pyrodex pellets. This is a reliable load that hits with authority and can stir up a hog's insides like a blender.

Shotgun slugs will also work, but select those that move fast and have controlled expansion. Both Remington and Winchester make some great slug loads that are far superior to the old Foster-type slugs. Don't think that you can just load up your old duck gun with slugs and go hog hunting. It doesn't work that way. With nothing more than a smooth bore and a front bead sight, you probably won't be able to keep three shots inside of a bushel basket at 25 yards. You're better off buying a shotgun that's specifically designed for slug use. Barrel rifling will stabilize the slug in flight and a good set of open sights or a scope will give you the necessary accuracy. With the right set up, it's possible to take a hog at 150 yards or farther with a shotgun. The rule of thumb when hunting with a shotgun is to hit a hog hard and keep on shooting until it's on the ground for keeps. Even then, watch it and be ready to shoot again if the pig even twitches.

Bowhunters face a real challenge when it comes to wild boar. Stalking close enough for a good shot is the least of your worries. Putting an arrow through the tough hide, protective shield and both lungs will demand the very best of broadheads. You can forget about all of those broadheads that feature replaceable cutting blades. I've seen too many break-up in a pig before they made it into the boiler room. Most bowmen who successfully hunt wild hogs favor two-bladed broadheads, with absolutely razor-sharp cutting edges. I like to let a boar quarter away from me, at no more than 30 yards, before I release an arrow. My point of aim is always a few inches below and behind the nearside front shoulder. This means the underlying keratin shield will not impact the broadhead. Furthermore, I like my arrow to penetrate both

Wild boar might be alien wildlife, but they've been in North America long enough to be considered "naturalized" citizens.

lungs and stay inside of the animal. This way the arrow keeps working in the wound, resulting in continued blood flow. If you've placed the arrow correctly, most of the time, the hog won't go very far. When things go bad, expect a long day of searching for a wounded pig. Like I said, pigs are tough!

Field Care: Even if you gut a boar quickly, the flesh can spoil faster than other field dressed game. The most important consideration is the prompt elimination any retained body heat. Hanging the carcass in the shade is a good move, but removing the hide will accelerate the cooling process. A skinned carcass must be protected from insects, so cover it with a protective bag. Moreover, make sure that it is hung where the cooling effect of even the slightest breeze can be exploited. As soon as possible, quarter the carcass or remove the meat from the bones and get everything refrigerated.

On the table: Wild pork is some of the tastiest and leanest wild game you can ever put a fork into. Since all of the fat is on the outside of the muscle tissue, rather than marbleized within the meat, there isn't any worry about ingesting high levels of fat. The flavor is so delicate that it goes well with any style of cooking. I use ground wild pork in Italian, Mexican and Asian recipes. Wild pork roasts, chops and other cuts are the best of the best game meat. Stop by my place sometime and I'll pull a package out of the freezer and we'll dine like royalty.

Isn't it time? While wild boar may be seen as unwelcome aliens by some I am reminded that the ring-necked pheasant was at one time also imported into this country. I don't think anyone wants to eradicate that game bird from the upland scene. Negative opinions about wild hogs are understandable, since they aren't nearly as pretty as many species of native game. No, I don't think anyone but a hog hunter would ever term a wild pig "nice looking." In fact, most members of the opposite sex are quick to put up a howl about any suggestion of a mounted boar head on the wall.

Regardless of their appearance, wild boars of every genetic mix are still top-notch game animals. Sure, they can root up and damage some areas, but that's just because they're not hunted enough to keep their numbers under control. Many farmers, ranchers, environmentalists and even game departments complain about wild boars, but those same individuals and agencies often do little to promote hunting as a management tool. The removal of hunting seasons and bag limit restrictions, as well as promoting hog hunting itself, have proven to be effective management tools.

The economic upturn that wild boars bring to many communities is extremely valuable. If you don't believe me, then just ask many of the hog guides and hunting operations in states where these irascible animals can be found. Without wild boar, there isn't enough turkey, deer, elk and other game to keep many of them in business. Boar have been a boost to local merchants, as well as outfitters and guides everywhere they are found.

If you're one of those who hasn't been baptized into the fraternity of wild hog hunters, then come forward and confess your interest. Most of us are thrilled to have someone with a strong back along to help pack a boar out of the backcountry. Hunting wild pigs really has everything you could ever ask for. And no other big game hunting activity is so generous with season, bag limit and license allotments. Isn't it about time you joined the congregation?

Photo by Durwood Hollis

This little desert hog was taken with a scoped single-shot pistol. Check out those sharp tusks!

LITTLE BIG GAME: JAVELINA

The javelina may not be very impressive in size, but hunting this desert ghost is big fun.

If there's one thing that characterizes hunting opportunities in the Southwestern United States, it's the diversity of native big game. Arizona, New Mexico, and Texas all have elk, mule deer, whitetail deer, antelope, black bear, and the diminutive javelina. Often overlooked by hunters as a game animal of any significance, nonetheless, hunting the little desert pig is a unique and rewarding experience.

Where are they found? The scientific listing divides javelina, or more correctly, the peccary, into three separate subspecies — collared (*Dicotyles tajacu*), white-lipped (*Tayassu pecari*) and Chacoan (*Catagonus wagneri*). The collared peccary ranges throughout the Chihuahuan and Sonoran deserts of southwestern Texas, New Mexico, Old Mexico and Arizona. The white-lipped peccary is found in the tropical regions of Central and South America. And the Chacoan variety makes northern Argentina, Bolivia and Paraguay its home. Not only are these animals widespread in their distribution, they are also quite numerous. In Arizona, an estimated 60,000 animals can be found. Texas can lay claim to more than 250,000 javelina. New Mexico has a much smaller population of desert pigs, but enough to keep things interesting. Equally sizeable populations are situated in other parts of their extensive range.

What's in a name? The colloquial name, javelina, is derived from a similar sounding Spanish word that characterizes the animal's spear-like tusks. The other common name, peccary, reportedly comes from a Brazilian Indian word, "pecari." This word is said to be descriptive of an "animal that makes paths through the woods." Javelina are also known as *Tayaussa*,

Photo by Duwane Adams

Bowhunter, Craig Hayward, teamed with guide Duwane Adams to take this nice javelina.

Photo by Durwood Hollis

Javelinas will chomp on succulent cactus pads. Their rounded bite marks are a dead giveaway.

musk hog and my favorite—desert ghost (they seem to have the ability to appear and disappear out of the desert at will).

Since javelina will aggressively defend their young and are extremely bellicose when wounded or cornered, they have a reputation for pugnacious behavior. An out-of-sorts javelina, with its hair standing on end and teeth "popping" is guaranteed to get your adrenalin flowing. Add a few other toothed individuals to the mix and you have a good idea how these little hogs got their fame.

It's all in the looks: A full-grown javelina stands about 20 to 24 inches at the shoulder and weighs 30 to 70 pounds. Males are slightly larger and heavier than females. The pigs have a long snout (which serves as a rooting tool), small eyes and pointed ears. The neck is almost non-existent. The short, stout legs end in cloven hooves that manifest two dewclaws (vestigial toes) on both front feet. Interestingly, there is only one dewclaw on each rear hoof.

The coloration of newly born javelina is tan to brownish, with reddish dorsal stripping. Adults have a salt and pepper look, which is the result of whitish bands on their bristly black hair. In the winter, when the pelage is dense and dark, a distinctive lighter colored "collar" can be seen on adults. During the summer months the darker hair is shed and the collar is sometimes not quite as visible. With their compact, rounded body, short legs, hoofed feet and flat snout, javelina resemble pigs. However, there are distinctive differences, including a powerful musk gland located on the back, about 8 inches above the tail. The odor that emits from this gland is always detectable, more so when the animals are excited. In fact, you often can smell javelina before you see them.

While it may look like a pig, the tiny javelina is only similar in general appearance and behavior. When compared to either wild or domestic swine, a javelina has 38 teeth, while there are 44 in true pigs. Javelina, also have no gall bladder. And there are significant differences in the structure of the leg bone. Of course, wild and domestic pigs don't have scent glands. These anatomical differences are why pigs belong to the family Suidae and the javelina has been placed into the separate Tayassuidae lineage.

If any relationship ever existed, wild boar and domestic hogs may be distant cousins of the peccary. In fact, the javelina is possibly part of a lineage descended from an ancient wild hog that once roamed this continent. The fossilized remains of that animal were discovered in Agate Springs quarry, Nebraska and date back some 25 million years. Interestingly, the fossilized skull of that animal measured nearly 3 feet in length. If, indeed, there is any genetic relationship, that would have been one giant javelina!

Growing up: A javelina reaches sexual maturity in about 10-months, to a year. The animals are capable of mating any time during the year and can produce two litters a year. However, most breeding takes place during January, February and March. The gestation period is close to five months (average 145 days). While the production of a single infant does occur, litters of two or three are more common. A mother javelina, unlike other mammals, doesn't use her tongue to clean her newborn young. She just uses her snout and rolls them in the desert sand. Initially, at the time of birthing the

pregnant female will distance herself from the herd. This apparently is done to prevent other adults from killing and eating the newborn. After a day or two, the mother and her offspring rejoin the herd. Still, the mother is extremely protective and will only allow older female siblings of the newborn around her babies. Immediately imprinting on their mother, the tiny babies instinctively follow her every movement. Within six to 10 weeks, the infants are weaned and eating everything other members of the herd devour.

The buffet line: At best, the javelina is an opportunistic feeder. Simply put, they will eat nearly anything, including flowers, nuts, fruits bulbs, berries, succulent plants, insects, worms, small reptiles, eggs and young of small ground-nesting birds and carrion. However, prickly pear cactus predominates in their diet. The animals will use their hooves to knock off the spines, allowing them to gain access to the fleshy pads. Evi-

Photo by Durwood Hollis

The author examines a javelina bed. Scraped from the hard earth, this shaded area held nearly a dozen desert pigs.

The secret to finding javelina is patience and a pair of tripod-mounted, high-magnification binoculars. Here, guide Duwane Adams is doing what he does best—finding game.

Photo by Durwood Hollis

dence of their feeding activities can readily be seen where cacti and other succulents occur. Even though the high moisture content of cacti allows the animals to live on the desert floor and surrounding mountain ranges, nursing sows must have water on a daily basis. This means that the presence of both food and water are essential to locating these animals.

Extended families: Javelina live in extended family groups known as herds, bands or sounders. Such groupings usually average six to 10 animals, although herds of more than 50 have been reported. Most herds consist of at least one dominant male, a few subordinate males and several females and young. Occasionally, a lone animal may be seen. However, it's herd movement that usually tips hunters off to the presence of these animals. Most of the time they are difficult to see. I know, because it was tough for me to pick them out. The very first animals I encountered in Arizona appeared to be nothing more than tiny glistening specks scurrying across the desert. The reason they seemed to shimmer was sunlight reflecting on their grizzled pelage (black with gray annulations or rings). Unless the animals are bedded during the heat of the day, herd movement will always give away their presence.

Nap time: Herds of javelina are most active when desert temperatures abate. During midday, the animals find a shady place to bed. Bedding areas can be quite extensive and are often used repeatedly. Rest periods may take place under an overhanging Palo Verde tree, in a mesquite tangle, against the side of a wash, ravine or even in rooted-out caves. Herd dominance usually determines the most favorable bedding area. Hierarchy is determined by sex and size, with the largest male taking his place in the linear ranking.

Your place, or mine? Herds have a distinct range or territory which covers from 1 to 4 square miles. While javelina will share water sources, territories seldom overlap. Territorial markings, produced by rubbing the scent gland on their rumps against rock outcroppings, trees and other established points, are aggressively defended. When one group encounters another, the members may bristle up, lay their ears back and clatter their tusks. When they fight, the tiny terrors charge each other head-on and usually lock-up jaw to jaw. These contests generally don't last long, but they are exciting to hear and watch.

I once watched two separate herds of javelina cross each others' paths as they both went to water. Two of the largest males dashed forward, engaged in combat and kicked up more dirt than a midday dust devil. Several others "popped" their teeth like castanets and assumed threatening postures. Apparently, this tumult wasn't all that serious, because it lasted only seconds. When things settled down, the javelina went about their usual business. More puffery than anything else, the skirmish served to protect individual herd rights of access to the water. In fact, this interaction might have been a regular occurrence between these two groups of animals. I don't know how the javelina felt about it, but it was entertaining to watch (at a distance, of course).

A hunt to remember: Hunting javelina is anything but easy. First, you have to locate the little desert hogs, something that can be a challenge. After you locate a herd, don't count on getting close being a slam-dunk! To demonstrate just how difficult this can be, let me share with you my first experience with these desert demons. I had made arrangement to hunt the Arizona Handgun, Archery and Muzzleloader (HAM) season for javelina with guide Duwane Adams. The logic in my decision centered primarily on the availability of nonresident Arizona hunting permits for javelina. It can be difficult to draw a jav-

The desert is vast and javelinas aren't very big. Finding a herd can be tough, even for the most dedicated hunter.

This is what javelina hunting is all about. Locked-in behind a set of big binoculars, it takes lots of persistence to find what you're looking for.

Photo by Durwood Hollis

elina permit during the general rifle season. However, with the exception of a few selected hunt units, there is a good chance of drawing a HAM permit.

At the appointed hour, I arrived at Duwane's home. After a hasty breakfast, we drove an hour or so. Finally, we arrived at the edge of a series of rugged desert canyons. Stepping off into the darkness, I did my best to keep pace with Duwane. I should mention that Duwane Adams is as lean as a rail. Even carrying a 40-pound pack, he can hike uphill and down for hours. While I was in reasonable physical condition, it was nearly impossible to keep up. Fortunately, we didn't have to hike more than a couple of miles from the truck.

Duwane uses high-magnification binoculars to spot game. No matter whether it's deer, elk, sheep or even javelina, his tactics are always the same. Our game plan consisted of gaining the high ground while it was still dark, finding an open glassing position and scanning relentlessly for javelina. Settling in just below the top of a ridge, Duwane set up a tripod and mounted a set of Zeiss 15x60 binoculars on the top. I had to be content with using my own 10x50 binoculars and no tripod. Before the day was over, I was to learn more about glassing than javelina hunting.

After about an hour of looking over the same patch of ground several times, I was ready to find another place to hunt. Duwane, however, still seemed interested. In fact, he pointed out two separate herds of javelina that I had completely overlooked. It took me about five minutes to find the group of eight animals that were right out in the open. A herd of javelina can easily disappear into the terrain. If it hadn't been for the sun reflecting off of their glistening hair, I would have never spotted the little hogs. Even after I found them in my binoculars, the animals were still difficult to keep track of. Apparently, the name "desert ghost" is well deserved.

Duwane continued to glass the two herds of javelina for the better part of an hour. Finally he said, "The pigs seem to be working their way down toward the bottom of that far arroyo. Let's see if we can get to them."

Once again it was backpacks-and-boot-leather time. It was several hundred yards to where we'd last seen the herd of javelina. After about half that distance, I learned that the desert is anything but flat! Struggling to the top of a narrow ridge, Duwane stopped momen-

tarily to see if the javelina were still on course. To both of our amazement, the javelina had disappeared.

"Let's sit down and see if they'll pop up again," Duwane whispered.

Right away, the tripod and big binoculars came out of Duwane's backpack. I joined the search, but after an hour of steady glassing, neither of us could claim success. The javelina had simply disappeared into thin air. Now that the morning sun was starting to warm the desert, it was possible that the javelina had simply bedded down somewhere out of sight. It was time for a change of plans.

This time, we rapidly traversed two deep ravines and a stretch of flat ground. This would have put us in position to see some of the country that hadn't been visible from our

It took a long, cross-canyon shot to put this desert tusker on the ground.

Photo by Durwood Hollis

Handguns of every caliber are popular firearms for javelina hunting. Even so, it still takes a firm grip and a steady eye to put the bullet on the tiny target.

original glassing location. Everything went as expected, that is with the exception of one event. While we were making it across the second ravine, we ran into a lone sow with a young piglet. There was no avoiding the confrontation. It just happened! To be sure, the mother and offspring boiled over the top of the ravine and disappeared from sight. By the time we made it to a vantage point, the entire herd was swiftly departing the countryside.

When we found the tracks, it was easy to figure out what had occurred. The group of javelina, minus the solitary sow and her offspring, had been bedded down under a mesquite tree at the edge of the second ravine. Apparently, the tiny hog was newly born and the sow wanted to be apart from the main herd. When we accidentally "bumped" the old gal and her piglet, their flight had alerted the rest of the herd. Our opportunity for success evaporated just as quickly as it had been manifest. Like I said, hunting javelina is anything but easy.

The best thing about hunting with someone who is familiar with the country is that hopefully there will be more than one opportunity. If at first you don't succeed, then this knowledge becomes critical. On any given weekend, you're likely to find Duwane Adams in the field looking for game. Of course, he isn't always hunt-

ing. As a guide, he needs to constantly polish his skills and search out new hunting locations. We had blown our first opportunity at javelina. It was time for Duwane to call upon his vast experience and locate another herd in the area.

On our way back to the truck, we came across several shallow caves in the bottom of one ravine. Rooted out by the javelina for bedding areas, the dugouts had been strategically positioned. No matter how the sun traversed the sky, the pigs always had daytime shade. When we investigated further, a heavy musky odor was easily detected. And a multitude of tiny javelina tracks were everywhere.

"They were here," Duwane remarked.

Twice, in the space of less than an hour, we had been on top of javelina without taking a shot. A casual observer might have questioned our hunting prowess. I was beginning to learn that what we had experienced was a common occurrence when pursuing javelina. To be sure, the lesson came with a considerable outlay of boot leather, sore muscles and perspiration.

Tired and thirsty, we finally made it back to the truck. With a promise from Duwane to "find more pigs," we were on our way to a new location. The new location looked a good deal like the old location, but there is a certain similarity about all desert locales. After another mile or so of uphill footwork, we found ourselves overlooking a substantial canyon. The best part was the shin dagger that grew in thick patches in several places. Shin dagger is the preferred food of the javelina and this place had the look of a fast food buffet line. Duwane assured me that he'd glassed several herds of peccaries in this canyon over the years. However, this day the entire area was devoid of desert pigs.

Mumbling something under his breath about his reputation being at stake, we returned to the truck and set out for another location. There wasn't much time to rest and the hiking was beginning to take a toll on my legs. Still, Duwane turned down a rocky path that barely passed for a road. Trying to keep my head from banging into the roof of the truck cab while we made our way down this particular road (if you could call it that), was a major endeavor. Fortunately, we didn't have far to go. Pulling up in a hail of dust and gravel, Duwane announced, "We're here!"

For the third time that day, we shouldered our packs and took off across the desert. And despite a rather serious hike of about 2 miles, it was the tripod and binoculars that made the day. Just minutes after he had settled in behind his huge Zeiss glasses, Duwane pointed in the direction of a small stand of cedars on the opposite hillside. Sure enough, a group of javelina was bedded down in the shade of one of the trees.

Glassing javelina at 300 yards is one thing, getting close enough for a shot with a handgun is another. An hour and about 250 yards later, we finally were able to find a position that offered a reasonable shot presentation. The only problem was picking out a target. The hogs were so balled up that it was hard to get a clear shot. Patience isn't one of my best virtues. And when it comes to hunting, I am often a victim of my own impulse to make things happen. In this instance, I didn't have to wait long. A brief scuffle broke between the pigs and they all stood up at one time. This afforded the opportunity to look the herd over. Two of the hogs were obviously larger than the rest. I had long since found a solid rest, so it was only a matter of deciding which of the two pigs to take. That decision was no problem. One hog had a very visible ruff of lighter hair around his neck—a mark of true maturity. Placing the crosshairs of my pistol scope right behind the animal's shoulder, I squeezed the trigger.

At the shot, the entire hillside seemed to erupt. Javelina scattered everywhere, seemingly running in all directions. Thinking I'd missed, I cursed my luck and was prepared to accept disappointment. It wasn't until I heard Duwane exclaim, "Great shot," that I realized the hunt was over. I finally had my javelina. Checking through the binoculars confirmed that the boar hog lay just a few feet from where the bullet took him.

After field dressing the javelina, I then learned the best thing about hunting little big game. Packing out a desert pig is a lot easier than dealing with any other big game animal.

Solid evidence: Javelina leave lots of sign behind. Evidence of their passing can be found in sharply pointed hoof prints that resemble petite deer tracks. Bedding sites are usually shaded and scoured clean of rocks and debris. Of course, javelina droppings are clearly evident in conjunction with tracks and beds. Since the peccaries prefer prickly pear cactuses, you can find evidence of feeding activities on the external margin of the fleshy pads. A javelina uses its hooves to knock off the spines, and then it will nibble on the ends of the modified leaves. You'll see rounded bite marks and lots of shredded fibrous material.

Since the desert environment tends to preserve everything quite well, don't be fooled by just any old set of tracks, rooted out beds or munched over cactuses. Old sign isn't worth spit, so don't waste your time on it. Look for tracks that are well defined, with sharp edges. Likewise, recent bite marks on cactuses, in conjunction with soft scat, usually mean that the desert pigs are about. A javelina herd is territorial. While these domains can vary in size, most average 750 to 900 acres. Just finding a herd of peccaries in an area of that size, given all the irregularity of the desert, can take all day. You'll need to cover lots of ground to find javelina and fresh sign is the most important key to that discovery. When you locate evidence of recent activity (less than one day old), then you can start your search in earnest. The little animals are good at hiding; so don't overlook anything that appears promising—including the shaded bottom of any washout, ravine or canyon.

Hog hotspots: Each of the three Southwestern states—Arizona, New Mexico and Texas—have certain areas that offer the best javelina hunting opportunities. In Arizona, the little desert dwellers primarily can be found from the upper Verde River Valley southeasterly through Bloody Basin, Tonto Basin and throughout the Globe-Miami Mountains. The Fort Apache and the White Mountain Indian Reservations also have javelina, but nowhere near the number of animals that can be found on the San Carlos Indian Reservation. The animals also inhabit the foothills of the Swisshelm, Tumacacori, Huachuca, Santa Rita, Canelo Hills, Santa Teresa, Sierrrita, Baboquivaris, Pinaleno, Tortolita, Catalina and Rincon Mountain ranges, south and east of Tucson.

The most huntable New Mexico javelina population can be found in the extreme southwest corner of the state. The Steins Pass region in the Coronado National Forest, the Burro Mountains in the Gila National Forest and the Pyramid Mountains south of Lordsburg all

Photo by Durwood Hollis

When you hunt javelina off the beaten path, a good backpack is all you'll need to get your little tusker back to camp.

have sizeable numbers of the tiny hogs. Other areas to check out can be found near Lake Valley and south of Deming, New Mexico. The Big Hatchet Refuge (a state Game & Fish Wildlife Area), south of Hachita, also holds plenty of pigs. And there's lots of good hog habitat in Grant, Hidalgo and Luna counties, however, make sure you have permission to hunt on private land in those areas.

Texas has the largest population of peccarys found in the United States. The animals are well distributed all across the southern half of the Lone Star state. While almost all of the hunting opportunities are on private ground, some public land javelina hunting is available. Hunting for the tiny tuskers at the Chaparral Wildlife Management Area (WMA) in Dimmit and La Salle counties and the James Daughtrey WMA in McMullen and Live Oak counties is conducted on a limited, special-permit basis. Unlimited permit hunting for javelina are available only on the Black Gap WMA.

Javelina Calibers: It doesn't take a whole heap of projectile weight and energy to successfully take a jav-

elina. Where allowed by game regulations, several .22-caliber centerfire chamberings with solidly constructed bullets will do the job. Even the mildest of the group — .22 Hornet, .218 Bee, .222 Remington and the 22 Remington Magnum—are all up to the job. The .223 Remington is another good choice. And any of the 6mm chamberings are more than enough medicine for javelina. Likewise, the .250 Savage, .257 Roberts and the .270 Winchester with 100-grain bullets are also favorites for this assignment.

Pistoleros are right at home in pursuit of the javelina. I've found a single-shot pistol with a telescopic sight much to my own liking for this sport. A host of caliber selections is available. The .243 Win., .250 Sav. and the 6.5mm TCU are some of my favorites. Of course, there's no reason why you couldn't take after javelina with an open-sighted revolver chambered in .357 Mag., .41 Rem. Mag. or .44 Rem. Magnum, if you were so inclined.

Regardless of caliber, most blackpowder shooters will use their favorite front-loading deer rifle for hunting peccaries. During Arizona's HAM javelina season, you'll see plenty of .50-caliber smokepoles in the field. My favorite charcoal-burner is a .40-caliber percussion rifle by the folks at Dixie Arms. The rifle weighs just 5-pounds and is a delight to carry in the field. With a patched 95-grain ball and 75-grains of Pyrodex, it shoots as flat as a slate billiard table. If there's a better black powder javelina rig, I haven't found it.

What you'll need: Never venture into the desert without an adequate supply of something to drink. Dehydration isn't fun; so don't even start down that path. A 1-quart canteen is about right for most hunts, but there are times when 2 quarts are just barely enough. A wide-brimmed hat and a long-sleeve shirt will keep the sun from burning you to a crisp. Since it can get cold in the desert when the sun goes down, don't forget to pack a light jacket or a sweatshirt. Other hunt essentials you won't want to forget are: A flashlight, lip balm, a sharp knife and toilet paper (plumbing emergencies do happen).

Outside of Texas, where baiting is common practice, most javelina hunting is a spot-and-stalk game. If you don't want to hike your heart out, then a pair of high-magnification binoculars should be part of your hunting gear. Prickly pear and lechuguilla (century plant) are favorite foods. Later in the day, scan under mesquite trees, in the bottoms of ravines and any other place where the animal might be bedded. Finding peccaries is something that takes lots of patience and hunting tenacity.

Calling all javelina: Peccary are very protective of their young. If a badger, fox or coyote grabs a little hog, it will squeal loudly. This sound can often be the catalyst that brings the entire herd to the fray. Knowledgeable hunters have found that there are times when javelina will respond to a predator call. Don't count on the call working every time, but when it does—be prepared. A javelina looking for a fight isn't anything to take lightly. The next time you go after desert hogs, a predator call in your pack could tilt the odds to your advantage. When the opportunity presents itself, give the call a try.

Field care: Field dressing a javelina is relatively easy. However, don't delay this important procedure. Even in the winter, it can get hot in the desert. An ungutted javelina bouncing around in the back of a pickup truck can be an unpleasant sight. Prompt field care is important to ensure that the meat doesn't spoil. Some folks go to a lot of trouble trying to remove the scent gland. My advice, forget about it! If you don't fool with it, there's no danger of spreading the musk to the meat. Anyway, when you skin the pig it will come off along with the hide.

While the largest of javelina probably won't weigh 40 pounds field dressed, using a packframe makes a lot more sense than just throwing the carcass over your shoulder. If you pack a javelina any distance, most likely your hunting buddies won't want to set next to you on the ride back to camp. Peccaries stink and there's no way around the musky odor. Of course, you can skin and bone-out the animal right in the field. Toss the meat into a plastic trash compactor bag before it goes into your pack and you'll eliminate most of the mess. While peccary meat isn't high on most folk's preferred table dishes, it does make great sausage—especially chorizo. Just don't forget to go heavy on the chili sauce.

Isn't it about time? If you haven't tried your hand at javelina hunting, then you've missed a special experience. Chasing after the little tusk pigs is just fun. If you use a blackpowder rifle, bow or a handgun, then the enjoyment is hard to equal. Even better, if you score, it's a snap to haul your trophy back to camp. And there's nothing like a mounted javelina head on the wall to get an after-dinner conversation started.

Photo by Durwood Hollis

In the field is where it counts. The right rifle, an appropriate bullet and a solid rest are all important.

CALIBERS FOR NORTH AMERICAN BIG GAME

Using enough gun is important, but putting your bullet on the target is vital!

Most hunters have their own opinions about what are the minimum and maximum calibers for North American big game. At the bottom end of the center-fire cartridge continuum, I can find no justification for using any chambering smaller than .243 Winchester/6mm Remington, firing a 100-grain bullet. At the other extreme, the .416 Remington, with its more than 2 tons of muzzle energy, isn't out of place on this continent. Many large animals can cling to life with remark-

Photo by Nosler®

With the right bullet design the .243 Winchester is perfectly adequate for deer and antelope. The new 90-grain Nosler® Ballistic Tip® bullet is designed to provide dependable terminal performance on big game.

able tenacity. Unless a bullet severs the spinal column, it can take an extended period of time for death to ensue. It's between bullet strike and system collapse that things can get *dicey*. And that's why you need enough gun!

And this opinion is not only shared by many, but is also based on several decades of personal hunting experience with a wide range of different calibers. Let's examine some groupings of selected big game chamberings.

.243 Winchester, 6mm Remington: These nearly identical .24 caliber rounds were both introduced in 1955 by Winchester and Remington, respectively. The .243 Win. was conceived as a light deer cartridge that also had the flexibility to be used on varmints. The 6mm Remington (then known as the .244 Remington) started out life primarily as a varmint caliber, but later the inherent capability of handling deer-size game came to the forefront.

Interestingly, the **.243 Winchester** is part of the .308 Win. family of cartridges. The simple act of necking the basic case either up, or down, has also given commercial life to the .260 Rem., 7mm-08 Rem., and the .358 Winchester. Factory-loaded, the .24 caliber, 100-grain bullet exits the barrel at 2,960 feet per second, generating 1,945 foot-pounds of energy. Interestingly, in my hands the .243 Win. has proven to be more effective in stopping deer, antelope and black bear in their tracks than many medium calibers shooting heavier bullets.

The **6mm Remington** is a unique design and not based on any other existing cartridge. A comparison between the two chamberings points to fact that the

6mm Rem. has a somewhat greater powder capacity and the slightly longer case neck. If you're a hand-loader, then these assets will be well appreciated. Factory loaded, the 6mm Rem. spits a 100-grain bullet out of the barrel at 3,100 feet per second, with 2,133 foot-pounds of energy. The differences between the .243 Win. and the 6mm Rem. are really insignificant. On deer-class game, all the way out to 300-yards, either chambering will put meat in the freezer.

.257 Roberts, .25-06 Remington: These quarter-bore offerings are often overlooked by big game hunters. Nevertheless, both chamberings are excellent deer, antelope and black bear calibers. And with the 120-grain loads they have proven effective on sheep, mountain goat and caribou as well.

The **.257 Roberts** enjoyed considerable popularity among American hunters from its 1934 commercial introduction well into the 1960s. Unfortunately, this caliber was underloaded by all ammunition manufacturers, making it a target for obsolescence when the .257 Weatherby, .264 Win. Mag. and the .25-06 Rem. entered the market in 1944, 1958 and 1969, respectively. The introduction of +P (additional power) ammunition for this caliber in the late 1980s, how-ever, rescued it from becoming outdated. The 100-grain +P load in this caliber moves out of the muzzle at an honest 3,000 fps, developing 1,998 foot-pounds of energy. And the 117-grain bullet leaves the muzzle at 2,780 fps, with 2,009 foot-pounds of muzzle energy. When used on big game, the greater bullet weight offered by the 117-grain load provides a clear edge over any of the 6mms.

The **.25-06 Remington** came into commercial existence in 1969. This necessitated very little in the way of cartridge development, since the round is nothing more than a .30-06 Spfd. case necked down to .25 caliber. At present, a number of bullet weights are factory-loaded. However, anything smaller than the 100-grain projectile is a varmint bullet and should not be used on big game. The 100-grain bullet steams out of the barrel at 3,230 fps, providing 2,316 foot-pounds of muzzle energy. The 117-grain projectile moves a little slower at 2,990 fps, with 2,320 foot-pounds of energy. And the 120-grain load is just a tad slower at 2,940 fps, but provides 2,382 foot-pounds of energy. Unfortunately, this caliber suffers from competition with the 6mms and the well-respected .270 Winchester. On one side of the equation, the 6mms can nearly equal the performance of the .25-06 Remington. Conversely, the .270 Win.

Winchester's Supreme Power-Point® ammunition has earned a solid reputation of dependable performance on a wide range of big game species.

with its 130-, 140- and 150-grain bullets is a more versatile big game round. Even so, this caliber is still chambered by all of the major firearms manufacturers and continues to remain popular with a small, but dedicated group of hunters.

.260 Remington, .264 Winchester Mag: Both of these 6.5mm chamberings offer peerless accuracy and negligible recoil. Despite these distinct shooting advantages mainstream American hunters have overlooked them, to a large extent. Let's examine them to see where they fit into the scheme of things.

The **.260 Remington** was first introduced at the 1999 Shooting, Hunting and Outdoor Trade Show. The brainchild of *Outdoor Life's* Shooting Editor, Jim Carmichael, this caliber is simply a .308 Win. case necked down to 6.5-caliber. Three different bullet weights are listed in the current Remington ammunition line-up, including: 140-grain CoreLoc®, 125-grain Nosler® Partition®, and a 120-grain Nosler® Ballistic Tip®. Velocity in these loads is 2,750 fps, 2,875 fps and 2,890 fps, respectively. This puts the .260 Rem. in same league with it near-siblings, the 7mm-08 Rem. and the .308 Winchester. When compared to other .308 variants, the .260 Rem. offers unmatched accuracy (1/2-inch three-shot groups at 100 yards are common) and superior sectional density. Now you understand why Jim Carmichael spent so much effort pioneering this chambering.

The **.264 Winchester Magnum** entered the commercial marketplace in 1958. It is one of four cartridges based on the belted .458 Win. Magnum case. Bullet weights from 85 to 160 grains can be used. However, the 100-, 120-, 129- and 140-grain projectiles will provide the best performance on deer, antelope and mountain game. The 100-grain load moves out of the barrel at 3,500 fps, with 2,721 foot-pounds of

Photo by Barnes Bullets

No matter what shape bullet you select, this is the kind of terminal performance you're looking for.

energy. The 120-grain bullet is also a real screamer at 3,200 fps, with 2,729 foot-pounds of energy. The 129-grain offering is only a tad slower at 3,100 fps, with 2,753 foot-pounds of energy. And the factory-loaded 140-grain bullet delivers an honest 3,030 fps at the muzzle, with 2,854 foot-pounds of energy. Despite all of the stunning velocity, this chambering does suffer considerable velocity loss in barrels less than 26 inches in length. I've used the .264 Win. Mag. on both mule deer and antelope and have found it to be my own personal caliber choice for open-country hunting.

.270 Winchester: This caliber holds such an important position in the pantheon of big game calibers that it deserves separate treatment. There is no doubt that in any survey of American hunters—particularly deer hunters—this chambering will be one of the five top choices.

While bullets used in the **.270 Winchester** are available from 90 to 150 grains, the best performance on big game will be found with the 130-, 140- and the 150-grain bullets. My preference in this caliber is the reliable 130-grain projectile. This little number exits the barrel at 3,060 fps, producing 2,702 foot-pounds of energy. Admittedly the .30-06 Spfd. parent cartridge, with its wider range of bullet weights, is a better heavy game caliber. In the right hands and with an appropriate bullet selection, however, the .270 Win. is more than adequate for nearly all North American big game. And if I could only have one rifle for the vast majority of my hunting, it would definitely be a .270 Winchester.

7x30 Waters, 7mm-08 Remington, .284 Winchester, .280 Remington, 7mm Remington Magnum: Since all of these chamberings share the same 7mm bullet diameter, I have opted to consider them as a single group.

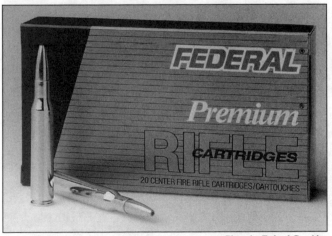

Photo by Federal Cartridge

The .270 Winchester is one of the best caliber choices for medium game.

Both the 7x30 Waters and the .284 Win. are probably the least known. On the other hand, the 7mm-08 Rem., .280 Rem. and the 7mm Rem. Mag. have all gained their share of the publicity spotlight.

The **7x30 Waters** is the creation of gun writer and ballistics authority, Ken Waters. Introduced by U.S. Repeating Arms (Winchester) in 1984 and offered in the Model 94 XTR Angle Eject lever-action, this caliber was designed to eclipse the performance of .30-30 Win. levergun chamberings. The 120-grain factory load leaves the muzzle at 2,700 fps, producing 1,940 foot-pounds of energy. While at first glance these figures look impressive, in my experience this caliber provides rather lukewarm performance on game. One of the problems is that because lever-action designs usually use tubular magazines, bullets must be flat-nosed to preclude accidental discharge during recoil. When compared to a pointed bullet, a flat-nosed projectile loses velocity at an accelerated rate. Used in a short-barrel levergun, the 7x30 Waters trajectory isn't much better than the .30-30 Win., 35 Rem., or the .38-55 Winchester. Furthermore, the 7x30 Waters is less effective with short-range target presentations than many slower levergun calibers. And it certainly isn't a long-range number by any means.

The **7mm-08 Remington** derives its life by simply necking-down the basic .308 Win. case. Interestingly, the factory-loaded 140-grain bullet, at a muzzle velocity of 2,860 fps, with 2,542 foot-pounds of energy, has better downrange performance than the 150-grain load in the parent .308 Win. chambering. While this enhanced efficiency isn't anything to write home about, it does demonstrate the superior design elements of the

Always fully examine your rifle before firing. It doesn't take much of an obstruction (in this case it was a small spider nest) to cause pressure to build inside of a barrel. When it does, look out!

Photo by Durwood Hollis

7mm bullet. Two factory loadings—120- and 140-grain bullets—are available in this caliber. The 120-grain load leaves the barrel at 3,000 fps, with 2,398 foot-pounds of energy. The 140-grain bullet performs nearly as well with a muzzle velocity of 2,860 fps and 2,542 foot-pounds of energy. The 7mm-08 Rem. is a fine deer, antelope, black bear and wild boar caliber, which can also be used on sheep and mountain goat.

The **.284 Winchester** is a weird little round that combines a .30-06 rim with a belted magnum case diameter. The rebated rim (actually smaller diameter than the case) makes this round look squat and fat. Despite appearances, the larger case diameter provides increased powder capacity for added performance in a short-action platform. The single factory load pushes a 150-grain bullet out of the barrel at 2,860 fps, with 2,724 foot-pounds of energy. When compared to the .280 Rem., this caliber is nearly its ballistic twin. In spite of this, the .284 Win., introduced in 1963, hasn't made much of an impression with big game hunters. While no current production rifles are chambered in this potent little number, should you run across a used Winchester Model 88, Savage Model 99 or a Browning BLR in this caliber, reach for your wallet and count your blessings.

The **.280 Remington** is nothing more than a .30-06 Spfd. case necked-down to .284-caliber. This chambering is really caught in a ballistics "no man's land." Velocity and energy are just a little better than the .270 Win. and slightly less than the .30-06 Springfield. A comparison of ballistics will bear this out. The 150-grain load is the only factory load that all three chamberings have in common. This bullet leaves the muzzle of the .280 Rem. at 2,890 fps, delivering 2,781 foot-pounds of energy. In the .270 Win. the same bullet weight exits the muzzle 40 fps slower, with a decrease of 76 foot-pounds of energy. And the 150-grain bullet out of a .30-06 Spfd. is just 30 fps faster, with an additional 50 foot-pounds of energy. Obviously, there isn't much difference between all three calibers.

The **7mm Remington Magnum** has been a tremendous commercial success ever since its 1962 introduc-

tion. This chambering is one of four belted magnums (.264 Win. Mag., 7mm Rem. Mag., .338 Win. Mag. and the .458 Win. Magnum) that are derived from the basic .458 Win. case. It also bears a close relationship to the .300 Win. Magnum. To a large degree, its success must be credited to the word "Magnum" tacked onto the caliber designation. The 140-grain load steams out of the barrel at 3,175 fps, with an impressive 3,133 foot-pounds of energy. Even the 175-grain bullet hustles right along at 2,860 fps, with 3,178 foot-pounds of energy. In between these two fine projectiles are the factory-loaded 150-, 160- and 165-grain loads. I've used this caliber extensively and have found it to be a fine long-range choice for nearly everything from deer to elk. Provided, that is, that premium quality bullets, in appropriate weights, are always used.

.30-30 Winchester: With a track record of more than a century of service and continued consumer demand, this chambering desires a category all by itself.

As a big game cartridge, the **.30-30 Win.** is best suited to target presentations not much father than 150 yards. Entering the commercial market in 1895, this round first saw service in the Winchester Model 1894 lever-action rifle. And today you'll find this same caliber still being chambered in the current U.S. Repeating Arms (Winchester) Model 94 levergun. Through the years, many other firearms manufacturers have also offered leverguns, bolt-actions, single-shot rifles and pistols in this caliber. Factory-loaded the 150-grain bullet exits the barrel at 2,390 fps, with 1,902 foot-pounds of energy. The 170-grain package isn't far behind at 2,200 fps, generating 1,827 foot-pounds of energy. As these ballistic figures bear out, unless you count cowboy movies, the .30-30 Win. doesn't have a lot going for it by way of extended-range performance.

.300 Savage, .307 Winchester, and .308 Winchester: All three of these chamberings are quite similar in that they offer near .30-06 performance in a short-action platform. The .300 Sav. is the oldest of this trio,

Photo by USRAC

The most popular deer rifle ever is the Winchester Model 94 lever-action (Legacy model pictured), chambered in .30-30 Winchester.

Photo by Durwood Hollis

Open sights or a scope, it will take range work to get your rifle shooting right.

dating to 1920. The popular .308 Win. began life in 1952. With its 1982 roll-out, the .307 Win. is the youngest member of the group.

The **.300 Savage** was developed expressly for the Savage Model 99 lever-action rifle. The intent was to provide levergun users with ballistic performance that rivals the venerable .30-06 Springfield. Factory-loaded, the 150-grain bullet features a muzzle velocity of 2,630 fps, with 2,303 foot-pounds of energy. Likewise, the 180-grain pill slips out of the bore at 2,350 fps, churning up 2,207 foot-pounds of energy. Both loads are a little less than 200 fps slower than comparable .30-06 Spfd. rounds, but for generations of hunters the combination of enhanced performance in an easy-handling levergun seemed to make up for any ballistic shortcomings. In the post-World War II era this caliber has largely been displaced by the .308 Winchester. Nevertheless, the Savage chambering in older rifles continues to be used successfully on most big game—including elk.

The **.307 Winchester** offers near .308 Win. performance in a rimmed cartridge configuration. However, due to a slightly shorter and thicker case, both velocity and energy figures are inferior to the .308 Winchester. The 150-grain bullet moves out of the muzzle at 2,760 fps, with 2,538 foot-pounds of energy. The 180-grain pill lags behind at 2,510 fps, but still offers 2,519 foot-pounds of energy. This is certainly a more adaptable chambering than anything in the .30-30 Win. class. And with the added velocity, the .307 moves the Model 94 levergun out of the brush and deep timber into mixed cover. I've used the .307 Win. on wild boar and found its performance outstanding—even on moderately long (250 yards) shots. That said, the .307 Win. hasn't really been much of a commercial success. Hunters apparently never fully understood the difference between the plodding .30-30 Win. and the sizzling .307 Win. in their favorite lever-action design.

The **.308 Winchester** is about 100 fps slower than the respected .30-06 Springfield. However, the case is 12mm shorter, allowing it to be chambered in a short-action platform. The 150-grain factory load exits the barrel at 2,820 fps, with 2,648 foot-pounds of energy. The 180-grain load is somewhat slower at 2,620 fps, but it generates 2,743 foot-pounds of energy. A highly accurate and flat-shooting round, the .308 Win. can easily handle shots out to 300 yards. Chambered in a lightweight, carbine-length boltgun, this caliber has been my own personal big game choice for more than three decades.

.30-40 Krag, .30-06 Springfield, .300 Winchester Magnum: *The Krag, also known as the .30 U.S. Army, was our first domestic small-bore military chambering. Likewise, the .30-06 Spfd. also hails from a military background. The .300 Win. Mag. has a different lineage, but it is just another ballistic step in this .30 caliber continuum.*

The **.30-40 Krag** is a real old-timer, emerging on the scene in 1892. The only current factory load is the 180-grain round at 2,430 fps muzzle velocity, with 2,360 foot-pounds of energy. Obviously less powerful than the .30-06 Spfd., nonetheless, it has earned a solid reputation on game at moderate ranges. In the mid-1980s, Browning brought out a classic reproduction of the Model 1895 levergun chambered in .30-40 Krag. I had the good fortune of using one of the first of these rifles on wild boar at California's famed Dye Creek ranch. On a 200-pound running hog at about 175 yards, the 180-grain bullet traversed the entire the chest cavity and exited the far-side shoulder. I've never had better performance from any other caliber, including some of the heavier magnums. While this aged veteran may lack the impressive velocity of many more modern chamberings, it still offers rock-solid perfomance.

The **.30-06 Springfield** also began life as a military chambering in 1906. Without peer for versatility, this caliber can be used on everything from varmints to the largest of North American big game. Bullet weights from the 55-grain (sabotted Accelerator®) to the 250-grain pill can be loaded into this caliber, making it the most flexible game cartridge ever designed. For most practical use, bullets in the 100- to 130-grain weights are suitable for small game and varmints. Projectiles in the 150- and 165-grain weights are just about right for deer, antelope, black bear, caribou and mountain game. The heavier 180-, 200-, and 220-grain factory loads are best suited for use on boar, brown bear, and elk. The two most popular game bullets, the 150- and 180-grain feature muzzle velocities of 2,920 fps and 2,700 fps and generate 2,839 and 2,914 foot-pounds of energy, respectively. As a single caliber recommendation for North American big game, you'd be right on target with this fine chambering. Furthermore, it does it all without the punishing recoil of many so-called "Magnum" chamberings. Enough said!

While the **.300 Winchester Magnum** cartridge case is just a tad longer (.12 inch) than the .458 Win. Mag. and its three spin-offs—.264 Win. Mag., 7mm Rem. Mag., and the .338 Win. Magnum—there is enough similarity in all other design features to suggest a strong family resemblance. Introduced by Winchester in 1963,

it quickly gained popularity with the big game hunting fraternity. Factory-loaded ammo comes in 150-, 180-, 200-, and 220-grain bullet weights. Deer hunters favor the 150-grain load that offers a sizzling 3,290 fps muzzle velocity, with 3,605 foot-pounds of energy. If a cross-canyon wind kicks up, then the 180-grain bullet with a muzzle velocity of 2,960 fps, generating 3,501 foot-pounds of energy, is probably a better choice. For game in the elk, moose and brown bear class, the 200-grain load with a muzzle velocity of 2,825 fps, churning up 3,544 foot-pounds of energy, or the 220-grain bullet with 2,825 fps at the muzzle, with 3,508 foot-pounds of energy, are better choices. The .300 Win. Mag. is fast enough and packs the necessary added energy to allow the use of heavier .30-caliber bullets for long-range target presentations. However, these gains in bullet speed and *punch* are offset by greater recoil. This alone can make the .300 Win. Mag. a difficult caliber for many shooters to master.

8mm Remington Magnum, .338 Winchester Magnum: *These two calibers are close enough ballistically to be considered near-siblings. With bullet diameters of .323 and .338, respectively, there isn't a whole of lot*

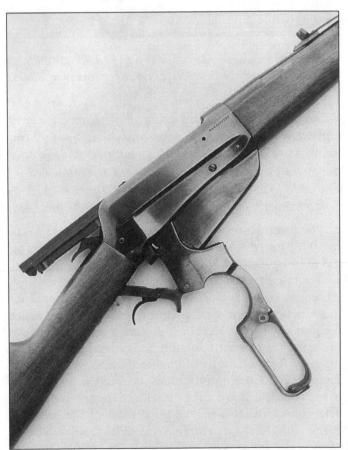

Photo by Durwood Hollis

Chambered in .30-40 Krag or .30-06 Springfield, even an old-timer like the Winchester Model 95 lever-action can deliver the goods.

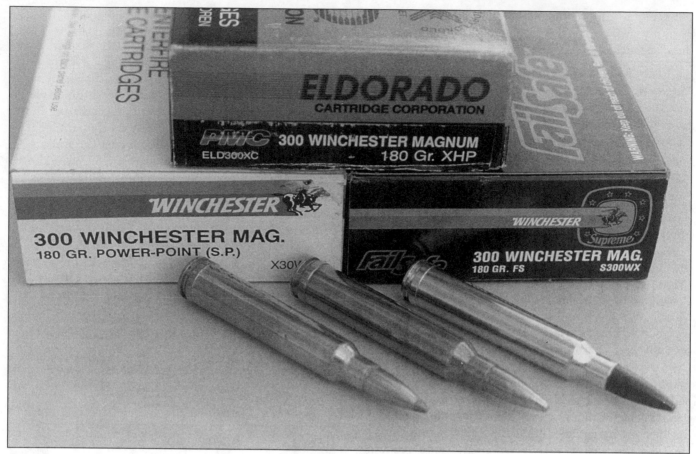

Photo by Durwood Hollis

The .300 Winchester Magnum is a fine choice for all North American big game. With its larger powder capacity it has a distinct advantage in velocity and energy over the .30-06 Springfield at all distances.

difference in terminal projectile performance. Overall cartridge case length is where their differences are manifest. The 8mm Rem. Mag. with its longer case necessitates the use of a full-length magnum action. The .338 Win. Magnum, however, is short enough to function easily in a standard-length cartridge platform.

The **8mm Remington Magnum** came to the market in 1978. Interestingly, Remington based the design on the .375 Holland & Holland Magnum. As a result, this necessitated the use of a magnum-length action, which increased bolt travel. Coupled with the fact that at its introduction there was a limited selection of bullet weights, the 8mm Rem. Mag. didn't actually make a big *splash*. At its introduction, many were left wondering how Remington would make such a dumb marketing mistake. Error in judgment, or not, the 8mm Rem. Mag. is still a fine caliber for large, heavy big game. The 185-grain factory load moves out of the barrel at 3,080 fps, with a *whopping* 3,896 foot-pounds of energy. To be sure, handloaders can choose from a wide range of bullet weights, including a 200-grain Nosler® Partition®, 220-grain projectiles from Sierra and Hornady, as well as a stunning 250-grain Barnes

X-Bullet®. Many have cited the lack of bullet selection as the main reason why the 8mm Rem. Mag. didn't catch on like the .300 or the .338 Win. Magnums. Certainly, there are a few more .30-caliber bullet choices, but that isn't true in the .338-caliber arena. Yes, there is only one 8mm Rem. Mag. factory load, but what does that matter if you have handloading capability? While the ballistic differences between this chambering and the .338 Win. Mag. are miniscule, nonetheless, it is still serious elk, moose, and big bear medicine.

The **.338 Winchester Magnum** is by all markers the quintessential North American big game caliber. Introduced in 1958, this chambering, along with the .264 Win. Mag., was based on the .458 Win. Mag. necked-down. While the .338 Win. Mag. has been overshadowed by other calibers as a deer and antelope chambering (the 180-grain Barnes X-Bullet®, with its enhanced sectional density it's a better long-range deer rifle than anything in the .30-caliber class), nevertheless, it's unrivaled as an elk, moose and grizzly bear round. This is true in useful trajectory, enhanced frontal presentation and sustained bullet penetration. The ever-popular 225-grain load lifts off at 2,780 fps, providing 3,860 foot-pounds of energy. Close behind

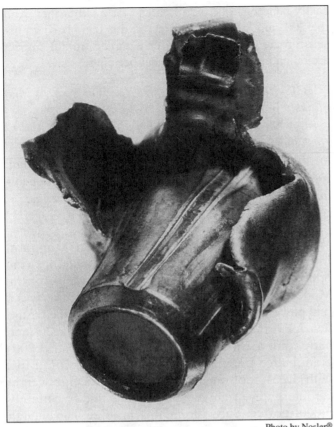

Photo by Nosler®

Capable of both controlled expansion and sustained penetration, the Nosler® Partition® bullet has a peerless reputation among big game hunters.

big game species in heavy cover. And despite the fact that there are more impressive bolt-action chamberings, in the handy Model 71 levergun configuration, this caliber is hard to beat as a close-range caliber or as a back-up rifle.

The **.35 Remington** dates to 1906 and has been chambered in bolt-, slide-, lever-action and semi-automatic rifles. And recently, both the Remington XP-100 and the Thompson/Center single-shot pistol have used this chambering. While not as commanding as the .348 Win., with its large diameter and heavier bullet, the .35 Rem. is a better woods caliber than many other short-range offerings. The factory-loaded 200-grain bullet moves out of the barrel at 2,080 fps, producing 1921 foot-pounds of energy. While not terribly impressive, these ballistics are plenty adequate for short-range work on deer and black bear.

The **.356 Winchester** was introduced by Winchester in 1980 for their Model 94 XTR Angle Eject levergun. Big brother to the .307 Win., with whom it shared the initial caliber entry stage, this chambering is quite capable of handling game as large as wild boar, bear and elk at moderate ranges (250 yards). The 200-grain factory load hustles right along with a muzzle velocity of 2,460 fps, with 2,688 foot-pounds of energy. The

is the heavier 250-grain bullet with a muzzle velocity of 2,660 fps, with a devastating 3,921 foot-pounds of energy. I've used both the Winchester 220-grain Power-Point® and the Remington 225-grain CorLoc® bullet in this chambering for elk with matchless performance—even well beyond the 300-yard mark. And that's a lot to say about any caliber.

.348 Winchester, .35 Remington, .356 Winchester, .358 Winchester: Here's a grouping of very similar calibers that have a lot of bullet weight and frontal area to offer. The .348 Win. and the .35 Rem. are excellent "up-close-and-personal" (under 150-yards) rounds for any North American game. The .356 Win. and .358 Win. are both fully able with the same class of game, but at greater (200-275 yards) distances.

The **.348 Winchester** began its commercial career in 1936 as a chambering for the Winchester Model 71 lever-action rifle. This is an extremely robust rimmed cartridge for a levergun chambering. While 150-, 200- and 250-grain factory fodder was initially available, only the 200-grain load can now be found in Winchester's ammunition line-up. Exiting the muzzle at 2,520 fps, with 2,820 foot-pounds of energy, the 200-grain bullet is definitely the best choice for any

Photo by Durwood Hollis

When chambered in a single-shot pistol (Thompson-Contender pictured), the old .35 Remington is both handy and effective on deer, black bear and wild boar.

250-grain factory fodder moves out at 2,160 fps, and offers 2,591 foot-pounds of energy. This is another caliber that I've put to considerable use with great success. Fired from a levergun with a 20-inch barrel, this chambering is hard to beat in mixed cover. Furthermore, when the flat-nosed .358-inch bullet hits something, in most situations, it's "lights out."

A mid-1950s introduction by Winchester, the **.358 Winchester** is based on the .308 Win. case necked up to .35 caliber. Like other .35 caliber near relatives, the .358 Win. comes into its own in a carbine-length rifle—especially a lever-action. The 200-grain factory load starts out of the barrel at 2,490 fps, with 2,753 foot-pounds of energy. That's a little less speed and energy than the .348 Win. and a little more than the .356 Winchester. However, the bullets used in the .348 Win. and the .356 Win. have inferior ballistic characteristics because of their abbreviated, flattened design. This alone gives the .358 Win. a decided performance edge, especially at distances beyond 150 yards. An excellent round for use both in the woods and mixed cover, it can

Photo by Barnes Bullets

Another great projectile choice is the Barnes X-bullet®. With its solid copper construction, both expansion and weight retention are outstanding.

easily handle shots to 250 yards—or a tad farther. And the 200- and 250-grain bullets in this chambering possess greater weight and offer a larger frontal impact area than anything in the .30 caliber class.

.350 Remington Magnum, .35 Whelen: At first glance, one would envision considerable differences existing between these two calibers. The .35 Whelen is as sleek looking as one would expect of a chambering based on the parent .30-06 Spfd. case. Conversely, the squat, rotund .350 Rem. Mag. is the exact opposite in appearance. In truth, however, they are nearly ballistic twins.

The 1960s gave birth to many revolutionary ideas, one of which was the **.350 Remington Magnum**. Introduced in 1965 as one of two chamberings (the other was the 6.5 Rem. Mag., now obsolete) for the Model 600 Magnum, short-action, boltgun, this was a real powerhouse of a caliber. Interestingly, the ballistics for this number were charted out of a 20-inch barrel, not a 26-inch barrel. The factory-loaded 200-grain bullet features a muzzle velocity of 2,710 fps, with 3,261 foot-pounds of energy. In a lightweight carbine with an abbreviated barrel, this is certainly lots of power! Sure, the .350 Rem. Mag. has enough recoil in such a combination to give you a headache, but so what! For those who hunt on their feet, deep in remote back country, this little number is serious big game medicine.

The **.35 Whelen** is nothing more than the basic .30-06 case necked up to accept .35 caliber bullets. Whether or not Col. Townsend Whelen (U.S. Army) participated in the development of this chambering while he was the commanding officer at the Frankford Arsenal in the 1920s, or it was simply named in his honor isn't really all that important. What is significant is that this chambering offers outstanding ballistics in a non-belted, standard-length case. Existing solely as a wildcat chambering for more than half a century, it was finally brought into the Remington ammunition line-up in 1987. Two bullet weights—200- and 250-grain—are available factory-loaded. Featuring muzzle velocities of 2,675 fps and 2,400 fps, with 3,177 and 3,197 foot-pounds of energy, respectively, both are fine loads for large, heavy game. Unlike the limited overall magazine length of a short-action rifle chambered in .350 Rem. Mag. (Remington Model 600 Magnum or Model Seven), a standard-length action chambered in .35 Whelen provides enough room to seat bullets farther out in the case neck, or allow for the use of a slightly longer projectile—like the all-copper Barnes X-bullet®. The additional velocity and enhanced sectional density provided by such loads are significant assets over similar weight bullets in the .350 Rem. Magnum. Since it offers solid ballistic performance, without the

The new Nosler® 300-grain bullet for the old .45-70 Government chambering is a real performer on big game.

Photo by Nosler®

punishing recoil of a belted magnum, many prefer the Whelen chambering for elk, moose and grizzly.

.375 Winchester, .444 Marlin, .45-70 Government, .450 Marlin Magnum: Despite their differences, all of these calibers offer similar performance. All three are short-range numbers, whose performance potential is best realized at shooting distances less than 150 yards. Within this parameter of operation, however, they are quite suitable for any North American big game species—including moose, elk and bear.

The **.375 Winchester** is one of several calibers expressly developed for the U.S. Repeating Arms (Winchester) Model 94 Big Bore lever-action. Introduced in 1978, there has never been a large demand for this chambering. Nevertheless, the .375 Win. is a great woods number that offers respectable performance on deer, black bear and possibly even moose at ranges under 150 yards. The 200-grain bullet moves out of the muzzle at 2,200 fps, with 2,150 foot-pounds of energy. The 250-grain isn't far behind at 1,900 fps, with 2,005 foot-pounds of energy.

Another *heavy hitter* is the **.444 Marlin**, a 1964 introduction by Marlin to be used in the Model 336 levergun. Firing the same flat-nosed 240-grain bullet as the .44 Rem. Mag. pistol cartridge, the .444 Marlin adds new dimensions of velocity and potential energy.

Factory-loaded, the 240-grain projectile moves out of the barrel at 2,330 fps, with 2,942 foot-pounds of energy. With a frontal impact area substantially larger than any of the .35 caliber chamberings, the .444 Marlin should provide superior initial impact. However, due to a less than aerodynamic bullet design, it runs out of steam beyond 150 yards. I've used this caliber on wild boar and have been impressed at its short-range knock-down power. Likewise, this chambering should provide similar performance on deer and black bear at suitable distances.

Joining the U.S. Military in 1873, the **.45-70 Government** was the primary military ammunition for nearly a score of years. This was orginally a black-powder caliber, hence the designation .45-70 which stood for .45-caliber, loaded with 70-grains of black-powder. Furthermore, depending on the particular bullet weight—330-, 350-, 405- and 500-grain—that figure was also added to the early nomenclature (e.g. .45-70-405). In addition to its military service, no doubt the .45-70 Gov't. was also used by buffalo hunters. By the 1930s, however, this old warrior was well past it prime. And it wasn't until recently that there was a resurgence of interest in this caliber. Two factory loads are available—300-grain and 405-grain—at 1,880 fps and 1,330 fps, with 2,355 and 1,590 foot-pounds of energy, respectively. Of course, handloaders can improve on these figures in modern rifles. While its rainbow-like trajectory inhibits shots much beyond 150 yards, it is pure dynamite within that boundary.

Basically, the new **.450 Marlin** chambering is the old .45-70 Gov't. chambering with a big dose of stimulant. While .45-70 ballistics can be enhanced by handloading, such a practice is safe only in firearms of modern manufacture. There are still enough older single-shot and repeating rifles in .45-70 that improving on the ballistics with modern powders could be a risky venture for any ammunition firm, not to comment on the litigation that would follow subsequent use of such fodder. What Marlin has accomplished with the .450 Magnum is to bring to fruition the potential of the antiquated chambering in a shorter, belted case that cannot be fired in older .45-70 rifles. The 350-grain bullet leaves the muzzle at 2,100 fps, developing 3,427 foot-pounds of energy. As you can see, the .450 Marlin Magnum is just an old warrior in a new uniform.

.416 Remington Magnum: There are few game animals in North America that necessitate the use of this cartridge. The grizzly bear, as well as its cousin the coastal brown bear, are two that come to mind.

Bear hunters are wise to use an appropriate caliber and the **.416 Rem. Mag.** is all that—and then some! Introduced in 1988, the .416 Rem. Mag. is formulated on an 8mm Rem. Mag. case, necked up to accept .416 diameter projectiles. Factory-loaded the 300-, 350- and 400-grain bullets leave the barrel at 2,530 fps, 2,520 fps and 2,400 fps, respectively, with each generating in ascending order 4,262, 4,935 and 5,115 foot-pounds of energy. The former editor of *Petersen's Hunting Magazine* and one of this nation's most experienced hunters, Craig Boddington, once told me that a "grizzly or brown bear can soak up bullets like a big sponge and keep on coming." That being the case, the use of the .416 Rem. Mag. as a North American dangerous game cartridge is well justified.

British Big Bores: *Of the many fine chamberings the Brits have developed over the years, the .300 and .375 Holland & Holland Magnums have made it to these shores. The .300 H&H Mag. is getting a little "long in the tooth" and is no longer chambered by domestic firearms manufacturers, but the .375 H&H Mag. is still an American favorite for large, heavy big game.*

Photo by Bob Robb

Hunters who go after brown bears aren't a bit shy about using the .416 Remington Magnum.

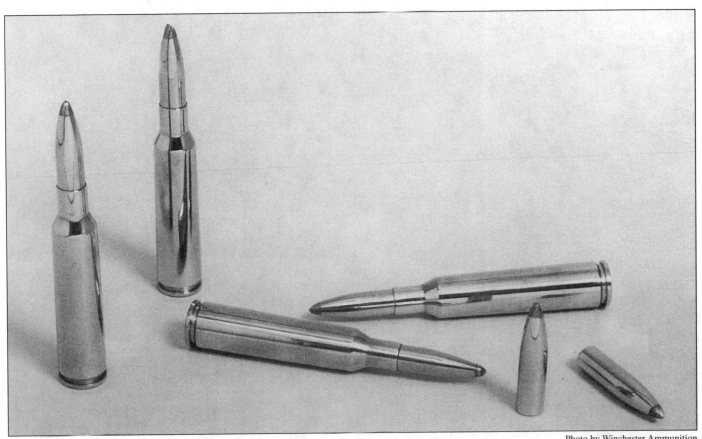

Photo by Winchester Ammunition

Long a favorite of Scandinavian hunters, the 6.5x55 Swedish Mauser is one of the most accurate chamberings available. The Winchester Super-X®, 140-grain, point soft-point load is just right for medium-size game.

Dating to 1925, the **.300 Holland & Holland Magnum** was the consummate .30-caliber magnum for a number of years. Overshadowed by the 1944 development of the .300 Weatherby and the 1963 entry of the .300 Win. Mag., nevertheless, it continues to be an excellent long-range caliber for most North American big game. The .300 H&H Mag. drives a 150-grain bullet at 3,190 fps, with 3,390 foot-pounds of energy. Both the 180- and 220-grain loads are equally as impressive offering 2,880 fps and 2,620 fps of velocity apiece, with 3,315 and 3,350 foot-pounds of energy, respectively. This caliber is no longer available in newly manufactured domestically produced rifles, but if you can find one on the used gun market don't hesitate to lay your hands on it.

The **.375 Holland & Holland Magnum** dates its birth to 1912. Popularized as an all-around caliber for hunting in Asia and Africa, in North America it is occasionally encountered in elk camps. Those hunting in Alaska and Canada favor it for use on moose and grizzly. The two most popular bullet weights in this caliber—270- and 300-grain—exit the muzzle at 2,690 and 2,530 fps individually, generating 4,340 and 4,265 foot-pounds of energy, respectively. One of my good friends, Frank Baratti, used this chambering

to take an enormous elk in British Columbia (how fitting) a few years back. When it took two solid hits to bring the bull down, Frank certainly didn't feel overgunned. Is the .375 H&H Mag. too much gun for North America? When it comes elk, moose, and the big bears, I don't think so!

Continental Favorites: *There are several European calibers that have found a home in North America. The 6.5x55mm Swedish Mauser, 7mm Mauser, and the 8mm Mauser are chamberings that you often encounter in hunting camps across the nation.*

The **6.5x55 Swedish Mauser** began life as a late 19th Century military chambering in rifles used by the Swedish army. In sporting dress, Norweigans, Finns and Swedes use this caliber on everything, including deer, boar, and moose. There are several suitable bullet weights available for this chambering, including 100-, 120-, 129-, 140-, 156- and 160-grain projectiles. However, Federal, Remington and Winchester make a solitary 140-grain load, which features a muzzle velocity of 2,550 fps, with 2,020 foot-pounds of energy. Because many of the older surplus rifles in this caliber can't handle high-intensity loads, modern 6.5x55 ammunition is purposely under-

Winchester was one of the first in the new millennium with a new magnum caliber. The .30 Short Magnum is just that offering.

The European firm of Norma Precision recently introduced the high performance Oryx bullet to the North American market. Obviously, it can get the job done.

loaded. Of course, this is a situation easily rectified by handloading. Personally, I favor the Norma 129-grain load because it moves a little faster and is more useful at long range. Nevertheless, any of the 140-grain domestic loads can handle moderate (250 yards) target presentations.

7mm Mauser (7x57mm): This is an old-timer that saw its birth in 1892 as a military chambering. As a big game round, the 7mm Mauser, loaded with your choice of 140-, 145- or 154-grain bullet, is a fine caliber for antelope, deer and black bear. And the 175-grain load will work on caribou and even elk at medium ranges. All three of the lighter bullets exit the muzzle at 2,690 fps, and they generate an additional 100- to 150-foot-pounds of energy as the bullet weight increases. The 175-grain load moves out at 2,440 fps, with 2,313 foot-pounds of energy. Chambered in a lightweight single-shot or boltgun, this caliber provides adequate punch with mild recoil.

8mm Mauser: This was the military chambering of the German Army during both world wars. Dating to 1888, it has also been a European sporting favorite for more than a century. There is only one domestic factory load, a 170-grain bullet departing the barrel at an anemic 2,360 fps, with 2,100 foot-pounds of energy. However, continental ammunition firms (Norma, RWS, etc.) load several different bullet weights from 159 to 227 grains. The 159-grain European loading is right on par with our domestically-loaded 150-grain, .308 Win. load. Obviously, the 8mm Mauser is adequate for most North American game.

Hot Steppers: Both Remington and Winchester appear to be in a race to outdo one another with their respective developments of new high-velocity magnum chamberings. Certainly, all of the Remington Ultra-Magnums fit this category. As well, the newly developed Winchester .270, 7mm and .30 Short Magnums are other entries in this fray.

Remington 7mm, .30, and .338 Ultra Mags: It would seem that Remington has a lock on innovative 7mm developments. Their new 7mm Ultra Mag is no exception. This hot number pushes a 140-grain bullet out of the muzzle at 3,475 fps, generating 3,646 foot-pounds of energy. The .30 Ultra Mag is right in the same ball park with a 150-grain bullet exiting the barrel at 3,450 fps, with an incredible 3,964 foot-pounds of energy. And for you big-bore fans, the .338 Ultra Mag hurls a 250-grain bullet out of the barrel at 2,860 fps, churning up 4,540 foot-pounds of energy. When compared to standard magnum calibers, the Ultra Mags provide a flatter bullet path and significant energy intensification. However, all of this comes with greater recoil and muzzle blast. Both factors must be considered and dealt with honestly, before you decide to move up to any of these chamberings.

Remington 7mm and .300 SA (Short Action) Ultra Magnums: In 2001, Remington used their successful Ultra Mag concept and expanded it into the development of two new short action, Ultra Magnum cartridges—the 7mm Remington SA (Short Action) *Ultra Magnum* and the .300 Remington SA (Short Action) Ultra Magnum. Chambered in Remington's handy Model Seven bolt-action carbine, both of these new non-belted chamberings provide velocities and energies previously only found in a long-action platform. The **7mm Rem. SA Ultra Mag** fires a 160-grain bullet out of the muzzle at 2,960 fps, producing 3,112 foot-pounds of energy. The **.300 Rem. SA Ultra Mag** pushes a 180-grain bullet out of the barrel at 2,960 fps,

Winchester is one of the major ammunition firms that loads the 7mm STW cartridge.

The Winchester Model 70 bolt-action rifle is the choice of many big game hunters. Mated with the right scope, it is capable of wringing the best out of any caliber.

generating 3,501 foot-pounds of energy. These are extremely efficient short-action cartridges that equal the ballistic performance of the 7mm Rem. Mag. and the .300 Win. Mag. chamberings, respectively. And this velocity and energy both come together in a highly accurate, short-action boltgun. Remington's Model Seven is one of the finest little rifles I've ever used. Now chambered in significantly enhanced, smooth-feeding, non-belted magnum chamberings, it's going to be a "hard act to follow."

Winchester .270, 7mm and .30 Short Magnums: Winchester Ammunition has recently developed three short magnum cartridges. U.S. Repeating Arms Company (USRAC) and the Browning Arms Company are both chambering all of the Winchester Short Magnums in lightweight, short-action platforms. The Winchester **.270 WSM** exceeds the performance of the venerable .270 Win., regardless of bullet weight comparison. The 130-grain pill exits the barrel at a velocity of 3,275 fps, with 3,095 foot-pounds of muzzle energy. Likewise, the 140-grain bullet offers a muzzle velocity of 3,125 fps, generating 3,035 foot-pounds of energy. And the 150-grain bullet steams out of the barrel at 3,150 fps,

with 3,034 foot-pounds of energy. The **7mm WSM** is like the famed 7mm Rem. Mag. in both velocity and energy production. The 140-grain bullet in this caliber leaves the barrel at 3,225 fps, producing 3,233 foot-pounds of energy. The 150-grain and 160-grain bullets are equally impressive exiting the barrel at 3,200 fps and 2,990 fps, with 3,410 and 3,176 foot-pounds of energy, respectively. The **.30 WSM** provides greater velocity and energy than the .300 Win. Mag., and does so in a beltless 2.1-inch case. All three WSM chamberings should be of interest to those that want magnum performance with a reduction in overall gun weight and barrel length.

Other Choices: Cartridge designers: Roy Weatherby, Layne Simpson and John Lazzeroni have contributed excellent chamberings to the North American big game hunting scene. All of these creations are a step above (sometimes well above) similar Remington and Winchester magnums. Whether or not enhanced velocity and energy means a great deal at practical target presentations is a debatable point. For those who want something more, however, there are plenty of additional choices.

Weatherby Magnums: If you're a fan of the non-magnum 6mms, then the **.240 Wby. Mag.** will be of interest. The factory-loaded 100-grain bullet virtually explodes out of the muzzle at 3,395 fps, with 2,559 foot-pounds of energy. A simply awesome long-range antelope and mule deer cartridge, this little number can get the job done. The **.257 Wby. Mag.** is another hot little round that pushes a 100-grain bullet out of the barrel at an impressive 3,602 fps, generating 2,882 foot-pounds of energy. An absolute death ray on deer and antelope, this takes the quarter-bore concept into a new realm. Like its siblings, the .257, 7mm, .300 and .340 Wby. Mags., the **.270 Wby. Mag.** is based on a necked-down .300 H&H Magnum case. This screamer moves a 130-grain bullet out of the barrel at 3,375 fps, producing 3,283 foot-pounds of energy. If you're a .270 Win. fan, then this is more of the same—to the maximum. In the same class, the **7mm Wby. Mag.** blows a 139-grain bullet out of the muzzle at 3,340 fps, with 3,443 foot-pounds of energy. Those who are devotees of the 7mm will be thoroughly enchanted by these ballistic figures. The **.300 Wby. Mag.** has been the flagship of this line of chamberings for many decades. The 150-grain bullet in this caliber features a muzzle veloc-ity of 3,600 fps, with 4,316 foot-pounds of energy. Of course, the entire range of .30-caliber bullets, with anticipated gains in both velocity and energy, can be loaded into this Weatherby creation. As an elk, moose and big bear chambering, it's hard to beat the **.340 Wby. Magnum.** Driving a 250-grain bullet at 2,980 fps, with 4,931 foot-pounds of energy, this caliber is definitely a .338 Win. Mag. on steroids. The recoil is something else—but what did you expect?

Shooting Times Magnums: Gunwriter Layne Simpson designed a pair of chamberings, both of which are based on the 8mm Rem. Mag. case, suitable for use on North American game. The **7mm Shooting Time Westerner (STW)** delivers impressive ballistics that put it well ahead of the 7mm Rem. Magnum. The 140-grain bullet in this caliber exits the barrel at 3,450 fps, with 3,700 foot-pounds of energy. Lagging slightly behind is the 160-grain load at 3,250 fps, with 3,250 foot-pounds of energy. I've used this chambering on antelope in Wyoming's Red Desert where it's tough to get close and it has put trophies on my wall and meat in the freezer every time. While 7mm STW has been brought into the factory chambering and ammunition fold, the **.358 Shooting Times Alaskan**

Photo by Federal Cartridge

In their Premium ammunition line, Federal offers the Barnes Expander™ sabot-encased shotgun slug.

The new Nosler® Parition-HG™ .50-caliber hunting sabots have made a strong impression with blackpowder hunters.

(STA) is still waiting for such acceptance. A-Square loads a 225-grain bullet in this chambering that hauls its tail out of the muzzle at 3,056 fps, with an incredible 4,655 foot-pounds of energy. When it comes to Alaskan game, or for that matter, any North American big game, the .358 STA can "deliver the goods."

Lazzeroni® Magnums: John Lazzeroni has given a whole new definition to word "Magnum" when it comes to cartridge designations. His little .257-caliber Scramjet® takes a 100-grain bullet and blasts it out of the barrel at 3,721 fps, producing 2,722 foot-pounds of energy. Likewise, the .284-caliber Firebird® launches a 140-grain bullet at 3,687 fps, churning up 4,372 foot-pounds of energy. The .308-caliber Warbird® spits a 150-grain projectile at a muzzle velocity of 3,775 fps, with 4,372 foot-pounds of energy. And the .338-caliber Titan® blasts a 200-grain bullet out of the barrel at 3,450 fps, generating an awe-inspiring 5,287 foot-pounds of energy. Of course, there are other bullet weights in each caliber that exhibit over-the-top ballistics. The calibers that I've mentioned here are only part of the long magnum line of Lazzaroni proprietary cartridges. Equally as impressive are an additional grouping of short, fat case designs. No, you can't walk into any sporting goods store or gun shop and purchase one of these whiz-bang rifles, let alone some shells. If you're

Blackpowder Bores

The three most popular frontloader bores are the .45, .50 and .54 caliber. The .45 caliber is strictly a deer and pronghorn antelope bore, while both the .50 and .54 bore are capable of handling any North American big game animal. Since the same bullet weights are available in the two larger bores, both are equally as effective in the field. Using similar weight projectiles, the .50 caliber has a slight advantage in penetration, while the .54 caliber has marginally better frontal impact. Patched balls, conical bullets and sabot-encased bullets are available for blackpowder shooters. Balls are usually faster, but they lack the terminal performance of a bullet. A wide range of bullet designs are available for the frontloader. And the recent development of pelletized Pyrodex® makes loading an easy chore. Drop the required number of pellets down the bore, seat your bullet of choice, slip a new cap in place and you're ready to go. It's as simple as that. Hunting with a smokepole is lots of fun. With special hunting seasons, often during the rut, it can be the best of all big game hunting experiences.

interested in maximum velocity, accuracy and quality control, then one of John Lazzeroni's creations might just be right for you.

The final shot: This review of calibers for North American big game has been extensive in its depth. However, other chamberings could have also been included. The firms of SSK Industries, Dakota Arms, North American Shooting Systems and A-Square all have impressive proprietary cartridge developments. For my part, I've been more than satisfied with the performance of any number of standard domestic calibers. The ability of the revered .30-06 Springfield on any big game species is difficult to duplicate. And what better deer chambering and antelope chambering is there than the .270 Winchester? When it comes to high velocity, my interest stops at the .264 and .338 Winchester Magnums. Moreover, the extra few yards of meaningful trajectory that other magnums provide just doesn't seem to be worth all the added recoil and muzzle blast.

So there you have it! In the final evaluation, it isn't the caliber that's important. You're the person behind the trigger and that's where it all begins and ends. If you can't hit what you're aiming at, then all the pool-table-flat-velocity and near-nuclear energy doesn't mean a thing. And that, my friend, is what it all boils down to.

Shotgun Slugs

The development of shotguns for big game hunting has come a long way over the past twenty years. Even with good open sights, smoothbore big game hunters of bygone eras couldn't count on much accuracy out of Foster-type slugs beyond 75 yards. Rifled shotgun barrels made a significant improvement in that performance. Furthermore, the ability to mount a scope directly over the bore was another shotgun enhancement. Enter the aerodynamic, sabot-encased shotgun projectile and things really got interesting. Using a modern shotgun designed especially for slug use, I've been able to achieve astonishing results at ranges exceeding 150 yards. And it isn't only a 12-gauge game anymore. Winchester Ammunition recently came out with a high-velocity 20-gauge slug that has been pure dynamite. In a recent field test, this 20-gauge slug was able to drop a sizeable wild boar at a measured distance of 160 yards. And similar results were seen when the slug was used on whitetail deer. In those jurisdictions that mandate the use of a shotgun for big game, no longer does the hunter have to feel like he's using an inferior firearm.

To a large extent, modern optics influence where and how we hunt big game.

BIG GAME OPTICS

Improvements in the design and manufacture of field optics over the last 50 years have made a real difference in how we hunt.

Looking back over the last half-century of big game hunting, the most visible difference between hunting camps of the 1950s and those of today is a widespread acceptance of optics. Without exception, any rifle purchased in the 1940s and 50s wore iron sights. Few, if any, were set up to accept scope mounts. To do so, one had to pay a gunsmith to have the receiver drilled and tapped.

One of the more popular scope mounts of that period allowed the user to pivot the scope out of the way when the need arose. A hinge on one side of the mount made the pivoting action a simple matter. One only had to

Photo by Durwood Hollis

Modern riflescopes are crafted from rust-free aluminum and titanium tubes and have internal windage and elevation adjustments.

Photo by Bushnell

Quality optics, like this Bushnell Elite™ variable 1.5-4.5x32 riflescope, have made a real difference in the way we hunt.

"unsnap" the scope from the retention points on top of the receiver mount, while it remained firmly contained in the mount rings. Once loose, the instrument could be rotated to the left side of the rifle receiver a full 180 degrees. This provided unobstructed access to the rifle's iron sights. Reportedly, the scope would return to its "zero" position when it was placed back into its original position on top of the receiver.

Of course, other "quick detachable" scope mounts also made their way to the market (some of which are still with us today). The reason for detachable, see-under or shoot-over scope mounts was the lack of trust in the optical sighting instruments of that day. All too often, condensation formed on the inside of optical lenses during cold weather. This necessitated keeping your rifle outside, rather than inside the warm confines of a lodge, vehicle or tent. If you weren't careful where you stored your rifle, it might just have a sheet of ice clinging tightly to it, making the action impossible to open until things thawed out. Just as bad, any amount of dew, rainwater or snow could freeze on the scope lenses overnight. And when you brought the rifle into a warm environment to thaw, the old bugaboo of internal scope condensation was right there to greet you. In light of all of these problems, it's easy to understand why hunters didn't trust their rifle scopes.

Photo by Durwood Hollis

Not only is the hunter's rifle equipped with a quality scope, he also is using a pair of binoculars.

Another difficulty early scope users encountered was the fact that scopes weighed entirely too much. The scope tube, most non-optical components and the mounts were made out of steel. A standard 8-pound turnbolt rifle, equipped with a scope, rifle sling and a full magazine of shells, could easily weigh 10 pounds—or more. Carrying one of those heavyweights was guaranteed to have you listing to one side like the Titanic after its encounter with the iceberg.

Another problem common to steel scopes was rust. Despite the moderate protection of a blued finish and reasonable care, most steel scopes eventually gained a little "character." To prevent tiny specks of rust accumulating on the finish, your scope had to be wiped down with an oily rag daily. Failure to perform this needed activity was a sure bet that the rust demons would pay you a visit.

Most early scopes provided only a set magnification. When variable magnification scopes finally appeared, the reticles (aiming points) often increased in size as the magnification was amplified. Even worse, the point-of-aim could shift considerably. These factors alone were enough to deter most hunters from acquir-ing one of the "new fangled" variables. And it would be years before optical engineers solved the problems inherent in the variable-power scope design.

Today, modern riflescopes and mounts are as tough as nails. I can remember watching a friend of mine come loose from the saddle, as his horse stumbled and fell down a steep slope. In the process, the horse rolled over his rifle at least once before everything came to a standstill. When it was safe to approach the animal, my companion, fearing the worst, pulled his rifle from the scabbard. Amazingly, both the rifle and scope looked unharmed. A quick check of the point-of-aim established that the rifle shot right where it did before the unfortunate mishap. Are modern scopes reliable? And can they handle the rigors of the hunt? You bet!

Despite all of the initial problems with riflescopes, some things haven't changed. The 4-power (4x magnification) scope is nearly as popular as it was a half century ago. Low magnification, fixed-power 2x and 3x scopes are still favored for close cover work. And fixed-power 6x scopes continue to be well-liked for open country deer and antelope hunting. Of course, significant improvements in variable-power scopes have

Photo by Bob Robb

In open country, an accurate rifle topped with a quality riflescope is paramount to success.

By using an extended eye relief objective, even pistol shooters can access the optical advantages inherent in a modern scope.

allowed those instruments to eclipse many fixed-power models in popularity. While the 4x scope remains the standard for most big game hunting venues, a 2-7x variable is identical in size and weight and offers target enhancement over a much wider range of magnification. For all of the same reasons, the 3-9x and 2.5-10x variables have gained in popularity over single-magnification, fixed-power models.

Fixed-power or variable: When you compare fixed-power and variable-power scopes, the differences are readily apparent. Fixed-power scopes are mechanically and optically less sophisticated and have fewer components than variable-power models. This relates directly to product development, raw material costs and manufacturing expense. The end result is seen at the retail point of purchase. Fixed-power scopes are more affordable than variable-power models. If you're on a tight budget (who isn't these days?), you're better off purchasing a top-of-the-line fixed-power scope, rather than selecting an inexpensive variable. This doesn't mean that a variable is inferior to a fixed-power. Just expect to pay more for the same quality in a scope that offers you a

range of magnification, over one that only provides a set magnification.

Even the point of manufacturing origin can influence the price of a scope. The price of a product made where skilled labor is less costly will, obviously be less than that of one made where the work force demands top wages. The same holds true for the cost of raw materials and manufacturing space. Import taxes, shipping costs and other fees can drive the cost of offshore products well beyond those of domestic origin. And this holds true whether or not that product is produced domestically or offshore. Quality optics are made in Europe, Asia, and here at home. The best values change from one year to the next. Rather than just accepting name recognition as indicative of quality and value, do a little comparison shopping. All manufacturers provide technical specifications of their optics, so read the fine print carefully.

Field of view: The diameter of the image (edge-to-edge), expressed in feet, transmitted through an optical instrument to the eye(s) is defined as the field-of-view. The greater the magnification, the narrower this field becomes. Conversely, as the magnification is

Photo by Redfield

Quality scope mounts, like these from Redfield, are critical to the maintenance of total optical alignment.

decreased, the field of view gets wider. A fixed-power scope has a set field of view. However, the same field of view seen through a variable scope will change in diameter depending on the magnification. The objective lens (the one farthest from the eye) can also play a role in the size of the field-of-view. In scopes of comparable magnification, the larger the objective lens will provide the greater the field of view.

How much magnification? Too much is just as bad as too little. Your selection of a scope must be based on two things: the useful trajectory of the caliber you'll be shooting and the range at which most targets can be expected. Calibers like .30-30 Win., .35 Rem., .348 Win., .375 Win. (not the magnum), .38-55 Win., .444 Marlin, .450 Marlin Mag. and the .45-70 are most useful under 150 yards. With the exception of low-light shooting situations (early morning, late evening, dark timber), iron sights are perfectly adequate for all of these calibers. Scope selection should not exceed 2x or 3x, or at the most, 4x magnification. Any greater target enhancement will only tempt you to exceed the ballistic performance envelope of your rifle.

The really big boomers, like the .416 Rem., .416 Rigby, .416 Wby. Mag., .458 Win. Mag., .460 Wby. Mag. and the .470 Nitro Express are considered dangerous-game calibers. Big-bore rifles are meant to break bone, churn up insides and divert charging animals at relatively close range. While several are capable of handling shots out to 250 yards, I don't know any professional hunter who would allow a client to shoot at something big and nasty that far away. Certainly, 2x and 3x magnification is enough for dangerous game. When used on African plains game, big bears and even elk, a scope of 4x magnification is

suitable, with any of the low-power variables offering greater flexibility in mixed cover.

Calibers like the .243 Win., 6mm Rem., .25-06 Rem., .257 Roberts, .270 Win., .280 Rem., .30-06 Spfd., .300 Win. Mag., .338 Win. Mag., and several others, are all capable of dealing with targets out to 300 yards. If you shoot one of these calibers, then select a scope that effectively handles the entire useful trajectory curve of that chambering. In my experience, a 4x scope doesn't allow precise bullet placement much beyond 200 yards. While a fixed-power 6x scope might be a better choice for long shots, it's too much magnification for close cover. The solution to this predicament is the variable-power scope. Certainly, the 2-7x and 3-9x variables are ideally suited to any of these calibers. And a 1-6x variable might be the hot ticket should you have to hunt aspen groves, dark timber or any other thick stuff.

This leaves us with the .264 Win. Mag., 7mm Rem. Mag., 7mm STW, Remington Ultra magnums, Weatherby magnums, the Lazzeroni chamberings and similar calibers. Here's where the 3-9x, 2.5-10x and the 4-16x variables are right at home on full-size rifles. If you own a rifle in one of these ultra-velocity chamberings, then it probably deserves all the glass up top you can handle. After all, why come to the party and then not be able to dance? This doesn't mean that I am an advocate of long-range shooting, especially when it's possible to close the gap. However, sometimes you just can't get close. In those instances, extra magnification can help you to put your bullet where it needs to be.

Magnification mastery: On one occasion, I watched through my binoculars as a hunter blundered into a nice mule deer buck at scant yardage. He

Photo by Aimpoint

Aimpoint revolutionized the optical sight market with their innovative "red dot" sights. Extremely useful anywhere the shooter needs rapid target acquisition.

Rubber-armored binoculars are built to withstand field abuse. Used day-in and day-out, this new generation of binoculars is the best of the best.

Photo by Durwood Hollis

snapped the rifle to his shoulder and the sound of hammer contact with the primer was heard. All of this didn't seem to affect the deer, who just stood looking at the orange-clad intruder. Cycling the bolt on his rifle two more times, the hunter kept up the barrage until he was out of shells. While he was reloading, the deer finally got tired of all the commotion and ran off. Curious, I made my way over to where the action had taken place.

"I don't know how that buck got away. My gun must be shooting off," the frustrated hunter exclaimed.

I noted that the hunter had a 4-12x variable mounted on his trusty bolt-action rifle. One quick glance at the scope told the story. The magnification adjustment sat on 12x. His sin? He had simply forgotten to turn the scope down to a lower setting. When he attempted to

shoot, he found it impossible to form an adequate target image. The high magnification kept his rifle bouncing on and off the target. On 12x magnification, any slight movement was bound to send his bullet whizzing off to points unknown. It was a hard lesson for him to learn, but one he will never forget.

If you own, or are contemplating the purchase of a variable-power scope, then magnification mastery is the key to effective operation. When you're afield, keep the scope set at its lowest magnification. If you have a close-range shooting opportunity, then you'll be prepared. On a longer range target, you can increase the magnification as needed to provide an adequate target picture. In most cases, you won't have to hurry a long shot. You'll have time to crank up the magnification, get a stable rest and make the shot. Enough said!

Reticles: The aiming point within the scope's eyepiece is the reticle. This usually consists of two very fine lines that intersect in the precise middle of the field of view. This reticle, or crosshairs as they are known, can take several forms. Varmint and target shooters want the thinnest reticle possible. European hunters, who legally can hunt at night, generally like a thick reticle that is easily seen in low light. Similarly, those who pursue dangerous game also prefer a reticle that can help them with target acquisition.

All the rest of us seem to prefer what has come to be called the "plex" reticle. This consists of a pair of moderately coarse crosshairs, which step-down in thickness just before they intersect, forming a precise aiming point. The thinner section of crosshairs covers (subtends) the target at a known distance, usually 100 yards. This data is published by the manufacturer and allows the hunter to use the fine section of crosshairs as a makeshift rangefinder in the field. For example, if the thin crosshairs subtends 4 inches at 100 yards, at three times that distance the same section will subtend 16 inches. The kill zone on an average deer is about 18 inches from top to bottom. If that zone fits within the section of fine crosshairs, then the buck is about 300 yards away. All of this isn't quite as precise as it sounds, but it can help you estimate the distance from the scope to the target.

Other useful reticle configurations are standing post, point and crosshair, plain crosshairs, crosshairs and dot and a free-floating dot. The post, as well as the post and crosshair allow maximum visual acuity and an instantly accessible aiming point. Since the heavy post stands out against the aiming point, it draws the eye to the target without hesitation. In heavy cover, where running shots may be the norm, both the standing post and the post and crosshair are quite useful. Target and varmint shooters often favor reticles featuring plain crosshairs, crosshairs and a dot, or a free-floating dot. These reticles provide the ultimate in a precise aiming point. However, the shooter must have enough time to form an appropriate target image. At the bench, or while varmint shooting, the aiming point is extremely small. A heavier reticle might cover up too much of the target. When I am shooting ground squirrels, I want to see the squirrel, not just a fuzzy outline. When it's big game I am after, then give me all the reticle possible.

In the mist of Alaska's coastal islands, this hunter uses his binoculars to cut through the fog.

Photo by Bob Robb

For viewing distant objects, binoculars are an essential component of the hunt.

Most of the time an animal doesn't just stand there and let you dope the wind, estimate range, and then compensate for bullet drop.

Aiming point adjustment: Positioned in the center of the scope body are two aiming point adjustments— one on top, the other on the side. To prevent unintentional movement, removable caps are used to cover the adjustment knobs/screws. The topmost adjustment is used to move the elevation (up-and-down), the side adjustment controls windage (side-to-side).

When you mount the scope on the rifle, the scope must be aligned with the bore. "Bore sighting," as it is referred to, is the process of aligning the scope aiming point and the bore. You can do this yourself by using a boresighting device that inserts into the muzzle of the rifle. When the device is in place, a grid pattern can be seen through the scope. To bore sight the scope, simply adjust the elevation and windage until it is appropriately centered on the bore sight grid. When you go to the range, prior bore sighting will most likely put you on the target at 100 yards. Once you're on the target, then it's only a matter of using the elevation and windage adjustments to get the rifle shooting where it is aimed.

To adjust the aiming point, move the elevation and windage as needed. For example: If your bullet strikes the target low and right, the reticle should be adjusted up and left. Since the adjustments are incremental (one "click" of the adjustment usually equals 1/4 inch of bullet movement at 100 yards), the use of grid-style targets makes adjustment quick and easy. Once you've got your rifle shooting where you want it, replace the adjustment point covers and you're ready to go hunting.

Eye focus adjustment: The eyepiece (lens closest to the eye) of some scopes can be adjusted to compensate for the differences in the focal length of the eye. To accomplish this, mount the rifle to your shoulder, loosen the objective lens locking ring and turn the objective bell until the image is clear and sharp. When things look right, tighten the locking ring on the objective bell.

Lens coatings: No matter how precisely ground the finish on a piece of glass, it will still reflect a certain amount of light. The reflective loss degrades the image transmitted through the glass. Riflescopes have a number of glass lens elements. When light enters the objective lens (the one farthest away from the eye), some of

Photo by Bushnell

These rubber-armored Bausch & Lomb (now Bushnell) Elite binoculars are typical of what quality optics should be.

that light is lost through reflection. A loss of approximately 5 percent at each atmosphere-to-glass surface can be expected. When you multiply that by the total number of such surfaces within the lens system, the total can amount to significant image degradation. To optimize the amount of light transmitted through the scope, the manufacturer applies a thin anti-reflective or dielectric coating to the surface of all atmosphere-to-lens surfaces. This is an expensive process, but necessary if the scope is to be useful in low-light environments (early morning, late evening and in deeply shaded areas).

Scope finish: Many scope manufacturers offer a choice of gloss, matte or brushed aluminum finishes on their products. Certainly, the finish on a scope doesn't contribute to its optical quality. The only reason to offer these choices is to match the finish of the firearm you're using. Only one finish—a moderate gloss—was offered for years. Then the custom makers started producing rifles with matte finishes. As a response to demand, scope manufacturers jumped on the bandwagon. More recently, stainless steel rifles have become popular. A scope with a gloss or matte finish doesn't look out of place on a stainless rifle. However, one with a plain or brushed aluminum finish is thought by some to be a better selection. It's all a matter of personal taste.

Binoculars: Like riflescopes, the use of binoculars wasn't all that widespread in hunting camps 50 years

ago. Even where they could be found, only instruments of moderate magnification were used. High-magnification binoculars (10x, 12x and 15x) were thought to be too big and heavy for consideration as "hunting" instruments. All of this has changed over the years as developments in optics have evolved.

The advent of affordable, high quality binoculars has made a dynamic impact on the hunting market. At the same time, interest in using binoculars as more than just viewing instruments began to develop. Some individuals discovered that locating game with binoculars was better than tramping all over the countryside. As this success became manifest, others began to look at binoculars as something more than just a weight around their necks.

Binoculars are nothing more than two individual monoculars joined along a shared axis. The joining of the monoculars allows the eyes to perceive the same viewed optical data simultaneously. This connection point between the monoculars allows the individual optical components up and down movement. This is done to compensate for the positioning of each individual's eyes. Furthermore, the joining of the separate monoculars provides an image that is far easier to perceive and with less eye strain.

Instrument configuration: Binoculars feature two different prism systems—offset and inline. The offset system uses a porro prism design. This is the most familiar instrument configuration and is easily identified by "Z" shape of each monocular half. The inline system uses a roof prism design and is characterized by straight monocular barrels.

The porro prism binoculars offer a wider range of tolerance when positioning the internal glass prisms in relation to one another. Greater latitude means less manufacturing cost and more affordable binoculars at the retail level. Conversely, internal prism-mounting tolerances within the straight monocular barrels of the roof prism design are extremely critical. The precise mounting of each prism adds to manufacturing cost and the ultimate retail price of the instrument. Additionally, the inline mounting of the prism results in a 10 to 12 percent reduction of ambient light transmission.

When comparing the two different instrument designs, a couple of important considerations emerge. Porro prism binoculars provide outstanding image resolution, excellent light transmission and a very affordable price. However, the offset monocular barrels add to the overall size and weight of these instruments. Image resolution and light transmission in roof prism binoculars is more than adequate for field use. Even though roof prism binoculars are more costly than comparable porro prism instruments, the smaller size and lighter weight are often seen as more important considerations.

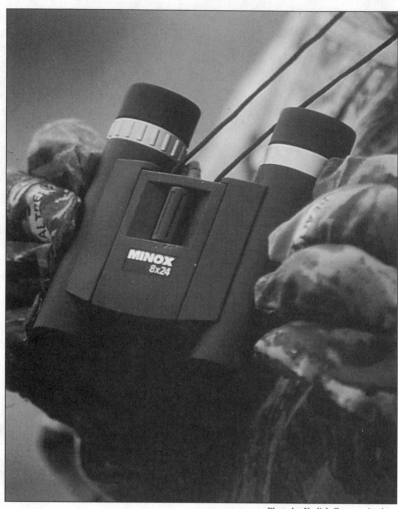

This pair of Minox 8x24 BR binoculars fit both your pocket and your budget.

Photo by Kodiak Communications

Lens coating: All of the same requirements for anti-reflective lens coating that apply to riflescopes also pertain to binoculars. This is a time-consuming and expensive process. The fewer lens surfaces that receive this treatment, the less time is spent in the production of a particular instrument. While the manufacturer may advertise binoculars as having "coated lenses," the coating may have only been applied to the surfaces of the external lenses. The rest of the air-to-glass lens surfaces within the prism system may be uncoated. The instrument may well wear an attractive price tag, but the viewed image will be significantly affected. When you select binoculars, look for the instruments that have "fully coated lenses." This statement alone provides a measure of assurance that all air-to-glass lens surfaces have received the necessary dielectric coating.

Exit pupil: The amount of light transmitted through an instrument's prism system is dependent on the size of the exit pupil. This can be determined by dividing the amount of magnification into the diameter of the objective lens. The exit pupil is the resultant number. Using a pair of 7x35 binoculars as an exam-ple, you simply divide the magnification of seven into the 35mm objectives and arrive at 5mm as the size of the exit pupil. The pupil of the human eye can contract to as small as 2mm and expand as large as 7mm in diameter. This happens naturally to allow the eye to formulate a visual picture. Early in morning and late in the evening, the pupil of the eye will expand to 5mm, or a little wider. If your binoculars don't provide a corresponding exit pupil, insufficient light will be transmitted through the prism system. The resultant image will be dim and unclear. This is the reason why binoculars with small diameter objectives (8x20, 9x25, etc.) and correspondingly small exit pupils are not very useful in low light. Furthermore, the field of view in these instruments is extremely small. These pocket-size binoculars may be just fine for casual use in full daylight conditions, but they are not adequate for serious work at the edge of day. The most optimal exit pupil is about 5mm in diameter (i.e. 7x35, 10x50, 15x60, etc.). Even if more light than needed is transmitted through the prism system, your own pupils will constrict to compensate. The bottom line in this discussion is that more exit pupil is better than less!

Focusing systems: Three types of focusing systems—central, individual eyepiece and pre-set—are found in binoculars. Central-focus binoculars use a rounded focus adjustment projection in the center of the instrument. This focus adjustment control is connected to a worm gear that moves both eyepieces simultaneously. To focus the instrument, the focus adjustment control is rotated. An additional adjustment may be found on one eyepiece to compensate for any minor differences between each of the viewer's eyes.

Individual-focus adjustment binoculars feature an adjustment on each individual eyepiece. To bring the instrument into clear view, the user must adjust each eyepiece individually. This helps keep moisture out and is often found on binoculars used in marine environments.

Pre-set focus binoculars have no provisions for focus adjustment. The instrument has been designed by the manufacturer to be useful over a wide range of viewing distances. When you're in the saddle, the continual movement of the horse makes it difficult to focus binoculars effectively. The same thing is true when attempting to use binoculars from an idling vehicle. In these instances, binoculars of the pre-set focus variety can be heaven sent.

Binocular selection: What kind of binoculars you select is dependent primarily on your hunting style. For many years, I used a pair of tiny binoculars that easily slipped into my breast pocket. Since most of my hunting took place deep in the backcountry, those little wonders suited my purposes. The binoculars were light and easy to carry, but lacked adequate light transmission. Like many who eventually come to realize the importance of optical data, in time I gravitated from compact to full-size binoculars.

When it comes to hunting, there's room for nearly every kind of binoculars. I carry a pair of pre-set binoculars in the truck and on horseback. Tiny pocket-sized binoculars are never far from my reach when stalking. Compact binoculars of moderate magnification are about right for heavy cover. For serious glassing, tripod-mounted, high magnification (12x50, 15x60) binoculars are the only instrument that can do the job.

Another feature of binoculars that deserves consideration is protective rubber armor. A textured rubberized covering over the instrument body protects it from

Situated above a broad valley, this hunter uses a spotting scope to evaluate the trophy quality of a distant animal.

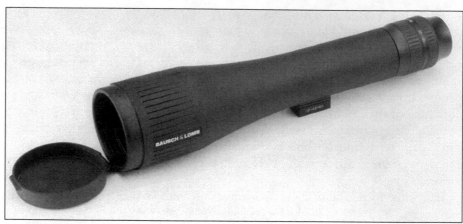

Those who hunt sheep and mountain goats rely on a spotting scope for trophy evaluation. Likewise, antelope hunters will find this type of scope useful under some situations.

Photo by Bushnell

most shock. If this feature is available, make sure your binoculars are so equipped. Eyecups that can be rolled down, or rotated in and out, to accommodate glasses also make real sense. This will allow you to position your eyes closer to the eyepiece when you're wearing sunglasses or corrective lenses.

Carrying binoculars: All binoculars come with neck straps. The first thing you'll want to do is throw away any neck strap that is narrower than about 1-1/2 to 2 inches in width. Narrow neck straps, even with lightweight binoculars, will rub your neck raw. A better choice is to replace the neck strap with a fabric-covered, wide neoprene rubber strap. Most camera shops carry a selection of these straps and they're well worth the money. The wider strap distributes the weight over a wider area and soft material eliminates chafing. Small to medium-size binoculars can be tucked into your shirt or open coat. Larger binoculars can be slung under your arm, or slipped into a pack. Having a pair of binoculars banging up and down on your chest isn't fun, so you might even consider some type of binocular restraint system. Several are available, so pick the one that fits your frame comfortably.

Using binoculars: Get to your glassing site well before dawn. This may well mean exiting a warm sleeping bag while other hunters in camp are still fast asleep. You may have to eat a cold breakfast, drive to your chosen hunting location in the dark and climb the slopes with the aid of a flashlight. All of this is necessary if you want to get where you need to be before first light.

When you find an adequate glassing position, settle in quickly with as little noise and disturbance as possible. Some type of foam pad will make the ground more comfortable. A back rest (rock, tree, stump, whatever) is something else you might want to consider. Don't position yourself directly on top of a ridge or other location where you'll be silhouetted against the horizon. When your outline is visible, any movement will

attract the attention of game. A better position is just below the top of a ridge, or somewhere else that you'll blend into the terrain.

Serious game detection with binoculars takes time—lots of time. I've been with professional big game hunting guide, Duwane Adams, when he has spent the entire day glassing from one location. Should a client get bored and want to move, Duwane is apt to remind the client in no uncertain terms that he's working. I never give up glassing an area until all of the visual data is exhausted. Even then, the entire procedure is repeated over and over again. Animals get up, move about and the visual data changes. Even the position of the sun can illuminate what had been hidden by shade only moments before.

After the first couple of hours of daylight, a heat mirage will begin to reflect from the ground. The heat waves from this illusion will prevent extended-distance viewing. This means that initially you'll want to use your binoculars at the extreme edge of the magnification potential. I've spotted game with my binoculars more than a mile away from my glassing location. While the opportunity to hunt that game may not be immediately available, that visual data may come in handy later on in the afternoon, or on the following day. When you use your binoculars, place a mental grid on the view area. Try to visualize looking for a single individual seated in a set of bleachers, on the other side of a football field. Start at the top of the imaginary bleachers, then glass from left to right, slowly looking along the entire length of that row. When you've finished with the top make-believe row, then drop down to the next level and glass from right to left. Repeat the process over and over again until you reach the bottom. Carefully move through the various levels of vegetation by using the focus adjustment to work your way visually through each layer. Take your time. Productive work with binoculars isn't a race.

When it first gets light, start glassing the south, southeast and southwest slopes. Visually pick apart anything that looks promising. While you may find game standing out in the open, more likely what you find are bits and pieces. Since everything in nature grows straight up, a horizontal line deserves careful examination. Likewise, any reflected light deserves scrutiny. And even the slightest movement in the viewing area should draw your attention. Look for anything that is out of place, off-color and not easy to visually comprehend. Keep looking until you determine the nature of what you're seeing. Whatever it is that caught your eye might be what you're looking for.

Once the sun has cleared the horizon and starts its trek towards mid-morning, it's time to shift your glassing efforts to the north, northwest and northeast slopes. Here's where real glassing determination kicks in. Since these slopes usually catch the greatest amount of moisture, the vegetation can be thick. This is just the kind of habitat that game likes to use for bedding areas. If you find what you're looking for, then you have lots of time to formulate a stalk. And if you can't get in position to make a shot, back off and try again the next day. If not disturbed, most animals will bed repeatedly in the same general area.

When the afternoon shadows start to lengthen, game will begin to drift out into the open. You'll want to glass the edge of cover thoroughly right up to dark. Don't give up early. Some times things develop in the very last minutes of daylight. Remember, persistence is the name of this game. When you begin to trust your binoculars, instead of putting all of your confidence in boot leather, then you'll become a real hunter.

Safety considerations: A riflescope isn't a pair of binoculars, so don't use it as such. I can well recall an occasion when a fellow hunter came over the opposite ridge and noticed my blaze orange hat. He immediately pointed his rifle right at me, looked through his scope and then waved. I didn't like the idea of a loaded rifle being pointed directly at me. Needless to say, when I encountered the same guy later on, I let him know my feelings on the subject. Using his riflescope as binoculars was an unsafe, stupid move on his part. Don't you be guilty of the same thing!

Protect your investment: Optics are costly, so watch how you handle them. Clean the lenses by using specially formulated lens cleaner and lens paper (available at camera shops). Blow off any dust or debris, then moisten a couple sheets of lens paper with lens cleaner (not window cleaner) and lightly wipe the lens clean. If you want to scratch the lenses on your optics, then just keep on spitting on them and wiping them with your shirttail. If not, then use the right lens cleaning gear.

Final word: Quality optics are expensive. Cheap companions, cheap cigars and cheap gear are things to avoid. Cheap is cheap. Quality is something that you won't find in bargain-basement optics. So go all the way and buy the best you can afford. You won't regret that purchase.

Photo by Durwood Hollis

Wool outerwear, a knit cap and insulated boots are this hunter's choices for cold weather wear.

THE RIGHT CHOICES: CLOTHES AND BOOTS

Clothes and boots may not make the hunter, but they make a difference!

The prospect of being subjected to adverse weather conditions—including unbearable temperature extremes—with unsuitable apparel is just one of the many challenges of hunting. I've found myself in this situation—more than once. To make my point clear, let me share with you a couple of my poor choices in outerwear.

In the middle of the summer, a friend and I decided to embark on a wild boar hunt. The area we selected was a range of rugged hills that were foreboding at best. Wearing our usual tightly woven cotton jeans and smartly tailored long-sleeved shirts (hunters have to look good), the two of us set out

Photo by Durwood Hollis

These elk hunters are wearing full-length waxed cotton dusters for rain protection.

This bowhunter's outer layer is a hooded camo outfit made out of quiet Saddle Cloth®.

Photo by Images Group

well before daylight. A couple of hours past dawn the ambient temperature was already well past the 90-degree mark. We ran into hogs early on in the hunt and both of us managed to score. It took about two hours to bone out the meat, load our packs and head back to the truck. Along the way, we both consumed two quarts of water each. The fact that we were packing out 50 pounds of boned-out wild pork each didn't help the situation. By the time our vehicle came into sight, we were drenched in sweat and thoroughly overheated. If we had been wearing lightweight, open-weave, loose-fitting clothing, the movement of

air would have allowed perspiration to evaporate quickly. This alone would have provided an enhanced cooling effect. We just hadn't given enough thought to our choice of clothing.

On another occasion, I set off on an elk hunt fully prepared for inclement weather. Carried in my pack was some of the best high-tech rain gear money could buy. When storm clouds appeared, it didn't bother me in the slightest. After all, I was prepared. When the storm reached biblical proportions, however, everything started to leak. Within minutes, my clothing was wet. Once my cotton jeans and flannel shirt were soaked, they quickly became instruments of hypothermia. It didn't take long to feel more like a cold, wet dog, than a successful elk hunter (I did manage to take a 6x6 bull). As you can imagine, returning to camp was a very uncomfortable experience. I was so cold that it took nearly an hour in front of a roaring campfire and hot meal for me to stop shivering. Where I made my mistake was not testing my rain gear before I needed it. Once the integrity of my protective outerwear was compromised, things went from bad to worse.

In both of these instances, my own poor choice of clothing and protective outerwear nearly put me in the hospital—it could have killed me. The tightly woven fabrics and a tailored look might have been fashionable, but lighter weight material and a looser fit would have been more suitable for hot weather. Nothing will put you out of the game faster than overheating. Recent accounts of sports deaths point to the fact that core body temperature cannot exceed certain parameters without resulting in dire consequences. Just as compromising, untested rain gear combined with cotton clothing was another poorly conceived idea. As I learned the hard way, confidence in advertising hype won't keep you dry. Mix inadequate rain gear and wet clothing with plummeting temperatures and you can have a disaster. Simply put, your choice of clothing and footwear is all-important to survival in the outdoors.

Layering: One of the most important outdoor apparel lessons is how to wear your clothing in layers. This is as critical to those who hunt in hot weather, as it is when the mercury is falling. Pronghorn antelope

Photo by Filson

Wool pants, like these from Filson, are warm when wet and as "tough as nails."

Photo by Filson

When the weather turns cold, your first layer of protection should be long underwear.

use body hair to release body heat, or trap warmth. When the hair is erect and open, internal heat is easily dissipated. When the hair is held tight to the skin, body heat warms the trapped air, which serves as insulation. Layering works in a similar manner. Multiple articles of clothing allow you to take off, or add, as needed to maintain an even body temperature. It's as simple as that!

When it's hot, mesh undergarments combined with a lightweight shirt and trousers can promote increased air movement across your skin. When you perspire, that air movement allows the moisture to evaporate. The evaporative effect is your own personal air-conditioning system. When evening comes and the sun goes down, the addition of a light jacket serves to constrict air movement. This acts as a form of insulation, helping your body warm the contained air.

Internal body heat management in cold weather can be accomplished just as easily with additional layers of clothing. In the predawn hours, you'll probably need to wear everything you own—including a

A medium weight, long-sleeve shirt can handle broad temperature extremes.

Photo by Filson

heavy jacket or coat. As the daytime temperature moves upward, or your level of activity increases, articles of clothing can be removed one piece at a time. When the mercury starts to drop, or you slow down, a reverse layering technique can be employed.

Underwear: Beginning with the articles of clothing that are closest to the skin, your selection of underwear can facilitate cooling, or serve to retain body heat. Special fabrics, that move perspiration from the skin to the outside where it quickly evaporates, are designed to prevent heat build-up. Hot-weather hunters will find that this is essential for core temperature management. Underwear made for hot weather is the best choice for comfort on the trail when temperatures soar.

If cold weather is on the docket, then long underwear is the way to go. Even hunting in an early season, you'd be surprised how fast the temperature can

Photo by Filson

This Filson Double Mackinaw wool coat has lots of pockets and a collar large enough to keep your neck warm.

drop once the sun is down. Cotton long underwear may be priced attractively, but it absorbs and holds perspiration. Once cotton gets wet, it just stays damp. And when it's wet, it's like a built-in refrigeration system! Interestingly, silk long underwear is lighter than cotton, dries quickly and is extremely warm. Other choices in fabrics are wool/cotton blends, synthetics and lightweight fleece. Long underwear is made in a wide variety of weights, so choose the one that best suits your level of physical activity. Since long underwear can get a bit funky after a few days of constant wear, buy two sets so you'll have a change. A final reminder: Dark colored underwear will hide the grime of hunting camp better than solid white.

Pants: Hunting trousers are one of the most important clothing choices you can make. Cotton jeans are *de rigueur* for Western hunts and for more reasons than just fashion. Jeans are comfortable and they wear like iron. The only drawback is that the fabric can make a lot of noise in the brush and it absorbs moisture like a sponge. Once wet, it can take cotton jeans a long time to dry. Even worse, the evaporative effect can be bone-chilling. Modern fabrics,

In addition to a complete camo outfit, this bow hunter is wearing knee-length rubber boots to keep his trail scent-free.

Photo by Images Group

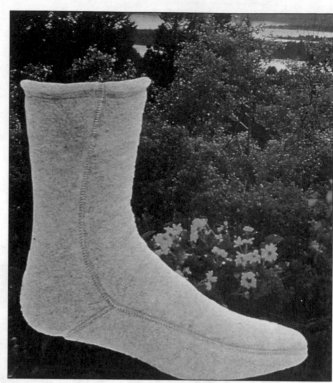

*When it comes to maximum foot comfort,
it's hard to beat fleece socks.*

Photo by Wyoming Wear

like Saddle Cloth®, have brought jeans to a new level of comfort and quietness. Add a fleece or flannel lining and you're ready for even extreme temperatures. Tight-fitting jeans may be the height of fashion in the city, but in the outdoors you'll want as much room as possible. When selecting a pair of hunting jeans, look for those styles that feature "relaxed" or "loose" fit. And a zippered fly, rather than one that buttons, is easier to deal with when an emergency arises (if you know what I mean).

Photo by Filson

*Lugs and "bobs" are the best combination
for hunting boot soles.*

When it's hot, make mine a wide brim, woven straw hat.

Photo by Durwood Hollis

Fleece trousers are another option, especially for bowhunters who are looking for the ultimate in quiet clothing. But fleece isn't as tightly woven as wool. Without a windproof liner, or something worn underneath, even a gentle breeze can pass right through the fabric. This isn't a problem for early-season hunts, but later on in the year it can make a difference. One drawback to this fabric, fleece isn't as tough as cotton denim or wool. One good fall and you can tear a knee out of a pair of fleece trousers easily. However, it is extremely quiet. This alone can be the overriding reason for its selection.

Wool trousers and cold weather are made for each other. Wool is tough as nails and even when wet it's still warm. Not everyone likes the feel of wool against his or her skin, but wearing long underwear prevents most direct contact. Since wool shrinks when washed, most woolens must be dry-cleaned. Some new wool blends can be machine washed, however, which eliminates all of the usual special care considerations. When you're in the market for a pair of wool trousers, look for the ones that offer this easy care feature. I've owned a pair of wool Malone pants for the better part of 40 years. And even though rough treatment should have long since destroyed them, they are still in good shape (no holes or tears). The initial cost of those trousers was more than I could afford at the time. Factored out over the number of years that I've own them, however, they turned out to be a bargain. Wool trousers are still expensive (what isn't these days?). If your funds are tight, then check out your local surplus store for the best buy in new or slightly used military-issue wool trousers.

Shirts: Shirts of all fabrics, colors and styles are available for outdoor wear. I am a fan of long-sleeved shirts because they offer protection to forearms, yet the sleeves can be rolled up when it gets warm outside. Pockets are important, just make sure they feature reliable closures. The outdoors isn't a place to be bound up by a tight-fitting shirt, so leave the tailored look at home. Another important feature is a shirttail long enough to stay tucked into your pants.

All the same fabric features that are important considerations with trousers are equally as significant when selecting a shirt. When it's hot, light cotton or a specially-formulated synthetic is the right choice. Broad temperature extremes will dictate medium-weight cotton, fleece or wool shirts. And the most extreme weather is the place for a shirt made out of a heavyweight, wind-resistant fabric.

Pull-over or vest? The next layer in hunting apparel should be either a pullover or a vest. The long sleeves of a pullover will provide added warmth to the arms and shoulders. And a buttoned neck opening can offer a measure of heat regulation. Even nothing more than a warm sweater or sweatshirt is a good addition to your outdoor clothing selection. A vest is designed

This successful whitetail hunter wears insulated leather gloves to keep his hands warm.

Photo by Durwood Hollis

Photo by Durwood Hollis

In addition to his wool outer wear, leather chaps and pac boots, outfitter and guide, Tim Doud also wears a warm neck gaiter.

to provide warmth to the body core, while offering maximum movement and ventilation. Lots of pockets, including a large back pocket, can come in handy for carrying hunting essentials. And if the vest is blaze orange, then it meets most state safety requirements. I often use both a pullover and a vest together. Each one is yet another layer that can be taken off, or put on as the need dictates.

Jacket or coat? Jackets are usually lighter than coats and may be all you need for most hunting venues—except the most extreme situations. When you make a selection, be sure that it's quiet, roomy enough to cover several layers of clothing and has lots of outside pockets (including hand warmer pockets). Waist length is more comfortable if you have to sit in a vehicle or ride horseback. Likewise, a flap-covered, two-way zippered front closure will allow you to open your outerwear from the top, or bottom, as desired. A collar large enough to turn up

and cover the neck is another design feature that shouldn't be overlooked. And extra material in the elbows will prevent rips and tears should you suffer an accidental fall.

Footwear: More hunts are ruined because of bad boots than anything else. Once you have a flat tire on one of your two wheels, the game's over. Avoid cheap boots like a jug of inexpensive wine. How much should you spend on a pair hunting boots? Expect that purchase to set you back the better part of a week's pay. Furthermore, you might even have to buy a couple of different pairs of boots. The last time I checked, there were five pairs in my hunting gear. And that's just for starters!

There is a plethora of boot materials, designs and configurations. If you hunt in the tundra of the North Country, then you'll need a pair of ankle-fit, waterproof hip boots. Knee-high rubber boots are a solid choice for those hunting anywhere near standing water. And where mud and snow are part of the picture, rubber is right at home. Rubber also works to keep you from spreading man-stink all over the place.

Leather boots are always a good choice for relatively dry hunting environments. I say that because it's hard to keep your feet dry in leather boots when it's wet outside. Even the best leather waterproofing will eventually give out in a torrential downpour. Moisture barriers integrated into boot construction are helpful. After your boots get scuffed and dirty, I wouldn't count this particular technology as completely reliable. When rain is in the forecast, then rubber-bottom pacs are a better choice. And I don't

mean what you might select for a weekend at the ski resort. Hunting pacs are made specifically for serious hiking. The kind with removable inner liners is the one to buy. While you're at it, get an extra pair of liners. The liners will absorb moisture, so they need to be changed daily. Leather, synthetic materials, or any combination thereof can be found in a variety of boot offerings. Just remember, there's no substitute for quality.

The important part of boot selection is fit. It's always a good idea to purchase your boots a half size larger than street shoes. You don't want your feet

Whatever you wear, make sure it's the very best. This plaid outfit from Woolrich Woolens is just that.

Photo by Images Group

sliding around inside the boots, but a little extra room is a good thing. This will allow you to wear two pairs of socks. Just as significant, a little extra space will save your toes from hammering into the boots when hiking downhill. Other features like lacing hooks, rather than grommets, will eliminate the tedium of getting into and out of your boots. Furthermore, I've had enough problems with broken leather laces to last a lifetime. Long ago, I changed over to nylon bootlaces. The nylon material outlasts the best leather lacing many times over. You'll experience more trouble keeping nylon laces tied, but that's what double knots are all about. Double-knotting boot-laces is a small price to pay.

Boot soles are another footwear consideration. Lug soles are the ultimate ground-grippers and will keep you upright in tough terrain. When the ground gets wet, however, the same lugs can load-up with mud and snow. After that, you'll feel like the Frankenstein monster—all boot and no brains! My wet-weather footwear has soles with a combination of lugs on the outside and rounded "bobs" on the interior. The outer rim of lugs is just the ticket to help my boots bite into the ground. And the smooth, rounded interior portion of the sole eliminates clinging mud and snow.

Socks: You'll need at least one pair of socks for every day in the field. I usually carry a fresh pair along with me in my pack. When you wear boots, your feet can take a beating. You'd be surprised how refreshing it can be to change socks midday. Cotton socks might be great at the gym, but they aren't worth spit inside a pair of boots. Even the thickest pair of cotton socks will pick up foot moisture quickly. Once they're wet, cotton socks can become very hard. Hard, wet socks are a prescription for blisters. A synthetic blend, wool or fleece, is a better choice in sock materials. I like a wool blend because the material is resilient even after hours of use. And wool socks retain heat better than most. Recently, I've been wearing some fleece socks by Wyoming Wear (P.O. Box 3127, Jackson, WY 83001, 800/996-9327) that provide an excellent protective barrier between tender feet and the inside of my boots. The fleece easily wicks moisture to the outside where it can evaporate, so my feet stay dry. This material is the optimum in keeping my feet warm in cold weather and cool in hot. The material dries faster than cotton, wool or even acrylic. And I've found fleece to be softer and far more comfortable than any other sock material. When you purchase boot socks, get prepared for the expense. Good socks cost real money. Don't be surprised when the price for five pairs leaves little change from a $100 bill.

Belt, suspenders, or both? No matter how great the food is in hunting camp, I tend to lose weight after a few days. The up at 4 a.m., hike all day, then barely make it into bed by midnight routine is a real calorie-burner. After a while, there aren't enough holes in my belt to take up the slack in my trousers. I can recall one time when my pants got so loose I had a difficult time keeping them from falling down around my ankles. To solve this problem, I've taken to wearing suspenders in addition to a belt. When it comes to belts, just any old strip of leather or webbing won't do! Select a belt that fits the complete width of the belt loops on all of your hunting pants. A wider belt will handle the extra weight of a knife sheath, an ammunition holder or whatever else you decide to hang on it. The addition of a pair of suspenders (extra wide) can shift some of the weight off the belt to your shoulders. Suspenders might get a few laughs in the office, but in hunting camp they are the height of fashion and practicality.

Headgear: Some type of hat is essential for any kind of outdoor activity—particularly hunting. In hot weather a bill cap can keep the sun out of your eyes. A full-brim hat will do the same thing, as well as protecting the back of your neck from sunburn. Add a mesh crown for air circulation and you'll be ready for action. When the temperature starts to drop, it's time to pull out an insulated cap, a hat, or a knit stocking cap. A cap or hat is your first line of defense in heat conservation. Your head is like a radiator. If you cover it up, it retains body heat. Uncover your head and the opposite effect will take place. Are you cold at night in your sleeping bag? Pull a stocking cap over your head and ears and you'll feel the change almost immediately. Are beads of sweat starting to dot your brow? Remove your cap or hat and feel the heat radiate from your head. Used in conjunction with layered clothing, headgear is an internal thermal regulator. Simply put something on your head, or take it off, as the need dictates. Personally, I am a fan of baseball-style caps, but your taste may be different. One thing I am sure of, there's a style, color and size to fit every hunter in the crowd.

Gloves or mittens? If there's one *bête noir* in the hunting field, then it has to be cold hands. Insulated leather, wool and leather combination, and neoprene are all good materials for hunting hand coverings. Rain and snow are both hard on leather. In the wet, wool can soak up water like a sponge. I like neoprene gloves (skin diving suit material) with a silk liner for most of my hunting needs. Not only do neoprene gloves fit better than most others, they are warm and don't inhibit trigger manipulation. Gloves can help keep your hands warm, but mittens are best for really cold temperatures. A pair of insulated mittens, with a covered slot across the palms for quick finger access, is my choice for really cold weather hunting. While

The multi-compartment containment found in this bag is ideal for packing hunting clothing and gear.

Photo by Michael of Oregon

you're at it, buy two pairs so you have a spare set. If you don't think that an extra pair is important, then just misplace one glove some day. About the time your fingers turn to ice, you'll appreciate the significance of an extra pair.

All the rest: There are a couple of other items that need to be included with your hunting apparel. A neckerchief is a small square of cloth that plays a large role in the scheme of things. Rolled up and tied around your neck, the neckerchief will prevent shirt collar chafing. Dunked into a cold stream and tied around your head, it will serve as a cooling mechanism. It can also become an emergency bandage, eyeglass cleaner and dust mask.

Some type of leash connection between your hat and shirt is really handy to have. Clip one end onto the back of your cap or hat, and the other end to your shirt collar and let the wind blow. Likewise, a neck strap for your glasses is good insurance against loss. More than once, my glasses have fallen out of a breast pocket. Once on the ground, or in the open cavity of a big game carcass, glasses just seem to disappear. I've lost enough expensive pairs to pay for the airfare to a Canadian hunting camp. A neck strap is attached to every pair of glasses that I now own—enough said!

A neck gaiter is something most folks haven't ever used. While you can turn your collar up, or hunker down into your coat to keep the cold off your neck, the best way to keep warm is wearing a knit gaiter around your neck. Nothing more than a tubular piece of knit material, a gaiter can be a real lifesaver when it gets frosty. While we're on the subject of gaiters, a pair of boot gaiters will keep the snow and dirt out of your boots and off your socks. An inexpensive addition to any hunter's outerwear, boot gaiters are useful in all sorts of weather.

The best you can afford: I learned a long time ago is that it doesn't pay to be a miser when it comes to the purchase of hunting equipment. If what you select isn't the very best, then expect it to fail at a critical moment. You're better off waiting until you can afford top quality, than settling for something from the bottom of the barrel. My advice: Buy the best you can afford. Believe me. Good stuff can last generations. I am still using some of the same hunting clothing that my father bought in the 1930s. Decades of use have only made it wear better. If one of your children asks, "When you're too old to hunt dad, can I have it?" right then and there, you know that you've purchased the very best.

It can make a difference: In the corporate world it is often said "clothes make the man." Clothing (footwear and headgear as well) may not make the hunter, but the right choices can make the hunt a lot more enjoyable. There are occasions when your choices in this realm can mean the difference between a successful hunt and a failure. Sometimes they can mean the difference between life and death. Chew on that a while. It won't take long for you to understand just how important those choices can be.

Pack for success: Show up at some remote trailhead with a set of hard-sided luggage and your guide is likely to give you a couple of plastic trash bags and ask that all of your stuff be re-packed. In saddle bags, the cramped quarters of a small airplane, a boat, or even in a vehicle, the fit-anywhere nature of soft-sided duffle bags is the way to go. The features to look for in this type of bag are: lots of outside zippered pockets, reinforced stitching and the use of heavy-duty materials (Cordura® nylon, Ballistic Cloth® or heavy canvas) throughout. Two medium-size duffles are better than one huge bag.

The best way to pack all your clothing and gear is put the big items (trousers, shirts, coat, jacket, rain gear, boots, etc.) in the inside main compartment. Accessories like binoculars and cameras should also be packed in the main compartment and well-cushioned with clothing. All your other apparel (underwear, socks, etc.) can be distributed throughout the outside zippered pockets. Any toiletries, insect repellant, gun oil, and similar materials should be enclosed in a separate plastic bags to protect your gear in case of leakage.

As a means of security, the zippered tabs on the outside pockets should be closed shut with plastic, self-locking ties like the kind electricians use to bind wire together. This will keep any inquisitive baggage handler honest. When you arrive at your final destination, simply cut the ties loose. Don't forget to pack some extra ties for the return trip home.

Check everything twice: Even though you may have packed your bags several days before departure, it's a good idea to re-check everything. You'd be surprised how easy it is to overlook something important. Finally, make sure all of your documents (hunting license and tag, game regulations, airplane tickets, travel visa, etc.) are packed where they won't get lost. Once you're on your way, leave all the problems of home at home. And whatever you do, have a good time!

Photo by Durwood Hollis

The buck is down and the hunt is finally over. It's now time for a sharp knife to come into play.

GAME GEAR: FIELD DRESSING, SKINNING, TROPHY WORK AND HOME BUTCHERING

After the shot, the fun's over and the real work begins.

When your bullet, ball or broadhead is effective in making target contact, then the paradigm shifts to meat care. And this topic is one that seldom receives the consideration it deserves. However, what you do after the shot has a direct influence on the quality of venison that reaches your table.

Use caution: Make sure the animal is dead. Early on in my big game hunting career, I shot a buck and had to follow it for about 200 yards. When I found the animal, it appeared quite dead. I unloaded my rifle, leaned it against a nearby tree and validated my deer tag. Then, I rolled up my sleeves and prepared to field dress the animal. When I reached down to turn the animal on its back, it suddenly sprang to its feet. It was obvious that the deer was barely alive, but alive enough to have one last shot of adrenalin. Luckily, I managed to avoid the sharp antler tines. Another bullet put an end to the matter, but the experience left me somewhat shaken.

Never assume that any big game animal is dead. Make sure. Approach the downed animal from behind and look for any movement. If no physical activity is noted, then reach forward with your rifle muzzle or the end of your bow and touch the open eyeball. Should the eye blink, then immediately back off and quickly dispatch the animal. Whatever you do, never attempt to

Photo by Durwood Hollis

You may have to move the animal a short distance to where it's easier to deal with the field care chores.

Prompt field dressing is necessary to prevent spoilage.

cut the throat of a live animal. Such an action is an invitation to personal injury. Attempt to handle the animal only when you are sure it is dead.

Take your time: After you've established that the animal has expired, unload your firearm and place it in a safe place. Bowhunters will need to secure their bow and arrows in a similar manner. Take out your license or game tag, validate it and follow any other regulations regarding tagging harvested game. Roll up your sleeves and remove your watch.

Get comfortable: Move the animal to an area where you can work comfortably, preferably in the shade. If the carcass cannot be moved, then you're going to have to make the best of your situation. If the kill site is a steep hillside, you might want to secure the carcass to a stationary object with some rope. I once killed a bull elk on a slope so precipitous that had not the antlers hung up in some downed timber, the animal would have slid all the way to the bottom. In that instance, I tied the antlers to a couple nearby trees. Only then was

the animal stable enough to allow safe field dressing. The last thing I wanted was an unexpected ride downhill on a game carcass with a sharp knife in my hand.

Don't waste your time: Some folks believe that the external male sex organs and musk glands must be removed first. The penis, testes and musk glands will do no harm to the meat if you leave them alone. Besides, when you skin the carcass these organs and glands will be removed anyway.

Another useless act is throat cutting. When an animal is killed by a bullet or broadhead, the blood flows into the abdominal cavity. Think about it for a minute. Most animals expire because of blood loss. Cutting the throat of a dead animal serves no purpose (unless you want to ruin a perfectly good head skin cape). And we've already mentioned the danger of attempting to use a knife on a live animal.

Furthermore, it is not necessary to cut through the pelvic bone to extract the lower intestines, urine bladder and whatever else is down there. If you follow the easy steps outlined below, all of this material can be pulled up and out of the abdominal cavity. Using your knife to split the pelvis can damage the blade. Cutting through the bone with a saw can tear open the lower intestines and urine bladder, spilling feces and urine into the open cavity. And if you have to drag the carcass any distance, cutting through the pelvic area will expose the hams to dirt and debris.

Primary game care is a straightforward process that completely removes the digestive system, lungs, heart and other internal organs from the body cavity. This helps to cool the meat and inhibits premature spoilage. The four easy steps outlined below describe this procedure in detail.

Field dressing

Step one: If possible, turn the animal on its back and straddle the hind legs. Use your knife to cut around the external margin of the anus (include external genitalia if the animal is a female) to the depth of your knife blade (about 3 inches). This action frees the terminal end of the digestive system from the surrounding tissue.

Step two: Move forward and insert the tip of your knife through the skin into the bottom of the abdomen. Use caution not to puncture the underlying intestines and stomach. After the initial shallow incision, use two fingers to lift the hide up and away from the visceral mass while you're cutting through

Skinning is best done with a sharp knife and a steady hand.

Photo by Durwood Hollis

the hide. Extend this incision all the way forward to the sternum (bottom of the rib cage). A wall of muscle—the diaphragm—separates the abdominal cavity from the heart-lung cavity. This separation will be evident when you push the stomach down and toward the rear of the abdominal cavity. Use your knife blade to cut through the diaphragm, all the way around the interior circumference of the internal body cavity, down to the spinal column.

Step three: Reach forward with your free hand, past the heart and lungs, and locate the windpipe at the base of the throat. This will feel like a ribbed tube. Hold the windpipe with your free hand. Sever the windpipe with your knife, being careful not to cut yourself in the process (you'll be working blind inside the heart-lung cavity). Get a firm grip on the severed windpipe and pull it down and out of the heart-lung cavity. The lungs, heart, stomach and intestines are attached and should come out as well. Cut any away any connective tissue as you pull out the entrails. If you're fond of organ meats (heart and liver), cut them free before completely removing the entrails from the body cavity.

Step four: Reach down into the bottom of the abdominal cavity and get a firm grip on the lower end of the intestines. Pull the intestines and urine bladder up and out of the pelvic opening. If you've completely freed the terminal end of the digestive system (anus), then everything should come out easily. However, a little discreet cutting here and there may be necessary. Once the viscera are free, move them a distance away from the carcass. This will prevent you from stepping in the mess should you have to continue working (skinning, quartering, boning) on the animal. Furthermore, predators are always interested in an easy meal. When the gut pile is moved from the site of primary evisceration, it tends to draw hungry animals away from the field dressed carcass. Finally, lift the carcass off of the ground (if possible) and allow it to drain.

There are a couple of approaches to skinning, both of which have their purpose. Some folks are intent on removing the hide as soon as possible. This will certainly allow the meat to cool quickly, but in the high country exposed meat can dry out quickly. Prompt

Photo by Kodiak Advertising

There's a bag for everything—big and small.

Removal of the headskin cape is a tedious job. While your guide can handle this assignment, you should also know the basics.

Photo by Bob Robb

skinning is the appropriate action when the daytime temperature approaches triple-digit readings, but isn't nearly as essential in cold weather. Moreover, leaving the hide on the carcass will prevent meat shrinkage and insect damage. Whether you decide to skin the carcass right away, or delay until the last day in camp, this activity is an essential part of the overall game care process. The skinning process is easy, but takes some practice.

Skinning

Step one: Remove the lower leg hocks by locating the hock joint situated just below the main muscle mass of the front and back legs. There are two protrusions or prominent "bumps" located at the joint. Cut through the hide, completely around the circumference of the lowest protrusion. Set your knife aside and twist the hock from the leg. The front hocks will be the easier to remove. The rear ones may give you a little trouble. If you have problems, use a bone saw to sever each joint. Remove and discard all four lower hocks.

Step two: Using the tip of your knife blade, make an incision through the hide that extends upward along the rear margins of both hind legs to the point where the anus was cut free from the carcass. Repeat this procedure on both front legs, extending the incision along the rear margin of each leg, diagonally across the chest and joining the opening in the body cavity at the bottom of the sternum.

Step three: Starting at the rear leg hocks, free the hide from the underlying muscle tissue with a combination of careful knife work and lots of tugging on the skin. Avoid cutting through the large tendon that is connected to the hock joint. When you reach the base of the tail, sever the tailbone and use the tail as something to hold on to. Since the hide is looser on the back and sides of the carcass, the skinning will get easier as you work your way down the length of the body. Skin out both front legs. Continue skinning until you have reached the base of the skull. Cut through the neck muscle all the way around the base of the cranium. The head can be removed by twisting it free, or using a bone saw to cut the spinal column.

The final touch: Use a saw or an ax to cut through the pelvic bone, sternum and spinal column. You'll need to trim out any blood=shot or bullet-damaged meat. If you don't, you may have to throw out even more meat later on. Since the presence of fat is the reason for the "gamey" taste so often detected in venison, I suggest that you trim away as much as possible. Cover the carcass with an insect-proof meat bag and hang it in a cool, shaded location. Depending on the ambient daytime temperature, you can usually hang a field dressed, skinned carcass for three to five days. Cold nights are great for hanging meat. To retain the cold within the carcass during the day, make sure it remains in the shade and cover it with a tarp or an opened sleeping bag.

In warm weather, flies can slip into a meat bag through a tiny hole you may not have noticed. If the insects find moist meat anywhere on the skinned carcass, they will lay their eggs in that location. Should you note fly eggs (clusters of short, thin, white threads) anywhere on the carcass (particularly under the front legs and where dampness often persists), you must remove them before they hatch into maggots. A clean rag dipped in vinegar will take care of the problem. And if you happen to find a small cluster of maggots, don't toss out the entire carcass. Simply use the vinegar rag to wipe the offending insect larvae off of the meat. A few maggots aren't a problem, but spoiled meat can be. When you hang meat for any length of time, don't just walk away and forget it. Check the carcass daily and remove it to refrigerated storage as soon as possible.

Head cape removal: The decision to mount an animal head must be made at the very outset of field care.

Photo by Durwood Hollis

Essential game care tools include a knife, saw and sometimes even an ax. All of these sharp cutters are from Gerber Legendary Blades.

Photo by Bob Robb

Before you begin field dressing, make sure your knife is sharp. A few minutes on a pocket whetstone can help improve the edge.

Knife sharpening is easy and quick if you use the right method.

Step One: *Establish a sharpening angle between 10 to 20 degrees.*

Step Two: *Work the entire length of the blade edge along the whetstone in small, counter-clockwise circles.*

Step Three: *Flip the blade over and repeat the procedure, this time in small clockwise circles.*

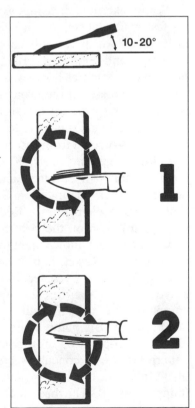

Line art: Buck Knives

You can remove the partial cape and leave it attached to the skull, or you can remove the entire cape. Both of these procedures are outlined below:

Partial head skin cape removal: To remove the head and cape, make a circular incision through the hide, completely around the carcass, just behind the front shoulders. At a point between the shoulders, following the line of the spinal column, slit the hide forward to the base of the skull. Skin the front legs, chest, shoulders and neck until you've reached the connecting point between the skull and the spine. Use your knife to cut through the muscle tissue of the neck down to the spine. Sever the head from the spine by twisting, or using a saw or an ax. This leaves the head and the cape in one continuous unit. Complete head skin cape removal will take more work. Unless you're familiar with this procedure, let your taxidermist handle it. Spread the cape out, hair side placed down and apply a covering of salt on the exposed underside. In a couple hours, the salt will have drawn out considerable moisture from the hide. Shake off the crust, roll the cape and head up, get them to your taxidermist as soon as possible. An alternative to this procedure is to eschew the salting, place the head and cape in a plas-

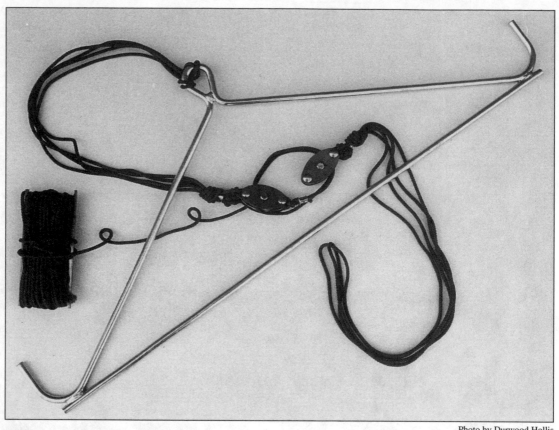

A small hoist and a gambrel hook can make the job of elevating the carcass a snap!

Photo by Durwood Hollis

tic bag, and freeze the whole works. An unsalted cape and head can be kept frozen for several weeks, giving you enough time to handle all the details related to future taxidermy work.

Complete head skin cape removal: The removal of the head skin from the skull is a demanding job. It's best to practice this procedure on a couple of representative animals (forked-horn bucks are great for cape skin removal practice), well before you attempt it on a valuable trophy. To cape an animal, make a single incision from the base of the skull to each antler (horn) base. Using a combination of discreet cutting and prying, free the cape from around the antlers (horns). Next, sever the ear cartilage under the hide, as close to the skull as possible. Separate the head skin from the skull by carefully working forward with the tip of your knife, turning the cape inside-out as you proceed. When you reach the eye socket, leave the eyelids and tear ducts intact (you'll have to pry mule deer tear ducts out of the skull with the tip of your knife blade). Cut the lips well inside the mouth and sever the nose free from the nasal cartilage. When the cape has been removed from the skull, turn both ears inside-out and leave the cartilage attached to one side. This will take extreme patience and prudent knife work. The lips must also be handled in a similar manner. When you're through, take a saw and cut the antlers (horns) free from the skull in one complete unit. To temporarily preserve the cape until

you can get it to your taxidermist, either salt it down and keep it cool, or freeze it.

Game care gear: There are several tools and items that can make field dressing, skinning and trophy work go faster. Of course, you'll need a knife and a sharpener. A saw or an ax will come in handy for dealing with bone and removing antlers or horns. Some type of hoist and a gambrel hook will allow you to elevate a deer-size carcass off the ground. A small tarp is handy if you have to work on the ground. And carcass cover bags (game bags) are essential to keep skinned meat clean and protected from insect damage.

Primary cutting tools: Knives come in two basic configurations—fixed-blade and folding. They really need no further identification. Small folders can be carried in the pocket. Larger folding knives are usually toted in a pouch on the belt. Some folders feature an attached clip that allows them to be secured to any convenient edge (pocket, belt, boot top, etc.). Lock-blade folding knives are easier to carry, but fixed-blade knives are far easier to clean up when field dressing is complete. You make the call.

Shape up: Big game hunters will be best served by either a clip-point or drop-point blade The clip-point pattern features a concave section, on the back of the blade, near the tip where material has been removed (clipped away). The best feature of this blade is an extremely fine working point. Highly adaptable to many cutting chores, the clip-point is a favorite among many hunters. The drop-point blade has a convex curve on the back of the blade, near the tip, that "drops" the point below the direct line of the back of the blade. The advantages found in this blade pattern include a reinforced tip and a sweeping cutting edge. Another blade pattern often seen is the trailing point. The design positions the blade tip above, or "trailing" behind the back of the blade. This blade has a pronounced sweep to the cutting edge, which makes it a better skinning knife than other patterns. The addition of a guthook, as well as a saw can add to the usefulness of any knife designed for big game work.

Carbon or stainless steel? The final knife consideration is the steel from which it's crafted. The basic two choices are carbon steel or stainless steel. The difference between these two is nothing more than the percentage of chromium in the metal. To qualify as "stainless," there must be 13 percent chromium present in the steel. Even the designation "stainless" doesn't

Quartering a game carcass will take more than a knife. Here outdoor writer Thomas McIntyre works on a wild boar carcass.

Photo by Durwood Hollis

When you have to drag a field dressed animal back to camp, save your back and use a game drag.

Photo by Durwood Hollis

mean "rust-free." All steel will rust, even stainless steel. The purpose of the added chromium in stainless steel simply provides an enhanced measure of rust resistance. While stainless steel predominates in the hunting field, carbon steel knives can still be found in hunting camps across the continent. As long as the user is the kind of person who cares for his carbon steel knife, the steel should remain free from the ravages of rust. If you're a little lazy about knife care, stainless steel is a better alternative.

Steel alternatives: There are a couple of other blade materials—ceramic and Talonite—currently available. The use of ceramic blade material was pioneered by Boker and has been popular with a number of hunters. Ceramic can hold an edge much longer than any steel and can never rust. The material is, however, relatively fragile and will break easily if any side load is placed on the blade. Should you drop the knife on a hard sur-

face, the blade can shatter. Once a ceramic blade gets dull, expect sharpening to be challenging.

Talonite is nothing more than a mixture of chromium carbides and cobalt. The chromium is extremely hard and the cobalt relatively soft. This combination of materials provides a blade that resists edge erosion, can be sharpened quickly and is absolutely rust proof.

Knife sharpening: There are lots of knife sharpeners out there. Each can provide satisfactory results—more or less. When you need a new edge in a hurry, the best way to go is a drag and scrape sharpener. Consisting of a pair of crossed carbide steel tips contained in a handheld fixture, this handy little sharpener will definitely scrape out a sharp edge quickly. Another quick way to sharpen your knife is with a diamond rod. The microscopic diamond dust bonded to the rod can work wonders on a dull blade. Other selections are "V" sharpeners, clamp-on sharpening guides and sharpening fixtures. Where you have electrical power available, the Chef's Choice electric knife sharpener can't be beat for an effortless and absolutely precision edge.

Rough cutters: A knife should never be used for rough cutting chores. Leave all of the bone-cutting to an ax or a saw. An ax cuts faster than a saw, but there are more safety considerations. Several cutlery firms produce these tools, with Browning (Folding Game & Camp Saw), Buck, Gerber (Back Paxe and Exchange-a-Blade Saw), Knives of Alaska (Hunter's Hatchet), McGowan Manufacturing (Firestone Belt Axe), Muela Cutlery, Outdoor Edge (Grizz Saw), Remington, Robertson Enterprises (Dandy Saw) and Turner Manufacturing (Uluchet®) all making some top-notch rough cutters. For

the last several years, I've used a Dandy Saw (P.O. Box 1711, Cody, WY 82414, 800/548-5748). Not only does it cut better than most other game saws, the laminated hardwood handle doesn't blister my hands. And when it comes to a game ax, the diminutive Hunter's Hatchet, by Knives of Alaska and the BackPaxe by Gerber are hard to beat. A saw is safer to use than an ax, but the ax cuts faster than the saw. It's up to you.

Off the ground: A hoist and gambrel hook is a handy combination that allows you to raise an animal carcass off the ground with minimal effort. Select a combination that is lightweight and as compact as possible. Even if you don't carry them with you in the field, both of these items are great assets for in-camp game care chores.

If you're a backcountry hunter, a pack frame will be an important consideration.

Photo by Jim Matthews

This successful deer hunter is on a real roll!

Bag it: You'll definitely need a cover bag to protect the skinned carcass, or individual quarters, from wind-blown debris and insects. Inexpensive cheesecloth game bags offer the most basic level of meat protection. Heavyweight knitted or woven game bags are a far better selection. Not only do these bags offer enhanced meat protection and insulation, they can be washed and used repeatedly.

Something extra: Another form of bug protection is pepper. A fine covering of pepper inside a dressed carcass will eliminate any insect worries. Likewise, a thin mixture of vegetable oil and red pepper sprayed on the carcass is another excellent bug shield.

Drag, tote or roll: Getting your trophy back to camp can be the embodiment of real work. Toss in a few uphill grinds and your legs and back will start complaining. Add a smattering of blow-down timber, snow, and mud to the situation and it will take all the fun out of hunting. While you can't avoid some of the work, your choice of game transport mechanisms can ease the pain.

Save your back: The most basic conveyance assist is a simple game drag. The first time I had to drag a deer back to camp, my belt served the purpose. I didn't

start off using the belt. The pain in my lower back from bending over and dragging the deer by its antlers was the first sign of trouble. Realizing that I had to take the strain off of my back, the belt seemed to be an easy solution. If I looped the belt around the buck's antlers, buckled it up tight and wrapped it around my wrist it would allow me to drag from a more upright position. Off came the belt and my plan was put into action. All of sudden, dragging got a lot easier and my back didn't ache anymore. Everything seemed to be fine, that is, until my trousers fell down around my ankles! Upon my return home, I fashioned a game drag out of a water ski rope handle and a length of nylon cord. You can devise your own game drag, or purchase one of the many that are produced commercially. Either way, you'll save your back, and keep your pants up!

Game frames: I haul most of my game to camp in pieces. Unless I am going to mount the head, all of the guts, bones and hide remain in the field (somebody has to feed the coyotes). This reduces the overall weight of an animal by nearly two-thirds. Most adult males can carry 40 to 60 pounds of weight on their backs, over irregular terrain, for a considerable distance. Sure, backpacking boned meat isn't a picnic. What game transport assignment (short of that involving a pickup truck) ever is? The primary piece of equipment is a pack tough enough to handle heavy loads. An external frame pack is probably the best choice, but some internal-frame models are also up to the chore.

You can avoid the entire mess associated with fresh meat by using plastic trash compactor bags. These bags are made out of thick plastic and won't tear or break easily. When you remove the meat from the bones, place it into a trash compactor bag, close the bag tightly and slip it into your backpack. When you arrive in camp your pack and trousers won't be all blood stained. Furthermore, in grizzly country it's a good thing to keep the smell of blood contained.

On a roll: If you hunt in the Rocky Mountains, no doubt you've seen more than your share of game carts. These ingenious wheeled game haulers come in an infinite variety of sizes and shapes and are often homemade. The best game carts I've used were commercially made. Don't expect a game cart to eliminate all of the problems associated with moving a field dressed carcass from one place to another. Used in country where the cart can be wheeled over an established trail, however, one of these conveyances can be "heaven sent."

Butcher blues: In most major urban areas, it's getting difficult to find a butcher shop that will handle wild game. Federal and state regulations won't allow a butcher to use the same cutting block, implements and other equipment for butchering both domestically raised and wild meat. If a butcher is going to cut and package wild game, completely sep-

arate equipment must be used. This means added cost, which is something that just isn't in most business plans. The result of all of this has been movement toward home butchering.

To get in this game, you'll need a couple of boning knives, a large plastic tub to hold meat, an oversized cutting board and a meat grinder. Converting a game carcass into packages of chops and ground meat isn't all that difficult. There are several illustrated books and videos that fully explain the process. Do a little reading on the subject, spend a couple of hours watching a video and you'll be ready for action. Don't worry about making a mistake. A meat grinder can turn a raggedly-cut steak into beautiful hamburger. While I occasionally employ the services of a commercial game butchering operation, most of the meat harvested through my hunting efforts receives its butchering treatment right in my own kitchen.

The final cut: When it comes to flavor, nothing is better than a tender piece of venison. Cooked to perfection and smothered with mushroom gravy, a cut of antelope, deer, elk, caribou, moose, and almost any other game I can think of is decidedly mouthwatering. Wild sheep, mountain goats, wild boar and even the feisty little javelina can be cooked in such a manner that it pleases the most discriminating palate. As my dad once said, "it's all good."

Wild game has been served at mealtime on this continent for more than 25,000 years. From the humble camps of the earliest Native Americans to the homes of modern hunters, game meat is a gourmet treat that is both good for you and good tasting.

Photo by Durwood Hollis

If you want to be as successful, then "Be Prepared."

BE PREPARED: GET READY FOR THE HUNT

Most problems encountered in the field are the direct result of a lack of pre-hunt preparation.

Looking back over years I've spent in the field with a rifle in my hands, it's easy to see that when things went bad, it was usually because of a lack of preparation on my part. In the outdoors, there's little room for error. The best way avoid problems is to understand where you're going, take adequate safety measures and have all the right gear when you get there.

On one occasion, I arrived at a remote hunting camp without a knife. Fortunately, I was able to scrounge around in an old cabin and come up with a paring knife. Absent a whetstone, I used a smooth rock to establish a passable cutting edge. And piece of cardboard secured with some electrical tape served as a makeshift carrying sheath. Had I not been able to locate this makeshift gear, the hunt would have, at the very least, been stalled for an entire day.

Okay. Anyone can forget a hunting knife, what about not carrying enough shells with you in the field? Yep. That was another of my own personal outdoor blunders. Setting off for a morning's deer hunt with a friend, I neglected to slip a few extra shells in my pack. Sure enough, I jumped a buck about two hours into the hunt. The first shot went right over the top of the deer. The second round was equally as ineffective. However, the third attempt dumped the little buck in the dirt. Approaching the animal, I was surprised to see it rise to its feet. It was then that I realized that there were no more shells in my rifle. Furthermore, there were no additional rounds in my pockets, pack or anywhere on my person. Faced with a wounded deer standing less than 50 yards from my position, I didn't know what to do. Fortunately, my hunting buddy had heard the shooting and headed in my direction. Topping a nearby

Photo by Durwood Hollis

Road emergencies can happen. Something to help dig, cut and chop may get you out of a difficult spot. Likewise, a multi-tool and a flashlight are equally as useful on or off the road.

ridge, he saw me point to the buck and then to my empty rifle. Taking the obvious course of action, he used his own rifle to resolve the problem.

These two incidents aren't the only ones in my hunting career. Suffice it to say that there is a great deal more that could have been brought out of the closet. Some of those experiences were funny and others were just really stupid. Over time, each one served to teach me a lesson.

Getting there: Some folks have a hard time just getting to the camp. Near my home is a major interstate highway which cuts right through several Western states. At the first grade of any significance, you'll see more than one group of hunters paralyzed along the side of the road with vehicle problems. I know, because I've "been there, done that!" It might be nothing more serious than a flat tire, but it stops the trip. While it's impossible to foresee all of the potential travel situations you may encounter, adequate vehicle preparation can take most of the uncertainty out of your travel

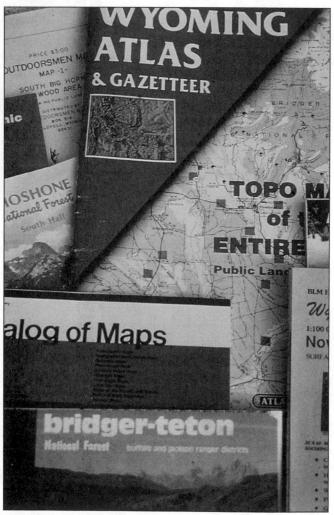

Photo by Durwood Hollis

Maps of every kind can help you negotiate your way on the highway or in the woods.

plans. New tires (including a spare that holds air), brakes, shock absorbers and hoses, as well as a complete engine tune-up will prevent most potential problems. While you're at it, put together a roadside emergency kit. This should include an assortment of tools (adjustable wrench, screwdrivers, a socket set, electrical tape and a roll of copper wire), tire chains that fit, a working jack, flares or reflective triangles, a pair of overalls, tarp, hand cleaner and a roll of paper towels. If you're traveling in another person's vehicle, encourage them to employ the same principles. These measures have gotten me out of more roadside problems than a fairy godmother. If your problems demand more sophisticated equipment and a skilled mechanic, then it's time to call the tow truck. When that happens, some extra cash or a credit card will be in order.

Making travel plans and securing airline tickets can be its own headache. Even the matter of transportation to and from the airport, secure parking (if you leave your vehicle), and getting your luggage on the right flight (things can get mixed up) all deserve due consideration and planning. Working with a booking agent who can also handle your travel plans is one way to go. Using a local travel agent is another option. And you can order tickets and book accommodations through the Internet. Whatever avenue you decide to take, make sure everything is in place well in advance of departure. Keep your ticket(s) and any other important papers where you can find them. Learn the route to the airport and allow more than enough time to get there. When you reach your final destination, store your return ticket(s) where they will be safe and can be easily located.

Maps and guides: If you're driving, a highway map will guide your way. Service stations still carry road maps, but they aren't free anymore. Likewise, some convenience stores also have maps. The best sources of free road maps are the weigh stations located along many major interstate highways at state borders. Other maps that you'll find useful are topographical maps produced by the U.S. Geological Survey (USGS), Bureau of Land Management (BLM) maps, U.S. National Forest (USFS) maps, and the *DeLorme Atlas and Gazetteer* (also available on CD-ROM, Delorme Topo USA™ 2.0). And there may be other published maps of specific hunting areas that are available in your hunting locale. Topographical maps can be found at backpacking shops and specialty map stores. Office locations for both the Bureau of Land Management and the U.S. Forest Service are listed in the government pages in the front of your telephone book. If you're interested in hunting an area a considerable distance from your home, telephone the local BLM or Forest Service office and ask for the address(es) and telephone number(s) in that region.

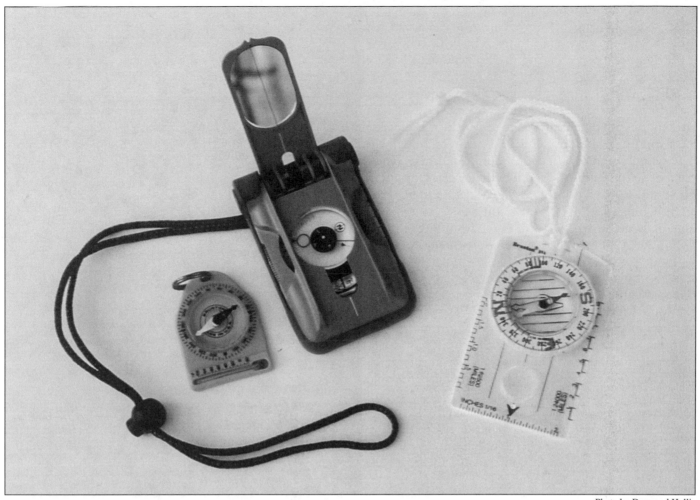

Photo by Durwood Hollis

No matter how simple or complex, a compass should be part of your equipment.

Photo by Durwood Hollis

Portable 2-way radios can help keep you connected with others in your hunting party.

Orienting instruments: Once you're in camp, getting around in the woods calls for the use of a compass or GPS (global positioning system) unit. I use my compass to plot out of the major terrain features that can be easily seen from camp. Knowing how each one lies in relation to camp means a return course will get me back to a warm fire and a hot meal. A compass is a relatively easy instrument to master. A more sophisticated approach is the use of a GPS unit. This technology employs contact between a hand-held instrument and a series of orbiting satellites. At first, a GPS unit can be intimidating. Once you understand how to work the instrument, the advantages become readily apparent. And the GPS system can work at night, something that leaves compass users completely "in the dark."

Keep in touch: Communication is an essential element of any hunt. The best way to keep in contact with your hunting partners is a two-way radio. There are several selections available, just make sure that each is compatible with the other. Handy accessories are a belt case and an ear-plug speaker. Most of these little radios have a two-mile line-of-sight transmission broadcast and reception area, but that's usually good enough for most needs. Whatever form of electronic communication you select, remember to pack lots of extra batteries. Some radios can eat up their power supply like a teenager at a fast-food joint.

Rifle gear: Setting up your rifle to function properly in the field takes a little doing. You'll have already put in some range time to get the old blunderbuss shooting where it should, so we won't deal with that issue here. If you haven't done so already, equip your rifle or hunting pistol with a carrying sling. Most rifles come from the factory with sling swivels already in place. If yours did not, have some installed, or do it yourself. A leather sling is traditional, but I prefer fabric-covered neoprene rubber or molded plastic. These synthetic materials aren't affected by wet weather, offer greater carrying comfort and can be easily obtained from many retail and catalog outlets.

Another good idea is to slip an elastic ammo carrier onto the buttstock of your center-fire rifle. This way, in addition to whatever is already in the rifle magazine, you'll have at least nine extra rounds readily available. And toting shells on your rifle is easier than having a belt carrier drag your pants down to the ground.

A soft gun case with lots of protective padding is sufficient for traveling by vehicle, but a hard case will be essential for air travel. And if your hunting plans

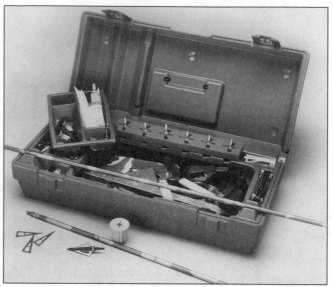

Photo by Ranging

Bowhunters have lots of gear they'll need to take to hunting camp. A tackle box can help keep everything together.

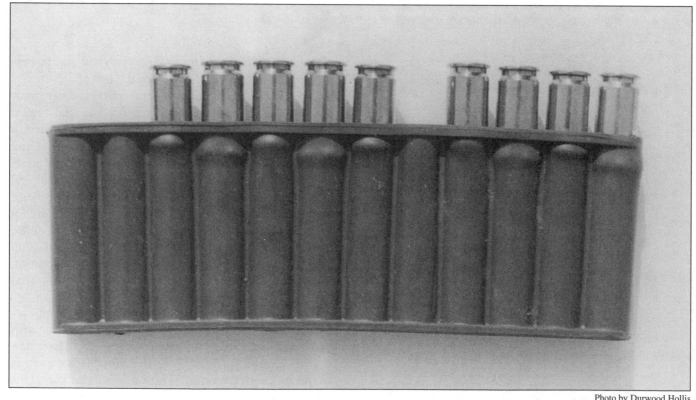

Photo by Durwood Hollis

Rather than bouncing around in your pocket, extra ammunition should be secured in a carrier.

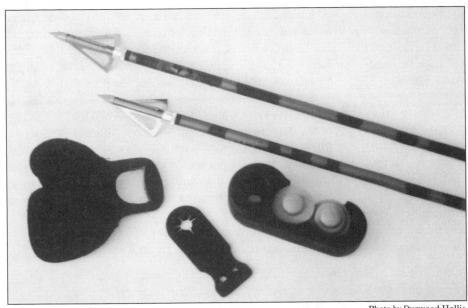

When you're in the field, a few extra arrows, finger tab (or release), a broadhead wrench and sharpener are all important.

Photo by Durwood Hollis

involve horses, then you'll also need a rifle scabbard. It's always better to bring your own scabbard than to depend on the outfitter or guide to have one you can use (they almost never fit).

A compact rifle maintenance kit with a cleaning rod, patches, oil and a multi-tool will come in handy—one time, or another. You don't have to bring everything you'd use at home, just pack the basics and call it good.

Don't forget to take along at least two boxes (40 rounds) of ammunition. Take the cartridges out of the factory boxes and repack them in plastic shell boxes. Black powder shooters will be better off using plastic "quick-loaders" (powder, cap and projectile all together), instead of packing a container of powder and

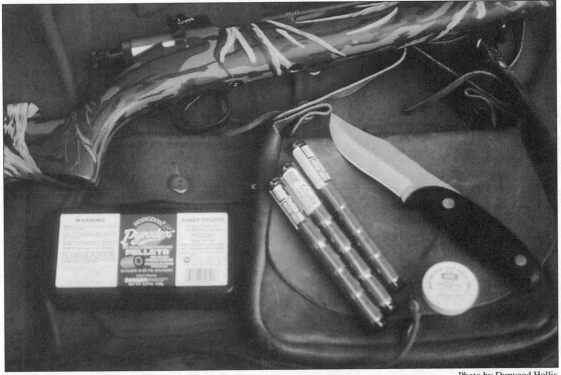

A "possibles" bag will help blackpowder shooters keep all of their accessories together.

Photo by Durwood Hollis

percussion caps. Black powder is highly explosive and no airline carrier will allow you to carry it with you. You may want to check with the airlines and see if "quick-loaders" are acceptable. If not, make arrangements at your destination to pick up whatever type of propellant you'll need.

Archery tackle: Most bowhunters shoot a compound bow. All of those pulleys and cables will need to be checked. While you're at it, have an archery professional tune your bow. Sure, it'll cost you a few bucks, but so what! When everything is tight and buttoned-down, then shoot your bow to ensure that nothing rattles or squeaks. A little lubrication here and a sound-dampening washer there should take care of any problem.

I like both a bow-mounted front sight and a string-mounted rear sight. Too many sighting pins can get confusing when it comes time to shoot. Some guys are fans of a single aiming point. Whatever kind of sight you select, make sure you can see the pins in dim light.

Some bow hunters like hip quivers (I don't). A bunch of arrows bouncing up and down and snagging in the brush isn't my idea of a good thing. If you use a hip quiver, then more power to you. A quiver attached to the bow is the choice of most veteran archers. You don't have to buy the quiver with a greatest capacity. Something that will carry half-a-dozen extra arrows is about right.

Arrows are another separate discussion. Most bow hunters select aluminum arrows (best economy), but

A hoist, gambrel hook, a couple of knives and a carcass bag will make game care chores a lot easier

Photo by Bob Robb

Photo by Durwood Hollis

Hunting season usually means cold, wet weather with the possibility of snow. The right clothing, as well as other gear will make the hunt more enjoyable.

the really serious shooters use carbon fiber (better penetration). About 24 arrows should be adequate for most hunting venues. When it comes to broadheads, there are so many choices that it's hard to pick a bad one. Just make sure that whatever you select is tough enough to hold together when it hits the animal.

The connection point between arrow shaft and broadhead is another important consideration. You can forget about plastic inserts (they break too easily). Spend a few extra dollars and go for titanium. Titanium inserts are less likely to fracture and will insure that the arrow and broadhead stay together. If the insert fails, then the arrow will fall out. Once the arrow is no longer working the wound, even with the broadhead remaining inside the animal, bleeding will slow down—or come to a stop.

Anything with nuts and bolts can loosen up. I would suggest that you pack a few tools that fit every adjustment point on your bow. A broadhead sharpener and wrench will also come in handy. If you shoot with a mechanical release, toss in an extra for good measure. And stuff a leather finger tab in somewhere just in case everything else fails.

A soft bow case usually provides adequate protection for vehicle travel. If you go by air, then you'll need a hard case. Most hard cases can hold a bow, quiver, extra arrows and all of your other archery tackle. Since air travel can be hard on luggage, buy the best hard case you can afford. And you'll need a couple of small padlocks to keep baggage handlers honest. Like rifle shooters, if time in the saddle figures into your hunting activities, then a scabbard for your bow will be necessary.

Black powder gear: Black powder and most black powder substitutes are corrosive in nature. If you don't clean the barrel of your front-stuffer after shooting, then expect a visit from the rust demon. Your rifle has its own ramrod, so you won't need a separate cleaning rod. You will need a patch jag and a caliber-appropriate wire brush to fit the ramrod, several solvent-saturated patches (saturate patches at home with your choice of solvent and put them in a plastic bag) and clean patches, toothbrush-size wire brush, oil and breech plug grease. While you're at it, toss in a few disposable gun wipes to keep your firearm clean and protected. In addition to cleaning supplies, you'll need a capper, a quantity of propellant and projectiles, as well as a bullet starter. A more complete assortment of black powder gear can be assembled to meet your own preferences, but these basics should get you through.

Game care gear: Hunting involves the harvest of a consumable product—venison! Game meat is some of the best tasting and healthiest protein you can eat. However, you just can't shoot an animal, field dress it, drag back it to camp and expect that steaks and chops are going to fall out when you skin it. I am afraid it doesn't work that way. If you don't know how to deal with harvested game, then learn! An entire chapter of this book is devoted to these activities, so spend some time reading it thoroughly.

Horse gear: Rifle and bow scabbards for horseback use have already been mentioned in this chapter. Other riding gear that you'll find useful will include pommel and cantle bags, as well as saddlebags. Leather is traditional, but you just can't use leather and not care for it. The best low-maintenance material is Ballistic® cloth or Cordura® nylon. Pommel bags are paired and slip over the saddle horn. These little bags are just right for

Photo by Durwood Hollis

When you're in the field, a canteen, first aid kit, whistle and lip balm should all be part of your personal gear.

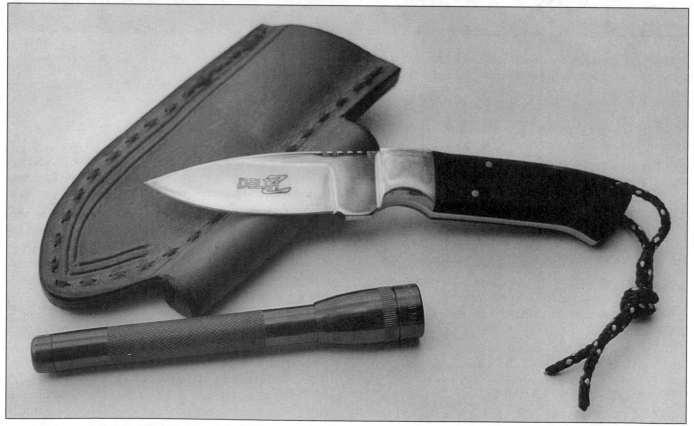

Photo by Durwood Hollis

A flashlight can be heaven-sent when nightfall comes. Carried in the same sheath as his knife, the author never leaves camp without one.

Photo by Bob Robb

Success requires planning.

carrying your camera or a pair of binoculars. A cantle bag fits right behind you and is attached with the leather strings that are on the saddle. This is where you'll find my lunch and rain gear. Saddlebags are also paired and fit behind the saddle. These bags have enough storage space to haul a down coat, extra socks and whatever else you'll need on the trail. Features to

look for are sewn-in padding to protect the horse and your equipment, zipper closures to prevent gear from bouncing out accidentally and reinforced stitching at every point of possible strain.

Some guys wear riding chaps to keep their legs dry when there's early morning moisture on brush and branches. Chaps also keep your pants from snagging in

Photo by Durwood Hollis

Packing your gear in two medium-sized duffle bags is better than trying to stuff everything in one big bag.

the brush. Leather chaps are tough, but heavy and difficult to hike around in. And it can get inconvenient putting chaps on and taking them off every time you want to go for a stroll. Cordura® nylon and waxed cotton chaps are lighter and easier to hike in, but they make a lot of noise in heavy cover.

Light source: A flashlight is indispensable. Pack a reliable flashlight, an extra bulb and some batteries. You won't need a torch of mammoth proportions. The small, aluminum Mini MagLite that operates on two AA batteries is just about the right size. Mine came with an extra bulb stored in the end cap, so I have an onboard replacement at all times. I carry the flashlight in a nylon webbing belt case. No matter where the hunt takes me, or what time of the night nature calls, that light is never far from my side.

Toiletries: Everybody is different, but hunting camp isn't a place to get seedy just because you can. While I might not shave for a week (acceptable), smelling like something the dog dug up (unacceptable) isn't part of my game plan. You might not be able to shower, but individually packaged wet wipes (the kind made for infant care) can help keep your body clean. Furthermore, wipes are better than toilet paper when it comes

to taking care of personal plumbing matters. A handful of wipes packed in a ZipLoc plastic bag should handle all of your intimate cleaning chores.

High altitudes are consistent with dry air. I don't know about you, but my lips can take a beating in this setting. For this reason, you'll never find me without something to keep my lips soft and pliable. Whatever you use, use it often and you'll prevent chapped lips. The same issue applies to my hands. No matter what I do, the constant exposure to dry mountain air turns my hands into alligator skin within a day. The best protective skin creams I've found are pure lanolin (available through your local pharmacy), a product called Bag Balm (try your local feed and tack store for this one), or wax boot waterproofing (carried at most sporting goods retailers). Until any of these products work their way into your skin, your hands will feel a little tacky. And you might have to use a cover scent to mask any odor, but you won't have chapped, cracked skin.

Other toiletries that should be a part of your personal kit are: toothbrush and toothpaste, deodorant, soap, comb or brush (if you still have hair), headache relief, something for nasal decongestion (especially if you have a problem with allergies), prescribed medications (bring just enough for the duration of the hunt) and a small pack of facial tissues. You'll also want to bring along a face and hand towel. Glasses are important, so pack them in with your toiletries. And don't forget to include an assortment of bandages (finger, knuckle, small, large and extra large) and antibiotic cream. Finally, a pair of tweezers and a fingernail clipper will both be greatly appreciated when the need arises.

Sleep well: You'll need a sleeping bag, but don't make the mistake of taking your child's slumber party bag to hunting camp. In the woods, nighttime temperatures can get cold—really cold! Your sleeping bag should be able to keep you warm at night, even when the temperature drops unexpectedly. Waterfowl down offers the lightest and warmest insulation, but a down bag can be expensive. And when down gets wet, it's worthless. A better insulation alternative is one of the newer high-loft synthetics. Best of all, synthetic insulation isn't affected by moisture. Rectangular sleeping bags are comfortable but, a close-fitting mummy style will be warmer. The secret to sleeping in a mummy bag is to let the bag move with you when you turn from side-to-side.

Final thoughts: You'll want memories of your exploits, so pack a camera and a couple of rolls of color print film. You can leave your expensive 35mm SLR, telephoto lens, digital camera and video recorder at home. A "point and shoot" camera is the right choice for a week in hunting camp. Most guys leave their cameras in the tent because of the weight. When your camera isn't with you, no pictures will be taken. A "point and shoot" camera weighs just ounces and is easily carried in your shirt pocket. This means that you're going to shoot more pictures, which is what you'll want to do.

There are times that you may be stranded in camp because of the weather. Without something to do, it can get really boring after a while. If you're a card player, then toss a deck into your gear. A pocket book, or two, can also be helpful in preventing boredom in camp and on a stand. A few business cards, a pad of paper small enough to slip into your breast pocket and a pen are other items of significance.

When it comes time to leave the comforts of home and head for hunting camp, you'll want to spend some time planning for that adventure. Thrown together haphazardly, your gear may not be sufficient to deal effectively with every big game hunting situation. You may not be able to plan for all contingencies, but prepare for the worse situation possible and hope it never materializes.

AFTERWORD

There was no logical reason for my presence in this remote wilderness. Even when you considered the rifle in my hands and the elk license in my pocket, none of it made good sense. While the mountains before me were magnificent in their grandeur, so are countless other locations in this world. If it was physical exercise that I wanted, certainly the health club near my home offers greater benefits. And the cost of prime beef in the local supermarket was far less expensive than the price of a guided elk hunt.

With the exception of those who live on the edge of civilized society, modern man really doesn't need to hunt for his existence. The assembly line production of domestic animals has long since eliminated the requirement to pursue and capture wild creatures. Our clothing, once made from nothing more than the skins of

Photo by Durwood Hollis

The hunt is over. What lies ahead is planning and preparation for hunts to come.

Photo by Ron Gayer

Photo by Durwood Hollis

beasts, is cut from mass-produced cloth and stitched by machine. The very button closures native peoples so painstakingly crafted out of antler, bone and horn are now just lifeless pieces of molded plastic.

Even the tools of the hunt—bow, arrows, rifle, bullets and powder—have all changed. Modern archers are content to use bows with pulleys, wheels and cable. Arrows are made from lightweight metal and extruded fiber and wear fletching of plastic. The sharpened points have only a passing resemblance to those once chipped from chert and obsidian. Likewise, riflemen shoulder firearms of stainless steel, with molded stocks as ugly as a mud fence. Instead of a hoary mixture of charcoal, saltpeter and sulfur, the smokeless propellants of this age are designed by computer programs and produced in tight unrecognizable granules.

Why then do men continue to hunt? Absent need, as well as a direct connection to the tools of his sport, Man the Hunter seems to be a relic from a time long past. Indeed, hunting has found itself on a long, downward spiral toward the backwaters of acceptable endeavors. There may come a time when such activities will be looked upon as a quaint undertaking that is no longer a part of civilized mankind's pantheon of recreational pursuits.

Even so, many of us still respond to an inner voice that seems inexplicably connected to our primal past. It was such a response that enabled me to endure mile-after-mile of equine travel through forested glades and along clear waters. And those selfsame urges had taken me to what seemed like the top of the world. And here at the edge of a remote treeless plateau, I had sent a jacketed-lead projectile on its deadly course. Deep in the bowels of the alpine meadow below, a bull elk lay dead at my hand.

Even though there never was a need, the venison from that animal will feed my family and others. The thick hide will become riding chaps and boot leather. And the head skin and antlers will keep the memories of this day alive. Indeed, the elk will have become a part of me and continue far longer than if he'd fallen prey to disease, the stress of winter, a hungry bear or mountain lion.

There is nothing that can plausibly account for my actions. Likewise, I have not been able to conjure up an acceptable argument to explain away the circumstances. And whether by my doing, or as a consequence of living in this wild place, death most certainly would have come to that elk and countless others. The truth, devoid of apologies, still remains. I stand accused, guilty and unrepentant.

There is a satisfaction that comes with knowing that the hunt has met with success. And that feeling is not easily attained by other accomplishments and deeds. It could be nothing more than deeply buried predatory instinct. Just as likely, that satisfaction is just the natural order of things. Today, natural man has given way to an unnatural creature that is hardly recognizable. On one hand he decries the pursuit of game as though it were an anathema, while all the time reaping havoc of every vile description on his fellows.

I want no part of the hollow rhetoric of this modern world that depicts the hunter as some primal ogre. I know better. For only in the forests and prairies of this great land are the answers to be found that were already there from the beginning. The facts are known. I am a hunter. And so I will always remain, even to my very core.

UNITED STATES GAME DEPARTMENT RESOURCE GUIDE

Alabama: Dept. of Conservation and Nat. Resources, Game and Fish Div., 64 N. Union St., Montgomery, AL 36130-1456, 334/242-3467

Alaska: Dept. of Fish and Game, Div. of Wildlife Conservation, Box 25526, Juneau, AK 99802, 907/465-4100

Arizona: Game and Fish Dept., 2221 W. Greenway Rd., Phoenix, AZ 85023, 602/942-3000

Arkansas: Game and Fish Commission, No. 2 Natural Resources Dr., Little Rock, AR 72205, 501/223-6351

California: Dept. of Fish and Game, License and Revenue Branch, 3211 "S" St., Sacramento, CA 95816, 916/227-2177

Colorado: Div. of Wildlife, 6060 Broadway, Denver, CO 80216, 303/297-1192

Connecticut: Dept. of Environmental Protection, Wildlife Div., 79 Elm St., Hartford, CT 06106-5127, 860/424-30011

Photo by Ron Gayer

Photo by Ron Gayer

Delaware: Dept. of Nat. Resources and Environment Control, Div. of Fish and Wildlife, 89 Kings Hwy., Dover, DE 19901, 302/739-5297

Florida: Game and Freshwater Fish Commission, 620 S. Meridian St. Tallahassee, FL 32399-1600, 850/488-4676

Georgia: Dept. of Nat. Resources, Wildlife Resources Div., 2070 U. S. Hwy 278 SE, Social Circle, GA 30025, 770/918-6400

Hawaii: Dept. of Land and Natural Resources, Div. of Forestry and Wildlife, 1151 Punchbowl St., Honolulu, HI 96813, 808/587-0166

Illinois: Dept. of Nat. Resources, Div. of Wildlife Resources, Lincoln Tower Plaza, 524 S. Second St., Springfield, IL 62701-1787, 217/782-6384

Indiana: Dept. of Nat. Resources, Div. of Fish and Wildlife, 402 W. Washington, Rm. W272, Indianapolis, IN 46204, 317/232-4080

Iowa: Dept. of Nat. Resources, Wallace State Office Bldg., Des Moines, IA 50319, 515/281-5145

Kansas: Dept. of Wildlife and Parks, 512 Southeast 25th Ave., Pratt, KS 67124, 316/672-5911

Kentucky: Dept. of Fish and Wildlife Resources, Frankfort, KY 40601, 502/564-4336

Louisiana: Dept. of Wildlife and Fisheries, P. O. Box 98000, Baton Rouge, LA 70898, 225/765-2346

Maine: Dept. of Inland Fisheries and Wildlife, 284 State St., State House Station 41, Augusta, ME 04333-0041, 207/287-8000

Maryland: Dept. of Nat. Resources, Wildlife and Heritage Div., Tawes Office Bldg., E-1, 580 Taylor Ave., Annapolis, MD 21401, 410/260-8540

Massachusetts: Div. of Fisheries and Wildlife, Field Hqs., One Rabbit Hill Rd., Westboro, MA 01581, 508/792-7270

Michigan: Wildlife Div., Michigan Dept. of Nat. Resources, Box 30444, Lansing, MI 48909, 517/373-1263

Minnesota: Dept. of Nat. Resources, Div. of Fish and Wildlife, Box 7, DNR Bldg., 500 Lafayette St., St. Paul, MN 55155, 651/296-6157

Mississippi: Dept. of Wildlife, Fisheries and Parks, 1505 Eastover, P. O. Box 451, Jackson, MS 39211, 601/432-2400

Missouri: Dept. of Conservation, P. O. Box 180, Jefferson City, MO 65102, 573/751-4114

Montana: Fish, Wildlife and Parks, 1420 E. Sixth Ave., P. O. Box 200701, Helena, MT 59620, 406/444-2535

Nebraska: Game and Parks Commission, P. O. Box 30370, Lincoln, NE 685043-0370, 402/471-0641

Nevada: Div. of Wildlife, P. O. Box 10678, Reno, NV 89520, 775-688-1500

New Hampshire: Fish and Game Dept., 2 Hazen Dr., Concord, NH 03301, 603/271-3211

New Jersey: Dept. of Environmental Protection, Div. of Fish, Game and Wildlife, P. O. Box 400, Trenton, NJ 08625-0400, 609/292-2965

New Mexico: Dept. of Game and Fish, P.O. Box 25112, Santa Fe, NM 87504, 800/862-9310

New York: Dept. of Environmental Conservation, Fish and Wildlife Div., 50 Wolf Rd., Albany, NY 12233, 518/457-5400

North Carolina: Wildlife Resources Commission, 512 N. Salisbury St., Raleigh, NC 27604-1188, 919/662-4370

North Dakota: Game and Fish Dept., 100 N. Bismarck Expressway, Bismarck, ND 58501, 701/328-6300

Ohio: Dept. of Natural Resources, Div. of Wildlife, 1840 Belcher Dr., Columbus, OH 43224-1329, 614/265-6300

Oklahoma: Dept. of Wildlife Conservation, 1801 N. Lincoln, Oklahoma City, OK 73105, 405/521-3851

Oregon: Dept. of Fish and Wildlife, P. O. Box 59, Portland, OR 97207, 503/872-5260

Pennsylvania: Game Commission, 2001 Elmerton Ave., Harrisburg, PA 17110-9797, 717/787-4250

Rhode Island: Dept. of Environmental Management, Div. of Fish and Wildlife, P. O. Box 218, West Kingston, RI 02892, 401/789-0281

South Carolina: Dept. of Natural Resources, P. O. Box 167, Columbia SC 29202, 803/734-3886

South Dakota: Dept. of Game, Fish and Parks, Information Services, 523 E. Capitol, Pierre, SD 57501, 605/773-3485

Tennessee: Wildlife Resources Agency, P. O. Box 40747, Nashville, TN 37204, 615/781-6610

Texas: Parks and Wildlife Dept., 4200 Smith School Rd., Austin, TX 78744, 800/792-1112

Utah: Div. of Wildlife Resources, 1594 West North Temple, Salt Lake City, UT 84114, 801/538-4700

Vermont: Agency of Nat. Resources, Fish and Wildlife Dept., 103 S. Main St., 10 South, Waterbury, VT 05671-0501, 802/241-3700

Virginia: Dept. of Game and Inland Fisheries, 4010 W. Broad St., Richmond, VA 23230-1104, 804/367-1000

Washington: Dept. of Fish and Wildlife, 600 Capitol Way N., Olympia, WA 98501, 360/902-2200

West Virginia: Div. of Nat. Resources, Wildlife Resources Section, State Capitol Complex, Bldg. 3, 1900 Kanawha Bl., Charleston, WV 25305, 304/558-2771

Wisconsin: Bureau of Wildlife Management, Box 7921, Madison, WI 53707, 608/266-2621

Wyoming: Game and Fish Dept., Cheyenne, WY 82006, 307/777-4600

CANADA GAME DEPARTMENT RESOURCE GUIDE

Alberta: Environmental Protection, Natural Resources Service, 9945 108th St., Edmonton, Alberta T5K 2G6, 780/427-3574

British Columbia: Wildlife Branch, Ministry of Environment, Lands and Parks, Parliament Bldg., 780 Blanshard St., Victoria, British Columbia V8V 1X5, 250/387-9717

Manitoba: Dept. of Natural Resources, Box 24, 200 Saulteaux Crescent, Winnipeg, Manitoba, R3J 3W3, 800/214-6497

New Brunswick: Dept. of Natural Resources and Energy, Fish and Wildlife Branch, P. O. Box 6000, Fredericton, New Brunswick E3B 5H1, 506/453-24440

Newfoundland and Labrador: Dept. of Natural Resources, Wildlife Div., P. O. Box 8700, St. John's, Newfoundland A1B 4J6, 709/729-2815

Northwest Territories: Dept. of Resources, Wildlife and Economic Development, Government of the Northwest Territories, 600, 5102-50 Ave., Yellowknife, Northwest Territories X1A 3S8, 867/873-7184

Photo by Ron Gayer

Nova Scotia: Dept. of Natural Resources, P. O. Box 698, Halifax, Nova Scotia B3J 2T9, 902/424-5935

Ontario: Ministry of Natural Resources, Natural Resources Information Centre, 900 Bay St., Rm. MI-73, Macdonald Block, Toronto, Ontario M7A 2C1 416/314-2000

Prince Edward Island: Fish and Wildlife Div., Dept. of Environmental Resources, P. O. Box 2000, Charlottetown, Prince Edward Island C14 7NB, 902/368-4683

Quebec: Ministére de íEnvironment et de la Faune, 150 boul, René-Lévesque Est. Québec City, Québec G1R 4Y1, 418/643-3127

Saskatchewan: Environment and Resources Management, 3211 Albert St., Regina, Saskatchewan S4S 5W6, 306/787-9034

Yukon Territory: Dept. of Renewable Resources, Field Services Branch, P. O. Box 2703, Whitehorse, Yukon Territory Y1A 2C6, 867/667-5221

Photo by Durwood Hollis

OUTFITTERS, GUIDES AND HUNTING OPERATIONS

Duwane Adams, Arizona Big Game Hunts, 204 Avenue "B," San Manuel, AZ 85631, 520/385-4995

James and Susan Boyce, Baranof Expeditions, Box 3107, Sitka, AK 99835, 907/747-3934

Tim Doud, Bliss Creek Outfitters, 326 Diamond Basin Rd., Cody, WY 82414,

Doug and Janet Gattis, Southern Oregon Game Busters, Box 1576, Medford, OR 97501, 541770-5050

Don Givet, Tejon Ranch, P. O. Box 1000, Lebec, CA 93243, 661/663-4208

Hawes Ranch Outfitters, 12057 - 121 Road, Ford, KS 67842, 620/369-2204

Multiple Use Managers, P. O. Box 669, Los Molinos, CA 96055, 800/557-7087

Scott Newman, P. O. Box 1357, Petersburg, AK 99833, 907/772-4878

Doug Roth/Craig Rossier, Camp 5 Outfitters, P. O. Box 121, Lockwood, CA 93446, 831/385-0358, 408/671-5844

Sandhills Ranch Properties, HC 91, Box 36, Gordon, NB 69343, 308/282-0457

Fred Webb, Webb Outfitting NWT Ltd., Box 313, Pritchard, British Columbia V0E 2P0, 250/577-3708

John R. Winter, Two-Ocean Pass Outfitting, P. O. Box 666, Thermopolis, WY 82443, 800/RANCH-09

Photo by Durwood Hollis

SELECTED U.S. GUIDES AND OUTFITTERS ASSOCIATIONS

Alaska Professional Hunters Association
P. O. Box 91932
Anchorage, AK 99509
907-522-3221
email:rfithian@alaskaprohunter.org

Colorado Outfitters Association
P. O. Box 1949
Rifle, CO 81650
970-876-0543
www.coloradooutfitters.org

Idaho Outfitters and Guides Association
P. O. Box 95
Boise, ID 83701
208-342-1919
www.ioga.org

Kansas Outfitters Association
2197 Kestrel Road
Hiawatha, KS 66434
www.kansasoutfittersassociation.com

Maine Professional Guides Association.
PO Box 336
Augusta, Maine (ME) 04332-0336
207-751-3797
www.maineguides.org

Mississippi Outfitters and Guides Association
www.msoutfitters.org

Montana Outfitters and Guides Association
P. O. Box 1248
Helena, MT 59624
406-449-9769
www.mog-montana.org

New Mexico Council of Outfitters and Guides
P. O. Box 93186
Albuquerque, NM 87199
505-822-9845

New York State Outdoor Guides Association
211 Saranac Avenue, #150
Lake Placid, NY 12946-1402
866-469-7642
www.nysoga.com

Oregon Guides and Packers Association
531 SW 13th St., Bend, OR 97702
800-747-9552
Fax 541-617-5027
www.ogpa.org

South Dakota Professional Guides and Outfitters
  Association
P.O. Box 703
Pierre, S.D. 57501
www.southdakotaguides.org
Texas Outfitters and Guides Association
P.O. Box 293141
Kerrville, Texas 78029-3141
830-238-4207
Fax 830-238-4207
www.texashuntingandfishing.com/toga/

Washington Outfitters and Guides Association
110 W. 6th Ave, PMB #398
Ellensburg, WA 98926
509-962-4222
Fax 509-962-4997
www.woga.org

Wyoming Outfitters and Guides Association
1716-8th St., P. O. Box 2284
Cody, WY 82414
307-527-7453
www.wyoga.org

HUNTING IN CANADA

Effective Jan. 1, 2001 non-residents entering Canada with firearms and without a Canadian Firearms License must complete a Non-Resident Firearms Declaration and pay a $50.00 Canadian fee at the point of entry. Non-Residents without a Canadian license who are borrowing a firearm must have an approved Temporary Borrowing License and pay a $30.00 Canadian fee, unless they are hunting under the direct and immediate supervision of a properly licensed individual. Canadian Customs offers preprocessing of declaration at selected points of entry. For additional information: forms and information 800-731-4000, www.cfc.gc.ca/visitors; customs information, 202-983-3500, www.ccra.gc.ca.

Photo by Durwood Hollis

SELECTED CANADIAN GUIDES AND OUTFITTERS ASSOCIATIONS

Saskatchewan Outfitters Association
3700-2nd Ave., West
Prince Albert, SK S6W 1A2
306-763-5334
www.spa.ca

Guide-Outfitters Association of British Columbia
Canada V6Y 4A4
604-278-2688
www.goabc.org

Photo by Jim Matthews

Enjoy Your Outdoor

Handgun Hunting
by Mark Hampton
Which handgun would you choose to take down an elephant, lion, cape buffalo, or jackrabbit? Learn which handgun calibers are effective for these animals and dozens of other wild beasts and wily varmints from around the world. Author Mark Hampton is an expert hunter who has owned a game ranch and taken more than 100 different species of game on six continents. Get practical advice on available guns, effective hunting bullet designs, handloading, and hunting accessories.
Softcover • 8-1/2x11 • 216 pages
200 b&w photos • 8-page color section
Item# HGHTG • $24.95

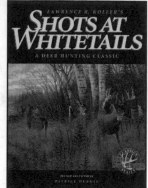

Shots at Whitetails
A Deer Hunting Classic
by Lawrence R. Koller
Revised and Edited by Patrick Durkin
Deer & Deer Hunting reintroduces the hunting classic *Shots at Whitetails* by legendary Adirondacks deer hunter Larry Koller. While guns and bows have changed since Shots at Whitetails was written in 1948, the deer remains the same elusive, majestic animal, thus keeping this oft-quoted book keenly relevant for today's deer hunters.
Hardcover • 8-1/4x10-7/8 • 314 pages
20 illustrations • 30 color photos
Item# SWTT • $29.95

Elk: Strategies for the Hunter
by Durwood Hollis
If you want to bag a trophy elk, author Durwood Hollis provides a detailed map to success. He'll guide you through the complicated process of applying for a license and hiring a guide and show you exactly what you need to succeed at elk camp. If you're serious about the most majestic animal in North America, this book is for you.
Softcover • 8-1/2x11 • 208 pages
125 b&w photos
Item# ELK • $19.95

The Complete Book Of Outdoor Survival
by J. Wayne Fears
Be prepared for the unexpected-and survive. Full of technical tips, useful skills, and real life examples, the practical information covered in this comprehensive guide benefits all outdoor enthusiasts from scouts and hikers to hunters and adventurers. Topics include edible plants, edible animals, smoking meat, making solar stills, and many more.
Softcover • 8-1/2x11 • 368 pages
550 b&w photos
Item# OTSUR • $24.95

Antelope Country
Pronghorns: The Last Americans
by Valerius Geist
Photography by Michael H. Francis
Professor Valerius Geist shares his fascinating insights into pronghorn antelope, the last surviving larger mammal of an era when the Great Plains was teeming with more species of wildlife than the African plains. Learn how the fleet, beautiful pronghorn was nearly wiped off the plains along with its bigger brother, the American bison, in the late 1800s, and then returned to abundance through myriad conservation efforts. The book is illustrated with striking photography by Michael Francis.
Hardcover • 8-1/4x10-7/8 • 176 pages
150 color photos
Item# ALPCY • $39.95

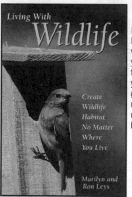

Living With Wildlife
by Marilyn and Ron Leys
If you are one of the millions of Americans who buy, build and hang bird feeders in order to bring the wonder of wildlife to your backyard this book is for you. Marilyn and Ron Leys take an in-depth look at the best ways to change the wildlife habitat in any yard, balcony or woodlot to attract the welcome guests, be they birds, butterflies or mammal, and repel those that cause problems. Several easy-to-read charts provide information at a glance on the best food and shelter, regardless of your location.
Softcover • 6x9 • 232 pages
150 b&w photos
Item# WILD • $16.95

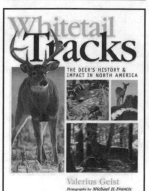

Whitetail Tracks
by Valerius Geist
Photographs by Michael H. Francis
This fascinating historical perspective on whitetails helps hunters and non hunters alike understand the effect humans have on the evolution of North America's number one big-game animal. You'll understand why hunting is a positive cultural force in shaping whitetail deer management today. Enjoy the stunning whitetail photos of Michael H. Francis while learning why whitetails continue to thrive.
Hardcover • 8-1/4x10-7/8 • 176 pages
150 color photos
Item# WHTPF • $34.95

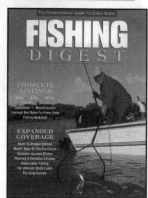

Fishing Digest
edited by Dennis Thornton
Reel in the latest gear, tackle, and equipment for your next fishing adventure. This comprehensive catalog lists rods, reels, depth finders, tackle boxes, boats, trailers, and other vital fresh water, salt, and deep-sea fishing equipment. Additional resources include helpful information for traveling anglers such as listings of more than 1,400 leading fishing guides and charters, fishing license fees and regulations for each state, top fishing resorts, and state and national parks. Information-packed articles report on hot fishing topics and successful tips and techniques needed to reel in the big ones.
Softcover • 8-1/2x11 • 352 pages
200 b&w photos
Item# FSH1 • $24.95

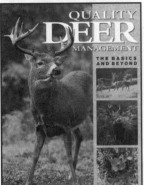